D1244394

EFFECTIVE NURSING LEADERSHIP

A Practical Guide

Virginia K. Baillie, RN, MA, CS

Therapist and Educator
Private Practice
Salinas, California

Louise Trygstad, RN, DNSc

University of San Francisco
School of Nursing
San Francisco, California

Tatiana Isaeff Cordoni, RN, MS, CNA

University of San Francisco
School of Nursing
San Francisco, California

AN ASPEN PUBLICATION®
Aspen Publishers, Inc.

1989

Rockville, Maryland
Royal Tunbridge Wells

Library of Congress Cataloging-in-Publication Data

Baillie, Virginia K.
Effective nursing leadership: a practical guide/Virginia K. Baillie,
Louise Trygstad, Tatiana Isaeff Cordoni.
p. cm.
"An Aspen publication."
Includes index.
ISBN: 0-8342-0036-8
1. Nursing services--Administration. 2. Leadership. 3. Interpersonal relations.
I. Trygstad, Louise. II. Cordoni, Tatiana Isaeff. III. Title.
[DNLM: 1. Leadership--nurses' instruction. 2. Nursing, Supervisory. WY 105 T875e]
RT89.T79   1989   362.1'73'068--dc19   DNLM/DLC
for Library of Congress
88-7759
CIP

Editorial Services: Susan Bedford

Library of Congress Catalog Card Number: 88-7759
ISBN: 0-8342-0036-8

Printed in the United States of America

1 2 3 4 5

To the hundreds of RN managers who have taught us what we need to know

to William and Mary Baillie, my parents; and to my mentors and colleagues who have supported my growth: Louise Trygstad, George McClendon, Robert R. Rynearson, Richard K. Gaines, and Lillian Archilles

—Virginia

to Warren and Jennie May Nigh, my parents; to Bruce, my husband; and to Dawn and Jay, my children

—Louise

to my family who support me in every endeavor: David, my husband; Mila and Keith Davis, my parents; Milla, Nancy, and Sheila, my sisters; and with loving memory to my dearest dad, Walter Isaeff, who brought a special joy to my life

—Tatiana

Table of Contents

Overview

The purpose of this text is to help the professional nurse leader increase her effectiveness by enhancing her interpersonal capabilities and skills. It is dedicated to present and potential nurse leaders who seek to become self-actualized and personally powerful. This book is written for those who want to change and to feel successful in the process.

The nurse leader may either occupy a management position or demonstrate leadership through other roles or activities. Not all managers are leaders nor all leaders managers. We often find ourselves leading without necessarily holding a management position in the organization. This book is for those in any position who wish to influence and motivate others; it is essential for those in management positions.

Today's nurse manager is confronted with increased role responsibilities and the need to act to accomplish the goals which are her responsibility. Often she does so with insufficient preparation, a lack of "learning time," and an absence of effective role models.

The information presented in the book is applicable to nurse managers and leaders in a variety of settings. However, because their need is the greatest, this book is particularly addressed to our RN colleagues who find themselves in management positions without the benefit of leadership education. It is also addressed to practicing RNs who aspire to management positions or to leadership positions that are clinical or professional, rather than managerial. We hope it will also be of value to staff developers working with RNs, both those in and those not in management positions, to help them acquire leadership education. Finally, this book is addressed to nursing students who have the benefit of concurrent nursing and leadership education.

This text is grounded in practice. It incorporates actual experiences of successful nurse leaders. What sets this book apart from other texts on nursing leadership is the authors' experience. These three colleagues share a similar mindset in the areas of recognizing, analyzing, and solving problems attendant to the development of nursing leadership and management resources. Two of the authors have led leadership workshops for several years and thus have been in contact with hundreds of nurse managers. The third author was director of staff development in a hospital with identified nursing needs. A three-year collaborative effort by the authors yielded a program which began with an assessment of individual care leadership competencies of the entire nurse management group in the staff development director's hospital. Workshops were developed and presented to meet identified needs. Evaluation demonstrated that the workshops (presented over a three-year period) increased leadership effectiveness, promoted personal growth, and were a source of satisfaction for the nurses who participated.

Leadership is an interpersonal process, and can therefore best be learned in an interpersonal setting. Because leadership in nursing is practiced with a work group, it is ideally learned with members of the work group. The work group provides a shared frame of reference and opportunities for continuing support in practicing leadership.

Because the ideal is often difficult to achieve, the reader is encouraged to form a group if her actual work group is not an available or feasible arena for learning. Three or four colleagues can learn together on their own. Or perhaps the staff development director could assist in the formation of a group of nurses from one setting who wish to develop their leadership skills.

Because individual learning precludes participation in group exercises and offering and receiving feedback, it is the least desirable form of learning. However, even the nurse learning alone can benefit from this book and learn to practice skills as opportunities present themselves in the work setting.

This book contains both individual and group exercises. That learning is enhanced when the learner participates is an accepted principle. The greater the interaction and practice with the material to be learned, the greater the learning will be. In many instances, the exercises are not specific to nursing. These exercises were selected when the focus was on learning the process, rather than the content. For example, because the NASA exercise in Chapter 8 is not related to nursing, it enables the learners to focus entirely on the process without being caught up in content. What is learned about process then can and should be generalized to the nursing work environment. It is helpful to discuss these generalizations and their applications after each exercise.

On two occasions the reader is referred to an outside source—an audiotaped listening test and a leadership evaluation. The first cannot be included in a book, and the second is not because of copyright restrictions. However, we have found both to be such outstanding aids that we would be remiss in not suggesting them. Alternative ways of learning are included, but the suggested sources remain the best.

This book is addressed to both women and men. We regret that our language does not have a unisex pronoun. For ease of reading we have selected the feminine pronoun, which remains accurate for more than 96 percent of all nurses.

This text attempts to expedite the dynamic process by which nursing managers and leaders acquire the core competencies essential to effective leadership practice. We anticipate that your current work dilemmas and constraints will become opportunities to transform values into action and visions of success into reality.

Chapter 1

Leadership and Management

Leadership is an interpersonal process. A leader interacts with group members to influence, motivate, and facilitate members to meet their potential. A nurse leader inspires others; improves their abilities; expands their horizons; brings out their best; builds on their strengths; catalyzes their hopes, aspirations, and expectations; and most importantly, renews their original commitment to nursing.

The statement, "Leaders are born, not made," is a myth. Some individuals appear to have a natural inclination for the leadership role and are more predisposed than others to assume command. However, although natural aptitudes can be sharpened and polished, learned leadership skills based on sound concepts are essential. Further development of leadership depends on consistent practice, role adaptation, positive association with effective mentors, and rewards. Leadership may be demonstrated by persons in any role.

In contrast to leaders who choose and achieve their roles, managers are assigned or appointed to their role. Management is of tasks and things. The individual nurse manager is both an investor in the organization and its goals and an integrator and interpreter of its major functions. She holds a professional role, an interpersonal role, and a business role. A manager's responsibility is to meet the organizational goals and perform the organizational tasks: developing schedules, controlling budgets, and giving patient care. However, because one person alone cannot meet all organizational goals, managers need to be leaders who can influence and motivate others.

The mission of a health care facility to carry out humanistic health care is reflected in the goals of the organization and is accomplished in part by each member of that organization. This mission is accomplished in an environmental system that is both complex and changeable. Each system, whether it be outpatient, inpatient, acute or long-term care, or community based, not only demands attention to task completion but also requires the leader to work effectively with the people who complete the task.

Figure 1-1 Dimensions of Management

Today's nursing manager must deal continually with three dimensions: (1) the job—the task that has to be done; (2) the mission—the goal of the organization; and (3) interpersonal relations—the people who do the job (Figure 1-1).

Most managers spend less time getting the task done and more time with the interpersonal relations; that is, working with people to get the task accomplished. Their success and effectiveness are largely determined by their abilities to share knowledge and develop staff. Thus, we can see the importance of leadership to the nurse manager's role.

The primary need in nursing today is for effective leadership. We have not adequately prepared the number of leaders needed to assume nursing leadership roles.

Presently, many institutions lack innovative nursing leadership for a variety of reasons including insufficient rewards, lack of mentors, insufficient knowledge and skill, poor role models, and insufficient role adaptation. Initial recruitment processes for managers generally focus on academic credentials, and although these are valid criteria for candidate selection, they do not by themselves guarantee leadership potential. Search panels comprised of administrative, medical, and nursing personnel must not be reluctant to select qualified applicants who advocate creative change.

Future Shock by Alvin Toffler (1972) and *Megatrends* by John Naisbitt (1982) present the message that the future is really now. To deal with today's rapidly changing, complex, and highly technological health care environment, we must not only appreciate our history as leaders but also engage in very effective planning for positive change.

HISTORY OF NURSING LEADERSHIP

The first groups that had a need for leadership and teamwork were the nomadic tribes. When the tribal system evolved into the ancient civilizations of Egypt and Greece, the need for leadership grew. Building the pyramids and temples of Egypt required scores of managers overseeing the actions of thousands of workers. The Greeks brought us the ideas of participation and consultation associated with democracy. The organization of labor further evolved during the Italian Renaissance with the development of the concepts of the assembly line, inventory, and cost control. It was during the Industrial Revolution, however, that the influence of the satisfaction of the employee on productivity was first considered.

Several schools of management and leadership have influenced our current beliefs. The classical theorists, Taylor (1911) and Weber (1957), described man as a logical machine, a rational instrument. This philosophy assumes that there is one best way to do every task and that organizations complete their tasks and fulfill their goals through the use of authority. Time and motion studies can therefore determine the most efficient means of task performance. Division of labor is based on specific rules and regulations and a specific hierarchy. Decisions are made from the top and communicated down. Employees are motivated mainly by money, and promotion is based on skill. The classical theorists further believe that employees:

- are naturally lazy and prefer to do nothing
- work mainly for money and status rewards
- are motivated to be productive primarily by the fear of being fired
- need supervisors to watch them closely
- have little concern about their immediate material needs
- enjoy being treated nicely
- naturally resist change
- are influenced by heredity

The classical theorists had a major influence on the structure of early nursing management. Nursing services historically have been directed by one person whose leadership was directed to supervisory personnel and then shared with staff. During periods of nursing shortages, public relations and personnel development departments argued that increased salaries and benefits would attract more nurses to work in medical centers. However, the increased benefits and salary did not increase either productivity or long-range employment for nurses.

In contrast to the classical theorists, Mayo (1933), McGregor (1960), and Argyris (1971) argue that employees are complex beings who are motivated by different reward systems. Satisfaction can be achieved on the job, especially through the work group, and individuals who become involved in work groups are more committed to the work group and to the organization. The real power to create change in an organization lies in interpersonal relationships.

The famous Hawthorne studies (Mayo, 1933) conducted in the 1930s bear out the assumptions of these theorists. The purpose of the studies was to test the effect of improved lighting on factory workers' productivity. In contrast to the investigators' expectations, both groups of workers—those with better lighting conditions and those working without the benefit of improved lighting—increased their productivity. The investigators determined that the increase in productivity came about because of the attention they paid to both groups of workers; that is, interpersonal relationships play a large role in productivity. The amount of reinforcement and support from management matters as much as the surroundings.

In contrast to "X managers" (those who follow the classical theories), the "Y manager" (McGregor, 1960) believes that people:

- are naturally active
- like to set goals
- seek many satisfactions at work and are stimulated by new challenges
- like to keep productive and involved
- seek self-realization and do not like monotony
- need to constantly grow and be encouraged

In the 1970s and 1980s, the process school of leadership and management developed. This school of thought supports the situational leadership approach—that there really is no *one* best form of leadership. Rather, the leader should adapt to the people being led and change his or her leadership style according to the degree of maturity of the employee (Hersey & Blanchard, 1977). Theorists of the process school believe that each individual has the power to encourage goal attainment or to hinder it.

Theory Z, developed by Ouchi in 1981, posits that when a management system provides (1) long-term support to employees, (2) mentorship, and (3) consensus in decision making, growth and development of the individual will be enhanced. As nurse managers, we may anticipate that with increased participation we can look forward to increased productivity.

Changes in nursing have paralleled these theoretical developments. In the early 20th century, such changes as finalization of nursing education and development of training programs in management science took place. The mid 20th century gave way to university education for nurses, human relations management, and rising technology. Currently, nursing leadership theories and concepts address humanization of the work place, worker participation in decision making, and effective use of resources in a tighter economy (Porter-O'Grady, 1986).

Recently, innovative approaches to leadership have considered the influence of personality on productivity (De Ville, 1985). Nurse managers are thus encouraged to coach more than supervise, to recognize behavior patterns that affect performance, and to inspire the staff to greater motivation.

In summary, managers in the past had more control and exercised more guidance over workers. Apathy, alienation, burnout, and crisis management often resulted. Today every aspect of health care is productivity and cost-effectiveness oriented. These goals are perceived as attainable through development and participation of employees—through leadership!

DEVELOPING NURSING LEADERS

To develop nursing leaders, we need to (1) value leadership, have a vision of the possibilities of leadership, and develop a strategic plan to attain those possibilities; (2) understand the leadership role and ourselves within this role (Chapter 2); (3) understand the working environment and the people with whom we work (Chapter 3); and (4) develop self and the skills involved in leadership (remainder of the book).

We need to understand and value the multiple payoffs of exercising leadership. Being a leader expands the role of the professional nurse. It sets the standard for professional practice and helps guide the practice of nursing. The positive use of control, power, influence, and leadership opportunities offers us the ability to develop and enhance our own professional repertoire of skills. Leadership therefore builds professionalism and pride, which are the sustenance of the professional practice of nursing.

Nursing leadership provides the satisfaction and feeling of competence that come from helping others reach their potential. Most of us entered nursing to care and to be caring. We find satisfaction in helping others, being challenged, and being competent. These same payoffs that attracted us to nursing are available from nursing leadership as we help staff help others. The additional payoff is that through leadership, we have a larger sphere of influence.

Each nurse leader will derive unique personal rewards from leadership. For example, the payoff of personal power often accompanies the nurse leader's influence to create planned change. To become empowered to effect positive change and growth is the height of self-fulfillment for the nurse leader. "Empowerment" through competence that enables you to transcend obstacles to progress, thereby smoothing the way for colleagues who may aspire to leadership, is very different from negatively exerted "power" for the purposes of self-aggrandizement.

We need to recognize and affirm the expertise of leadership. Nurses are famous for not giving support to one another (Storlie, 1982). We are so busy taking care of everyone else that we neglect one of the main responsibilities of leadership: support of each other! There is a correlation between lack of support and affirmation and the presence of competition with the dearth of nursing leadership.

Today's nursing leader needs a vision of what can be and the ability to communicate this vision to others. When we develop a personal vision and philosophy about our profession, we can examine choices and options in light of this question: Will it meet my personal, professional, and organizational goals?

Foundations for the future are based on long-term vision and strategic planning. Strategic planning identifies guideposts and opportunities for new solutions both to age-old problems and to some of the multifaceted dilemmas that confront leaders today. It requires a vision of what is possible, hope, commitment, planning, supportive structures and resources, and of course the opportunity for enactment.

We must develop ourselves as primary instruments of change—be "the change master." We must reassess ourselves, our profession, and the organizations in which we enact our roles in order to refine the means to assist ourselves, others, and the organization to respond creatively to challenges and crises. The effective nurse leader first identifies a need, defines a mechanism for change, and then becomes the instrument for its implementation.

We must develop systems, structures, and processes that promote creativity, enhance group synergy, and reinforce core nursing values. We must empower others to see and use that vision of what is possible in the design of professional and organizational values and structures.

Communication is the priority skill of leadership. Becoming a leader requires understanding our communication style: understanding how we express ourselves, how we make requests, and how we deal with conflict. Effective communication requires knowledge about group and individual behavior and the influence of our personal power on positive outcomes and change. In the past, limited emphasis in nursing was placed on communication. In today's high tech, high information society, the importance of effective communication cannot be overstated. As nursing leaders, we must have both healthy personalities and a communication system from which to envision, plan, and effect positive change.

Leadership requires us to have a healthy sense of self-esteem and self-confidence in our roles and the ability to share that on an interpersonal and group basis. As leaders, we can enhance group self-esteem by our role modeling of clinical competencies and skills and by our ability to communicate in healthy ways. Such aspects of self-esteem as connectiveness, uniqueness, and power can be applied on a group and individual basis. Involvement of both groups and individuals in projects of substance engenders an initial measure of self-esteem. Increasing challenges produce deeper convictions of self-worth, until ultimately groups and individuals can attain independently conceived objectives. Self-actualization denotes the transition from "follower" to "leader" status.

The nurse leader as a role model in her demonstration of expertise can motivate others to achieve their potential. She uses her power and influence to act as a mentor and to engender followership in others. The nurse leader is able to nourish and support others because of her understanding of self, others, and the environment in which they all work.

As nurse leaders, we need to be able to make effective decisions and manage our own stress and time. We need to be able to delegate, set limits, and discipline when necessary. In addition to her other skills, the manager/leader needs to know and work within the legal and institutional structure for employer-employee relationships; today this often means working within the structure of a union contract and negotiating this contract.

In a recent study of administrators in nursing education and inpatient and community facilities, critical competencies were identified for nurse administrators (Goodrich, 1982). Most of the critical competencies were leadership skills. The skills included group process, interpersonal relations, communication, decision making, motivation/support, power, delegation, supervision, knowledge of the change process, stress management, conflict management, priority setting, and time management.

This book is a guide to developing competencies needed for leadership. It begins with the development of self and role and then addresses the influence of the working environment. The interpersonal skills and individual competencies needed are presented in the remainder of the book.

REFERENCES

Argyris, C. (1971). *Management and organizational development: The path from XA to YB.* New York: McGraw-Hill.

De Ville, J. (1985). *The psychology of leadership: Managing resources by relationships.* New York: New American Library.

Goodrich, N. (1982). A profile of the competent nursing administrator. Ann Arbor, MI: UMI Research Press.

Hersey, Paul, & Blanchard, Kenneth. (1977). *Management of organizational behavior: utilizing human resources* (3rd ed). Englewood Cliffs, NJ: Prentice Hall.

Mayo, E. (1933). *Human problems of an industrial civilization.* New York: Macmillan Co.

McGregor, D. (1960). *The human side of enterprise.* New York: McGraw-Hill.

Naisbitt, J. (1982). *Megatrends.* New York: Warner Books.

Ouchi, W. (1981). *Theory Z.* Menlo Park, CA: Addison-Wesley.

Porter-O'Grady, Tim (1986). *Creative nursing administration.* Rockville, MD: Aspen Publishers, Inc.

Storlie, F. (1982). Power, getting a piece of the action. *Nursing Management, 10*(13), 15–18.

Taylor, W.F. (1911). *The principles of scientific management.* New York: Harper & Brothers.

Toffler, A. (1972). *Future shock.* New York: Bantam Books.

Weber, M. (1957). *The theory of social and economic organization.* New York: Oxford University Press.

Chapter 2

The Powerful Role of the Nurse Leader

Successful nurse leaders are not mere "passers-by" in the ever-changing health care arena but visionary activists who believe in involvement. They use leadership skills and clinical competencies to implement their roles. This chapter provides an overview of those skills required for the nurse leader to perform effectively.

The role of the nurse leader is multifaceted. As a nurse leader, you are an investor in the organization and its goals, as well as an integrator and interpreter of major functions related to task completion, interpersonal leadership, and alliance with the goal of the organization. The parameters of your role are extensive and its substance complex. In every situation, however, there is one constant: your role is dynamic!

To perform your role, you as the nurse leader must possess (1) clinical patient care management skills, (2) human resource management skills, and (3) operational management skills (Table 2-1). You must also understand that you are in a dynamic interaction with your working environment and that you affect the working environment and vice versa. You must understand that change can be both positive and negative and that you have a direct and positive influence in assisting that change to occur. How then do you as an individual nurse leader enact your role in developing and using the skills listed in Table 2-1?

ROLE ASSESSMENT

Effective nurse leaders implement their roles using the following planning strategies. They give themselves permission to collect, organize, and analyze data about their roles. These leaders use a consistent framework for role assessment. They identify those parts of the role that are important to them. They seek congruence from others on their role definition. If there is not

Table 2-1 Leadership Skills

Clinical Management Skills	Human Resource Management Skills	Operational Management Skills
Assessing problems and needs	Teaching	Budgeting
Identifying problems	Counseling	Controlling
Planning care	Facilitating	Staffing
Providing care	Leading rounds & conferences, staff education programs, and continuing education	Providing supplies
Teaching		Scheduling
Giving treatments and medication		Communicating
Leading clinical conferences	Career mobility	Coordinating
Evaluating	Peer review	Planning/evaluating performance
Coordinating care	Research	Auditing
Directing staff who are providing care	Training and coaching	Setting objectives and goals for future development
	Human relations	
	Motivation of staff	

Source: From *Nursing Management,* 2nd ed. (p.12) by Joan M. Ganong and Warren L. Ganong, 1980, Rockville, MD: Aspen Publishers, Inc. Copyright 1980 by Aspen Publishers, Inc.

congruence on key areas, they negotiate for their concept of the role. These leaders are thoroughly familiar with the description of their position and are capable of clarifying every facet of performance expectations, especially as these apply to their relationship with superordinates and peers.

If you are new to a leadership or management role, your orientation is a critical time to conduct a role assessment (see Appendix 2-A for assessment questions). A new manager/leader cannot perform effectively or develop a collegial network without an orientation that is clear and explicit about her responsibilities and areas of accountability. The orientation phase is essential to success and directly affects your potential for role congruency.

Both the experienced and the new nurse leader benefit by periodic analysis of their positions. Role analysis occurs at least annually as part of the evaluation process for the experienced manager.

ROLE EXPECTATIONS AND POTENTIAL CONFLICT

Role expectations are the rights, duties, responsibilities, and activities acceptable within the organization (Rheiner, 1982). These role expectations are what others expect we will do. They are set by "role setters"—those members of the organization who have direct contact with an individual in his or her performance. For example, nursing administration and leadership staff clarify with the employee all expectations of her role. Role conception (Rheiner, 1982) integrates the expectations that the individual employee has about her role in the organization with the expectations of others. Past experience may be an essential influence on the role conception and expectations of the role. Role conception functions to interpret one's role and reduce the possibility of future conflict.

Rheiner (1982) has developed a framework that describes the dynamic interaction between the role sender and role occupant. Both have role expectations. The degree of congruence between the sender and occupant will determine the effectiveness of role performance. As organizational goals change and as role senders change, the role occupant adjusts her personal role expectations. In this paradigm, the role occupant is adjusting to external changes. Conversely, by developing a tactical and strategic plan, the role occupant can successfully effect change in the sender's role expectations. By being aware of this dynamic process and having a strategic plan, you will be better able to effect role congruency and avoid role conflict (Table 2-2).

ROLE IMPLEMENTATION

As you become clear about your role's rights, duties, and responsibilities, role performance is initiated. Role performance (Rheiner, 1982) involves both the self-concept of an individual and the role expectations of the social system of the organization. When a merger between role expectation and role conception is strong, success within that role is possible. When there is a weak link between role conception and role expectation, we can expect both role pressure and conflict to occur (Figure 2-1).

Symptoms of role conflict include (1) a tendency to retreat from change, (2) a decrease in the willingness to risk and trust, and (3) a sense of failure. The effective nurse leader recognizes these symptoms and then negotiates between sender and self to reduce conflict in expectations.

Role pressure occurs as the individual realizes she is failing to meet expectations. Pressure can come in various forms; withholding of rewards, punishment, and ostracism from peers are examples. This pressure often leads to role stress.

Role stress is often predominant in today's organizations. If roles are ambiguous or incongruent, if the nurse leader feels overloaded with responsibility, or if role conflict exists, then role stress is certain to occur. Outcomes of role stress include burnout, decreased motivation, increased conflict with administrative staff, family or individual disturbances, loss of confidence in

Table 2-2 Role Theory

	Role Structure	
Role Senders	Role Occupant's Expectations	Role Performance

Members of organization in direct contact with role occupant
  staff
  peers
  superordinates
  staff of other departments
  physicians
 	
Hold expectations to evaluate performance of role occupant
 	
Strategic planning:
• implementation of role
• conformity
• responds to organizational needs and needs of employees
• seeks to decrease potential conflict
	Initial role concept developed through:
	  personal past experiences
	  position interview
	  position description
	  educational experience
	  literature search
	
	When self-expectations integrate with role sender expectations, role conception occurs
	
	Role occupant requires assistance from role senders to interpret and implement role
		Feedback:
		  degree of congruence between role occupant and role sender expectations
		
		Strong link:
		• congruence between role occupant's and role senders' expectations
		• results in role satisfaction
		Weak link:
		• disparity between role occupant's and role senders' expectations
		• results in role stress, conflict, ambiguity, overload, burnout

Source: Adapted from "Role Theory: Framework for Change" by Neil Rheiner, 1982, Nursing Management, 13. Copyright 1982 by Nursing Management. Reprinted by permission.

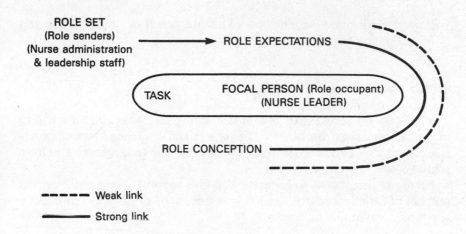

RESULTS: STRONG LINK between Role Expectation and Role Conception
= Positive Role Merger and Role Performance

WEAK LINK between Role Expectation and Role Conception
= Role Stress and Conflict with Decreased Performance

Figure 2–1 Role Performance. *Source:* From "Role Theory: Framework for Change" by Neil Rheiner, 1982, *Nursing Management, 13*. Copyright 1982 by Nursing Management. Adapted by permission.

---

self, deterioration of relationships with peers, and eventual withdrawal from the leadership role. Thus, to prevent role stress, it is essential to define the supportive skills that allow for effective leadership behavior and role implementation.

The following eight skills are supportive of role implementation. A description of each skill follows:

1. asking for and giving support
2. identification of supports and barriers to role implementation
3. establishing effective communication systems, role models, mentors, and networking associations
4. using techniques for goal setting and evaluation, e.g., management by objectives
5. determining your personal leadership style and adapting to workers' abilities, needs, and development
6. anticipating and planning for changes and challenges
7. evaluating own performance and seeking constructive feedback for self-development

8. appreciating and learning how to use the power of your own role and that of the organization

Skill 1: Asking for and Giving Support

In the process of assessing and implementing your role, you have had to request information from others. You have risked disclosing a lack of understanding of your role in order to achieve greater role congruence. You have asked for the support of others.

There are many ways to generate and give support. From a survey of a number of experienced managers comes this list of strategies to promote a supportive environment:

- Ask for direct help and be receptive when it is offered.
- Give help and support, especially to new members of the group.
- Assess individuals with whom you interact. Determine who is supportive, minimally supportive, or nonsupportive.
- List individuals with whom you desire to improve your relationship. List one action you would be willing to take to bring about this improvement.
- Maintain high-quality relationships by telling colleagues how much you value their support.
- Review your present network, determine how well it is working for you, and develop a plan to change it where necessary.
- Keep your energy exchange balanced; return favors and others' thoughtfulness.
- Thank individuals for their support both in writing and verbally.
- Use your network and encourage members of the network to use your support.

Skill 2: Identifying the Barriers and Supports to Your Role and Responsibilities

Barriers may block your way toward achieving an effective leadership role. Resistance to change is well documented in the literature. You may not be able to resolve certain controversial issues merely by making others aware of them. If you take time, however, to prepare the environment and strengthen your supports, natural resistance can be diminished and eventually dissipated. The following are examples of typical barriers:

- allowing past failures to guide the future through negative self-talk and feeling overwhelmed, e.g., no time, can't do it, it won't work, this place won't change.
- not planning for "what ifs" before implementing a project
- allowing others to set divisional/departmental responsibilities and objectives without your input
- engaging in undeveloped or underutilized negotiation of options
- failing to develop the talents of subordinates or peers
- using win/loss strategies to solve problems
- encouraging or participating in elitist or exclusive group decision making

This last barrier—elitist decision making—decreases your chance of sharing information through diverse discussion arenas. Further, overdependence on one group limits the number of creative options generated and can lead to a we/they attitude toward nongroup members.

An effective manager builds in supports to compensate for these barriers. Frequently, being aware of the barriers is itself a support. For example, if you have not developed the talents of subordinates, beginning that process will enable you to delegate effectively and complete more projects.

Gain support for yourself in your management role by implementing these support strategies:

- Encourage subordinates to submit a solution with each problem and to take time to evaluate conflicts before action.
- Balance constructive critical feedback with equivalent positive feedback.
- Seek out a reliable mentor for yourself to validate your ideas and secure honest opinions.
- Handle sensitive or volatile issues confidentially; apprise staff and colleagues of your expectation for reciprocal confidentiality.
- Encourage staff to validate communication for its clarity and congruence.
- Operate in an environment that allows disagreement but expects issues to be negotiated before implementation.

Think in terms of barriers and supports when you are implementing aspects of your role. Align your supports before starting a project. If you meet resistance, analyze the barriers. As you gain experience in conceptualizing situations in this way, the barriers and supports will become more obvious.

Skill 3: Establishing an Effective Communication System

A leader who uses listening/processing communication skills, rather than downward-dispensing informational strategies, can alter group attitudes and behavior. With a change of conflict resolution style, win/lose situations can become win/win opportunities. Effective communication can facilitate successful planned change. In contrast to the autocrat who demands adherence to self-perpetuating policies, a "change master" uses coaching, developing, and collaborating techniques with colleagues and subordinates to effect change. In addition, the effective leader uses her core attributes, such as integrity and openness in communication, to encourage intellectual and interpersonal exchange in work group development (Porter-O'Grady & Finnigan, 1984). Successful nurse leaders seek out role models and mentors and make consistent use of networking opportunities to support their roles.

Skill 4: Using Techniques for Goal Setting and Evaluation

Once your role assessment is complete, you can develop projects and goals that fulfill the various responsibilities of your role. Align these objectives with those of the organization, your department, and your subordinates to ensure support for them. Because alignment promotes role congruency, it is a factor in effective role performance. Make certain to include the most enjoyable aspects of your role in your objectives to ensure your job satisfaction.

Management By Objectives

A modern method for organizing your goals is *Management By Objectives* (MBO) (Drucker, 1954). Objectives written according to this format are behaviorally focused, goal directed, and well delineated through action plans. (See Appendix 2-B for guidelines for writing MBOs and examples of them.) Discuss your MBOs with the staff and your peer group to encourage their involvement. Post or publish the goals you and your group have attained. By sharing MBOs and celebrating achievements, you can engender support and interest in departmental and organizational progress. At the same time, you can appropriately counter any hidden resistance that may surface.

Achieving MBOs requires careful planning. (See Appendix 2-C for a completed fiscal year plan.) Use your annual calendar to circle in red key target dates for each objective. Insert checkpoints to track progress. Keep colleagues apprised of progress made, and modify your target dates as needed. Keep a record of all you achieve, including extraneous projects not specifically mentioned in your MBOs. This record will enhance your sense of accomplishment and communicate motivation while modeling professionalism and goal-directed performance to be emulated by others.

By establishing MBOs early in your employment, you as a new role occupant can circumvent role incongruency. Assumption of new responsibilities occurs more readily as your performance improves.

Skill 5: Determining Your Personal Leadership Style and Adapting to Employees' Abilities, Needs, and Development

Effective leaders are able to adapt their style of leadership to various situations. Using the same style in all events will lead to frustration on the part of the manager, the employee, and any other parties involved. Participatory management has many laudable characteristics, but will not work in all situations. Resolution of conflict and of some performance discrepancies often requires a more authoritarian approach. The amount of time available to make the decision often dictates the style of leadership used. Crisis management does not lend itself to a participatory approach. Under all circumstances, the experience, competence, and decisiveness of the effective nurse manager will determine the equity and justice of the appropriate decision. To demonstrate her proficiency, a nurse manager must positively influence staff members to be amenable to change. As staff members internalize methods of an effective but flexible leadership style, their involvement increases and their movement toward a designated goal quickens.

One innovative leadership approach developed by Blanchard is the Situational Leadership II concept (Blanchard, Zigarmi, & Zigarmi, 1985). It is an updated version of the original life-cycle theory of leadership developed by Hersey and Blanchard (1982). This practical and easy-to-understand approach to leadership can be used effectively within the health care setting. The Situational Leadership II model is discussed a great deal in leadership training circles and has been found to be one of the most effective models for leaders today (see Resources for obtaining further information on this model).

This model relates (1) the amount of direction and control (directive behavior) that a leader gives and (2) the amount of support and encouragement (supportive behavior) that a leader provides to (3) the competence and commitment (development level) that a follower exhibits in task performance (Blanchard et al., 1985). The leader uses directive behavior when she engages in one-way communication—spelling out the follower's role and

Table 2-3 Developmental Level

HIGH	MODERATE		LOW
High competence High commitment	High competence Variable commitment	Some competence Low commitment	Low competence High commitment
D4	D3	D2	D1

Developed ◄————————————————————————► Developing

Source: Reprinted by permission of Blanchard Training and Development, Inc., Escondido, California, © 1985.

---

clearly telling the follower what to do and where, how, and when to do it—and provides close supervision. The leader uses supportive behavior when she engages in two-way communication, listens, provides support and encouragement, facilitates interaction, and involves the follower in decision making. The development level of a follower is defined as the follower's (1) job knowledge and skills (competence) and (2) motivation and/or confidence (commitment). The more competent and committed the subordinate is, the more responsibility she can take for directing her own behavior. However, it is important to remember that development level is task specific; an individual or group is not developing or developed in any total sense (Table 2-3).

The Situational Leadership II model is congruent with the well-documented concept in the literature that there is no best leadership style. Four leadership styles are described in Exhibit 2-1. The successful leader is one who is able to enact a leadership style adapted to the particular requirements of a situation.

The question becomes: Which style to use and under what circumstances?

Exhibit 2-1 Leadership Styles

Directing (S1): High directive/low supportive behavior: Leader provides specific instructions (roles and goals) for follower(s) and closely supervises task accomplishment.
Coaching (S2): High directive/high supportive behavior: Leader explains decisions and solicits suggestions from follower(s), but continues to direct task accomplishment.
Supporting (S3): High supportive/low directive behavior: Leader makes decisions together with the follower(s) and supports efforts toward task accomplishment.
Delegating (S4): Low supportive/low directive behavior: Leader turns over decisions and responsibility for implementation to follower(s).

Using These Styles

As nursing leaders, we can use the Situational Leadership II model. First determine what you want to accomplish through your followers. Ask yourself, "What is the task or goal; what responsibility or task do I want to influence?" Second, specify clearly the level of performance that you want the staff member to accomplish in this task. Third, determine her development level in relation to that task. Does she have the necessary knowledge and skills (competence) and the confidence and motivation (commitment) to perform at the desired level? Fourth (Figure 2-2) draw a straight line from the development level continuum to the leadership style curve. The point where the straight line intersects the curve indicates the leadership style that is most appropriate for influencing that staff member to accomplish a particular responsibility or task (Blanchard et al., 1985).

Consider the following examples of the application of the Situational Leadership II model to the health care arena (refer to Figure 2-2).

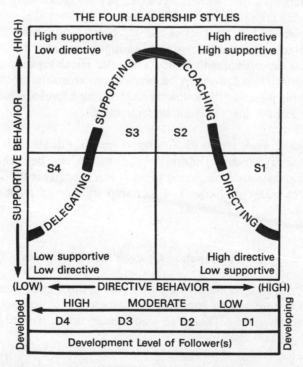

Figure 2-2 Situational Leadership II Model. *Source:* Reprinted by permission of Blanchard Training and Development, Inc. Escondido, CA, © 1985.

Example 1: You are working with a nurse's aide who is new to the organization and has never worked in health care other than her 6-month certification course. She is very willing (commitment) to do the task assigned, but her competence level is that of a beginner. She will benefit from your use of leadership style (S1), the directing approach.

Example 2: A new graduate nurse has worked for 3 months on your particular unit. She demonstrates some beginning skills, but often needs support and direction. As the head nurse, you may find the coaching leadership style (S2) to be the best form of leadership to use with this individual because she has some skills but low to moderate commitment.

Example 3: A clinical specialist has been assigned to your team. She holds a master's degree in her specialty and has 10 years' experience. She is new to the team and new to implementing a role never before used in your department. The supporting leadership style (S3) will be effective in this example because it allows for your appreciation of the follower's competency and her emerging and developing commitment to a new role.

Example 4: You are part of a group of head nurses involved in committee work. All individuals are highly motivated and have extensive experience in the leadership role. The delegating style of leadership (S4) will probably be most effective considering the high development level of the followers and their high level of education, as well as their low need for task direction.

In your small work group discuss some specific situations in which the leader has been frustrated. Determine what would have been the appropriate leadership style and compare it to what was used. This should help you find instances where a change in leadership style could most likely yield improved results.

Skill 6: Planning and Anticipating Changes and Challenges

In the future, an increasingly larger portion of the nurse leader's role will be devoted to helping and encouraging participants to respond to change (Porter-O'Grady, 1986). The nurse leader must anticipate and prepare for future changes and challenges.

Planning for change is an ongoing process (Schein, 1980). An essential first step is having well-developed support strategies. Consider these strategies in planning for change:

- Maintain a thorough, current understanding of the mission, plans, and goals of the organization to ensure that your unit goals are congruent with them.
- Be knowledgeable of plans for expansion, down-sizing, or elimination of roles and services. Effective communication of this information to staff can decrease anxiety when change occurs.
- Be confident of your role in shaping the future.
- Attack long-term problems that have depleted creative energy and disrupted unit synergy. For example, develop the following: a unit philosophy and objectives, decentralized orientation, an interview process and tool, and a standardized means of communication and feedback.
- Network with other managers within the organization and the community to validate health care trends.
- Maintain knowledge and expertise for your current role by reviewing current literature/journals, scanning tables of contents of publications, and getting on mailing lists of publishers involved with health care issues.
- Make time to read articles pertinent to your field.
- Develop contacts in many disciplines. Serve on interdisciplinary committees.
- Be open to diversity.
- Make time for moments of creativity and acknowledgment by actually scheduling them in your work schedule.
- Keep searching for new and better solutions to age-old problems.
- Allow for group thinking time.
- Develop discussion arenas to brainstorm for new solutions to age-old problems.
- Identify quality indicators of professional practice and incorporate these into your own practice.
- Analyze situations where individuals are successful, and incorporate similar attitudes and skills into your own experience.

Change in Organizations

Change is inevitable in any organization, although change for change's sake is normally not appropriate (Koontz & O'Donnell, 1968). For organizations to survive, they must learn to adapt to and plan for the changing cues in the work world (Hackman & Oldham, 1980). Often, if these cues are not recognized, the organization may seem effective and yet really may be dysfunctional. In nursing, signs of a dysfunctional response to impending change include increased absenteeism, turnover, boredom, complaints, mistakes, sabotage, job dissatisfaction, and burnout.

Change can be viewed as a dynamic form of energy that causes an interruption in a pre-existing steady state. For constructive organizational change to occur we must (1) diagnose the problem, (2) consider the etiology of the problem, and (3) decide on a treatment approach. For example, antibiotics may be an acceptable treatment for infection and yet if we have diagnosed the problem incorrectly and the patient only has a simple cold, the antibiotics will be ineffective. Likewise, if we give the antibiotics to a patient who is allergic to them, shock and death may occur. Therefore, the accurate diagnosis of the problem is essential. For constructive change to occur we must use appropriate resources to help analyze why and how change must occur. In other words, the cure should fit the disease.

There are certain times, both in our personal lives and in the life of an organization, when change is more acceptable. Consider the following principles of receptivity to change (Besse, 1957; Koontz & O'Donnell, 1968):

- Change is more acceptable when it is understood than when it is not. We need to clarify the change, the reasons for the change, and the etiology of the problem.

- Change is more acceptable when it does not threaten security than when it does. Certainly, the appropriate timing of change and an understanding of the values of our employees and our organization are essential. Change that is produced too rapidly without planning will threaten employee security and sabotage the effectiveness of the change.

- Change is more acceptable when those affected have helped create it than when it has been externally imposed. Participation in any decision-making process helps the employee own part of that decision. Therefore, change may be more successful.

- Change is more acceptable when it results from an application of previously established impersonal principles than when it is dictated by a personal order. Disregarding policies and regulations and introducing personal decisions without the involvement of staff and their participation will sabotage a successful change.

- Change is more acceptable when it follows a series of successful changes than when it follows a series of failures. It is more acceptable when it is inaugurated after prior change has been assimilated than when it is inaugurated during the confusion of other major changes. Change that is created too rapidly or amidst other failures confuses the employee and hinders the integration of the change itself. In a nurse leadership training session a colleague once remarked that in her organization she felt that change was created by everyone going to the train station, standing at the depot, and waiting for the train. The train would rush in, stop momentarily, and rush out of the train station. It would leave the staff and all the followers behind!

- Change is more acceptable if it has been planned than if it is experimental. Change requires constant evaluation, planning, directing, and controlling on the part of nurse leaders. It requires appropriate timing and clarification of role expectations and values. We have to also consider the problem behaviors that may occur when change is introduced, as well as the possible solutions. Effective planning can assist us in making these changes more acceptable.
- Change is more acceptable to people new on the job than to people who have been on the job a long time. As with personal change, the more we invest in one way of doing something, in one attitude, or in one value, the more resistant to change we are. When people are given the opportunity to face something with openness and clarity and a new start, change will tend to be more successful.
- Change is more acceptable if the organization has been trained to accept the change. Look at the history of your organization. How have other changes been adapted? What was the success rate? How do people view change? Discuss with your staff the value of change as you attempt to meet the challenges.

Planning and Implementing Change

If nursing leaders and managers are to be effective, they can no longer be content to let change occur as it will. They must develop strategies to plan, direct, and control change (Hersey & Blanchard, 1982). One of these strategies uses change cycles. It is normally easiest to present new knowledge; it is increasingly harder to change attitudes and individual behavior; and it is most difficult to change organizational and group behavior.

Change cycles are both participative and directive. Participative change cycles are implemented when new knowledge is shared and available to the group. Solutions are explored together, and the action is collectively determined. Examples of participative change strategies are management by objectives, decentralization of nursing services, and committee work designed to develop new policies and standards of care. These all employ participative change since they require consultation, feedback, and negotiation with others.

Directive change cycles tend to be forced on an organization or individual by an external source (Hersey & Blanchard, 1982). An example is a change of scheduling patterns that an organization management team directs to occur on a certain date for a certain group of people. There are times when directive change can influence the individual in a positive way and actually turn into a participative change cycle. However, participative change is usually more supported by the individual and tends to be longer lasting (Hersey & Blanchard, 1982).

A nurse leader recently discussed two examples of directive and participative change in her organization. On a particular Monday morning, staff were told that, effective immediately, their amount of vacation time would be decreased. This policy reflected a directive change. However, the administrative staff had not checked the existing vacation policy in the employee contract before announcing the change. Chaos and confusion among staff occurred. At this point, administrative staff met with a team of employees involved in negotiating contracts. The policy change was discussed, suggestions were introduced, and a participative change was then supported by both the staff and administration. Chaos and confusion were markedly reduced. Follow these 12 guidelines to increase the receptivity of your organization to change, thereby increasing the chances for the successful implementation of change:

1. Establish a common frame of reference among your staff. That is, speak the same language.
2. Develop a master plan with target dates.
3. Break the job or task into small pieces.
4. Involve staff in a participative mode when possible.
5. Define your constraints and barriers to implementing the change.
6. Identify and analyze solutions and choices.
7. Consider the ramifications of the change you are about to make.
8. Plan for evaluation to start in the beginning of the implementation process.
9. Make failure acceptable.
10. Bring out the hidden agendas of the participants.
11. Brainstorm. Many ideas in the beginning can facilitate the successful implementation of the change.
12. Consult a larger group or support group before making the final decision.

Skill 7: Evaluating Your Own Performance and Seeking Constructive Feedback for Self-Development

In a healthy professional situation, self-evaluation can be a most exciting activity. Periodic self-assessment is an important opportunity to review your accomplishments along a career path and to ensure appropriate monetary compensation for designated performance.

The process of self-evaluation begins long before a scheduled appointment with your supervisor. It starts with a thorough understanding of your position description. This document describes your areas of responsibility and accountability and is reviewed with your supervisor at the time of employment, during evaluation sessions, and at the time of role change. On these occasions, seek concurrence on the meaning and measurement of each aspect of the position description. Between evaluations, develop a quick and easy tracking system for all of your activities. For example, note daily on your calendar the projects you worked on that day. In developing your MBOs, build in incremental checkpoints with each target dated to ensure that goals are met in a timely manner.

Presently, many organizations require managers to prepare a self-evaluation. In preparation, gather the following materials and information:

- your position description
- a paragraph describing staff activities and accomplishments you have facilitated
- a summary of all special projects; attach copy of all proposals you developed
- a list of all committees on which you serve; specify your contributions and the outcome of the committee's work
- work accomplished for the organization and the community
- documentation for all CE classes attended within the evaluation period
- an annotated bibliography of all publications and presentations you have completed

After the materials are gathered, compare the accomplishments to the expectations indicated in your position's description, MBOs, and the standards agreed upon with your supervisor to measure your performance.

Be aware of any performance areas that may require improvement. Plan to address these areas constructively. Develop a well-prepared proposal for the correction of any performance deficiencies. To clarify your perspective, collaborate with a supportive colleague in preparing your self-evaluation. Such a collaboration can be mutually encouraging and creative.

Submit your self-evaluation along with the current fiscal year's MBOs and a draft of next year's MBOs. Keep a copy of all materials, as well as copies of supportive documentation gathered in preparing your evaluation. All materials should be in neat and legible form and placed sequentially in a binder. A formal package has a professional appearance, and the practice of preparing the material will be invaluable as you proceed to organize a professional portfolio for future career advancements.

The evaluation conference with your supervisor serves as a notation of "progress to date" on your MBOs and your areas of responsibility/accountability. Plans for the next year emerge naturally during the evaluation conference. Known changes in departmental and unit goals are incorporated and uncompleted projects continued through the following year's MBOs. During the conference, new trends in health care and budgetary constraints may surface to challenge you anew. Evaluation is an ongoing process, and the conference is an appropriate time to stop, reflect, and redirect.

Continuing Education and Self-Development

Many of the strategies for effective planned change require the nurse manager to remain up to date in her skills and thinking. Each individual is responsible for assuring her continued competency in a role beyond the level of licensure. Continuing education (CE) courses are an effective means of increasing clinical knowledge and developing an awareness of self in relation to others. Additionally, continuing education serves to expand your horizons.

How can a busy manager maintain role competency? *Develop a master plan.* At evaluation time, identify areas of performance with which you are dissatisfied. Seek out appropriate learning experiences to correct deficiencies or enhance your performance. Inform colleagues of your plan. Through networking you may discover an exciting learning experience that meets your needs exactly. Most staff development departments are an excellent resource for CE brochures and catalogues. Submit your name for inclusion on mailing lists of educational entities that specialize in subject content pertinent to your goals.

To stay abreast of trends, review regularly the contents of journals on health care and nursing. Photocopy pertinent or intriguing articles to read, and systematically set aside the time to do so. File articles by subject content for future referencing convenience.

Identify the current issues that you are facing in your work situation. Discuss these with your work colleagues and contemporaries outside the organization. They may confirm the appropriateness of your plans/decisions and contribute timely advice. Community-based special interest groups are a rich source of collegial expertise. One network of broad experience and a possible springboard to future professional opportunities is the local chapter of the Society of Nursing Service Administrators.

Skill 8: Appreciating and Learning How to Use the Power of Your Own Role and That of the Organization

You may now find yourself in one of the most exciting and powerful roles you have had thus far in your career: that of nursing leadership. In order to create positive working environments and effective health career delivery we must abandon our old attitudes and operate within the realities of the late 20th century. Nursing managers who are disillusioned and vehement objectors, or those who benignly stand by as observers, must and can be converted to courageous nurse leaders who can challenge the institutional status quo. Despite the limited opportunities for creativity, nurse leaders must unremittingly pursue their own agenda as visionary strategists. Although power is by no means the sole motivation in the nursing profession, it is a fact of life that influences the ability of the profession to grow, leadership to be enhanced, and patient care to be achieved (McFarland & Schiflett, 1979).

What We Know about Power

The concepts of leadership cannot be discussed in isolation; power is an important component. Leadership is often defined as the process of influencing and motivating an individual or group in efforts toward goal accomplishment. Power, then, is the leader's influence potential (Hersey & Blanchard, 1982). Given the relationship between leader and followers, the leader must understand how to use power effectively. We need power for several reasons:

- to control professional practice
- to be able to coordinate and direct care
- to get the job done with less stress
- to promote health legislation and our significant role as a provider of that health care

Power is a necessary means to a legitimate end: professional control over practice (Storlie, 1982). Given our need for professional control over practice, development of power is each nurse's responsibility. The use of power is not reserved only for nurse leaders at the highest organizational level but is also essential for nurse leaders at all levels.

We are often prevented from obtaining power because of our failure to support one another. Failure to support each other or misuse of power within our professional family has been one of the major deterrents to cohesiveness and power within the profession (Ashley, 1973).

Power can be seen as an energy. Using the analogy of a kettle full of boiling water, the steam that rises can be viewed as power. That steam then is energy, and the tea kettle is the organization within which we work. We might ask ourselves: How do we collect and use this energy? The energy of power flows and rarely remains in solid form. It can be used as rapidly and freely or with as much constraint as the leader and followers direct. Power is ideally a healthy and dynamic source of energy used to influence others (Clary & Luke, 1975). If allowed to flow unchecked, however, the energy may diffuse, dissipate, or be taken over by another, leaving the leader and follower without a substantial substitute. The nurse leader uses her power to create and define options necessary in the enactment of her role. The ultimate test of the leader is his or her wise use of power (Bennis, 1973).

To attain a clearer understanding of how you perceive and use power, complete Exhibit 2-2, an exercise on leadership and power.

As you ask yourself these questions about power and your powerful experiences, can you identify ways in which you truly use the power available to you? Can you name those people—mentors and role models—who support your use of power?

Types of Power

French and Raven (1959) describe six important sources of power.

1. *Expert power* is what all nurse leaders experience when they feel competent and in control of their particular areas of work or when they are utilized as resources to staff, patients, and families. Hersey and Blanchard (1969) indicate that a leader high in expert power is respected as possessing the expertise to facilitate the work behavior of others. This respect often leads to compliance with the leader's wishes.
2. *Legitimate power* is the power ascribed to an individual based on his or her position. A leader high in legitimate power induces compliance or influences others because they feel this person has the right, by virtue of his or her position in the organization, to expect that suggestions will be followed.
3. *Reward power* is based on the leader's ability to provide rewards for other people. Staff members believe that their compliance will lead to gaining positive incentives, such as pay, promotion, and/or recognition from the leader or the source of reward power.
4. *Coercive power* is usually associated with punishment or force. It is based on fear. A leader high in coercive power induces compliance because failure to comply will lead to punishment, such as undesirable work assignments, reprimands, or dismissal.
5. *Referent power* is based on the leader's personal traits. A leader high in referent power is generally liked and admired by others because of his or her personality. This liking for, admiration of, and identification with the leader influence others. Others often defer to the person with referent power based on his or her experience, knowledge, or information.
6. *Information power* belongs to those who hold the facts, figures, associations, and data necessary to do the job. This form of power can be given

Exhibit 2-2 Leadership and Power Exercise

Complete the following statements:
  I feel powerful when:

  I feel powerless when:

  Past power experiences have included:

  Current power experiences include:

  The most powerful influence in my life is:

  Behaviors that support my feeling personally powerful are:

  Power in my organization is best seen in the following ways:

or withheld, thus influencing outcomes when adequate, accurate information is required.

Many leaders possess more than one type of power, though there will generally be one that dominates or is most characteristic.

Power is demonstrated in organizations in various ways (Clary & Luke, 1975). Organizational power can be competitive. For example, hospitals that compete for existing resources, salaries, promotions, and staffing with other organizations use competitive power strategies. Power may also be experienced through collaboration. Organizations that share existing resources demonstrate collaboration. Organizations using catalytic power allow existing energy in the organization to be released. Catalytic power releases the expert skills and collective energy of the professional nurse leader group; its use is both wise and resourceful. Examples include:

- asking nurse leaders to be involved in community action projects
- encouraging nurses to serve as faculty/speakers in designated educational formats
- involving nurses in the whole picture of organizational growth and not limiting them to specifically-defined nursing care

Power often involves a struggle as the organizational goals and needs are weighed against group and individual goals and needs. For power to be used effectively, interpersonal relationships within the work group must be enhanced and needs and tasks coordinated.

Personal Power

When we express and demonstrate self-confidence and self-esteem coupled with a sense of goal direction, we exude personal power. The leader who accepts and learns from failures, welcomes challenges, takes risks, utilizes mentors and role models, and makes choices demonstrates personal power. Powerful nursing leaders have a positive regard for themselves, as well as for their colleagues and make consistent use of legitimate support and guidance. They seek out new challenges while working to achieve increased support and direction.

Strategies for Development of Personal Power. A variety of strategies can be used to develop personal power and obtain more influence in the work setting:

- To develop expert power, become competent in your own role and clinical skill.
- Develop your interpersonal ability to work with individuals and groups.
- Exhibit a willingness to give and receive feedback.
- Communicate what people need to know.
- Keep very personal data out of the work setting.
- Speak up. Don't be afraid to be right and don't be afraid to be assertive.
- Accept as well as give praise and recognition.
- Network.
- Don't let others take credit for what you do.
- Learn to say "no" without apology.
- When you must fire, demote, or transfer, do so quickly, fairly, and with documentation and support.
- If you work in an environment in which a clinical uniform is not worn, dress for business, not for a party. If in uniform, appear sharp and neat.

- Avoid symbols of powerlessness; for example, cluttered desks, pieces of paper everywhere.
- Don't ask permission for everything. Be selective.
- Take advice from "old hands" with caution.
- Be positive in your communications.
- Delegate to those who know how.
- Don't engage in petty criticism.
- Learn to speak in public.
- Recognize where your support is found in the organization.
- Do not allow yourself to be criticized in front of your staff.
- Note positive developments in writing. Discuss negative developments in person.

Teaching Your Work Group about Power

It is useful to teach your staff about power and its appropriate utilization. The following exercise (Exhibit 2-3) gives your group the opportunity to observe one particular team's use of resources that have been distributed unequally and to learn how to negotiate using expert, referent, informational, coercive, legitimate, and reward power. This exercise is especially useful within a staff development program or in a leadership training course. See the Resources list for information on obtaining this exercise.

Exhibit 2-3 The Unequal Resources Exercise

Group Size: This task may be done with clusters in groups of one to four members each. If more than one cluster of four groups is used, the facilitator may add the dimension of competition between, as well as within, clusters. The facilitator may ask several participants to be process observers.

Time Required: Approximately 1 hour, depending on the number and complexity of the tasks assigned and the ages of the group members.

Materials:

- scissors, ruler, paper clips, glue, black felt-tip markers, and construction paper in six colors
- Unequal Resources Task Sheet for each group.
- large envelopes to hold each group's resources; in the example below, the envelopes contain the following resources as designated by group

  Group I: scissors, ruler, paper clips, pencils, and two 4-inch squares of red paper and two of white

continues

Exhibit 2-3 continued

> Group II: scissors, glue and 8½ × 11 inch sheets of paper (2 blue, 2 white, 2 gold)
>
> Group III: felt-tip markers and 8½ × 11 inch sheets of paper (2 green, 2 white, 2 gold)
>
> Group IV: 8½ × 11 inch sheets of paper (1 green, gold, blue, red, and purple)

Physical setting: Table and chairs for each group. These should be placed far enough away from each other so the group's power position is not betrayed by casual observation.

Process:

1. The facilitator asks groups to be seated at their tables and then distributes an envelope of material and a task sheet to each group.
2. The facilitator asks the groups not to open their materials until told to begin the task. The facilitator then explains that each group has different materials but that each group must complete the same tasks. The facilitator explains that they may bargain for the use of materials and tools in any way that is mutually agreeable and emphasizes that the first group to complete all its tasks is the winner. (If clusters are competing, there will be both a group winner and a cluster winner.)
3. The facilitator gives the signal to begin and attempts to observe as much group and bargaining behavior as is possible so that he or she can supply some feedback during the final phase.
4. The facilitator stops the process when winners have been declared and groups have been allowed to complete ongoing tasks.
5. During the discussion, the participants may make process observations concerning the use of resources, sharing, bargaining, competition, group behavior, power, and the ethics of power.
6. The facilitator may alter the complexity of the task and the distribution of resources to fit many different types of groups and educational levels. As this is a teaching tool, an analogy may be drawn between this experience and how other groups or work teams relate to experiences of diminished power.

Unequal Resources Task Sheet

Instructions: Each work group is to be given a copy of these instructions. Each group is to complete the following tasks:

1. Make a 3″ × 3″ square of white paper.
2. Make a 4″ × 2″ rectangle of gold paper.
3. Make a four-link paper chain, each link in a different color.
4. Make a "T"-shaped piece 3″ × 5″ in green and white paper.
5. Make a 4″ × 4″ flag in any three colors.

The first group to complete all tasks is the winner. Using their power groups may bargain or negotiate with other groups for the use of materials and tools to complete the tasks on any mutually agreeable basis.

Process observers should be assigned for each group.

Source: Adapted from : J. William Pfeiffer and John E. Jones (Eds.), *The 1972 Annual Handbook for Group Facilitators.* San Diego, CA: University Associates, Inc., 1972. Used with permission.

This exercise is an excellent way to assess your own group's ability to collaborate verses compete. Discussion after the exercise can focus on the following issues:

- sources of power in each group
- the use of individual and personal power
- when power is shared
- what role is played by ethics and the use of power
- what happens when resources are unequal
- what the strengths and weaknesses were in negotiating for resources
- who helped and supported
- which group was able to amass the greatest number of resources and why it was able to do so

REFERENCES

Ashley, J. (1973). This I believe about power in nursing. *Nursing Outlook, 21*(10), 641.

Bennis, W.G. (1973). *Beyond bureaucracy. Essays on the development and evolution of the human organization.* New York: McGraw-Hill.

Bennis, W.G., & Benne, K (1976). *The planning of change.* New York: Holt, Rhinehart & Winston.

Bennis, W.G., & Thomas, J.M., Eds. (1972). Harmondsworth, England: Penguin Books.

Besse, R. (1957). Company planning must be planned. *Dun's Review & Modern Industry, 69*(44), 62–63.

Blanchard, K., Zigarmi, P., & Zigarmi, D. (1985). *Leadership and the one-minute manager.* New York: William Morrow & Co.

Clary, T., & Luke, R. (1975). Organizational and individual power. *Training and Development Journal,* April 1975, 41–50.

Drucker, P. (1954). *The practice of management.* New York: Harper & Row

Fiedler, F. (1967). *A theory of leadership effectiveness.* New York: McGraw-Hill.

French, R., & Raven, B. (1959). *The bases of social power.* Ann Arbor, MI: Cartwright.

Ganong, J., & Ganong, W. (1976). *Nursing management.* Rockville, MD: Aspen Publishers, Aspen Systems, Inc.

Hackman, R., & Oldham, G. (1980). *Work redesign.* Reading, MA: Addison-Wesley.

Hersey, P., & Blanchard, H. (1969). Life cycle theory of leadership. *Training and Development Journal,* May.

Hersey, P., & Blanchard, H. (1982). *Management of organizational behavior: Utilizing human resources* (4th ed.). Englewood Cliffs, NJ: Prentice-Hall.

Koontz, H., & O'Donnell, C. (1968). *Principles of management* (4th ed.). St. Louis: McGraw-Hill.

McFarland, D., & Schiflett, N. (1979). The role of power in the nursing profession. *Nursing Dimensions, 7*(2), 12.

Pfeiffer, J. W., & Jones, J.E. (1983). *The 1983 Annual: Developing human resources.* San Diego: University Associates.

Porter-O'Grady, T. (1986). *Creative nursing administration.* Rockville, MD: Aspen Publishers, Inc.

Porter-O'Grady, T., & Finnigan, S. (1984). *Shared governace for nursing: A creative approach to professional accountability.* Rockville, MD: Aspen Publishers, Inc.

Preston, P. (1981). Power: how to get it and keep it. *Occupational Health Nursing,* Sept. 1981, 12–18.

Rheiner, N. (1982). Role theory framework for change. *Nursing Management Journal, 13*(3),

Schein, E. (1980). *Organizational psychology* (3rd ed.). Englewood Cliffs, NJ: Prentice-Hall.

Storlie, J. (1982). Power—getting a piece of the action. *Journal of Nursing Management, 10*(13), 15–18.

RESOURCES

Situational Leadership II Developmental TASK Analysis II and Leader Behavior Analysis II is available from:

Blanchard Training and Development, Inc.
125 State Place
Escondido, CA 92025
(619-489-5005)

The organization also provides in-house training and leadership development programs.

The *1972 Annual-Developing Human Resources* Unequal Resources Exercise is available from:

University Associates, Inc.
8517 Production Avenue
San Diego, CA 92121

APPENDIX 2-A

Role Assessment Questions

The following list of questions provides a basis for developing an assessment tool for role analysis to use whether you are interviewing for a prospective new role or implementing and defining a new role in your current position.

QUESTIONS TO PROSPECTIVE EMPLOYERS OR ORGANIZATIONAL ROLE SENDERS

- What specific responsibilities of this position do you regard as most important? What are your additional expectations?
- How do you operate in terms of delegation of responsibility, and what is your general operating style?
- Are there any characteristics of an employee that are particularly distasteful to you?
- What is the degree of freedom with which an employee can act in terms of responsibility and accountability?
- What criteria will be used in the selection of a successful applicant?
- What criteria will be used in evaluating the performance of an employee in this position?
- Is there a current position description?
- How much orientation (time, process) is allocated for this position?
- What are your personal goals for the department?
- What are your goals for the area for which I would be responsible?

Source: © 1984 Tatiana Isaeff Cordoni.

- What do you envision that I would accomplish in this position within 3 months? 1 year?
- What impact does your organizational structure have on the position for which I am an applicant?
- What short-term and long-term problems exist in this department? What are the problems in the area for which I would be responsible?
- From your perspective, what are the major frustrations in the position for which I am applying?
- How would you describe the working relationships (of claimant groups)?
- What budget (resources) is (are) available to me in regard to staffing, salary, position category changes, use of consultants, purchasing equipment, and implementing planned change (growth or cutbacks)?
- How are new ideas accepted?
- What authority do I have for changes in my area in regard to policies, procedures, and performance expectations?
- Are there any identifiable roadblocks to change?
- What is the climate of interdepartmental relationships? How well do the disciplines mesh?
- What salary range and benefits exist for this position? How are salaries initially negotiated? How are they modified?

Appendix 2-B

Management by Objectives

In the process of developing objectives, keep notes as you are gathering data. Request clarification of details and examples of previously approved work. Share your philosophies with the role sender. This experience is stimulating, even for managers who have worked a long time in their roles. Use it as an opportunity to reconceptualize your role or reaffirm your commitment to it. The process is also a way to maintain a contemporary perspective. Review current literature and network with interest groups outside your organization to increase the breadth of your assessment.

INSTRUCTIONS

1. Pick four to six objectives.
2. Separate them into categories: operational or fiscal. (You need to have both.)
3. Place objectives in priority order within each category. (The highest priority is placed first.)
4. Assign a percentage weight to each objective to total 100 percent.
5. Base dates on the fiscal year.

The objectives in Table 2B-1 are examples to illustrate the flexibility and uniqueness you can have in developing objectives to meet your individual needs. There is nothing sacred about this list. The objectives fit under these eight categories:

1. unit philosophy (operational)
2. decentralized orientation (operational)

Source: © 1984 Tatiana Isaeff Cordoni.

3. developmental standards (operational)
4. HPPD (fiscal)
5. overtime (fiscal)
6. systems to enhance communication (operational)
7. unit developmental plans (operational)
8. certifications (operational)

Several terms can be used in the objectives you write. Instead of the word "develop," use:

- compose
- plan
- propose
- design
- formulate
- create
- prepare
- assemble

Replace the word "implement" with one of these terms:

- operationalize
- activate
- use
- schedule

Instead of the word "evaluate," you can use:

- judge
- appraise
- compare
- revise
- modify
- select

Table 2B-1 Sample Objectives

Priority	Operational Objectives*	Weight
	Unit Philosophy Develop (or revise) a written unit philosophy by(date)	
	Decentralized Orientation 1. Evaluate present decentralized orientation by(date)	
	2. Identify written outcome objectives, specific learning activities, and key resource people for each day of decentralized orientation by(date)	
	3. Sequence revised orientation program to accommodate the experienced specialty employee vs. a transfer employee vs. a new graduate by(date)	
	4. Implement revised decentralized orientation program by(date)	

Table 2B-1 continued

Priority	Operational Objectives*	Weight
	5. Evaluate effectiveness of revised decentralized orientation program by(date)	
	6. Develop A-V tape (or module) on (you select topic, i.e., shunt care, hemodynamic monitoring, CPM device, etc.) for decentralized orientation by(date)	

Developmental Standards

1. Assess unit staff to determine normal standard performance behaviors expected (clarify categories) at the end of orientation, 1 year, 2 years or longer by(date)
2. Form unit task group to (could fill in #1 objective or #3 objective) and recommend to nurse manager by(date)
3. Compose first draft of developmental standards (specifying expected performance behaviors of RNs, LVNs, etc.) at end of orientation, 1 year, 2 years or longer by(date)
4. Evaluate and revise present developmental standards into the following time periods (at end of orientation, 1 year, 2 years or longer) by(date)
5. Implement (can identify Phase I, II, etc.) developmental standards by(date)

Communication

1. Implement routine unit meetings every 6 weeks by(date)
2. Develop a standardized communication process for staff who are unable to attend unit meetings by(date)
3. Form a unit task group to recommend ways of improving unit meetings to nurse managers by(date)

Developmental Plans

1. Develop a written 6–9 month unit developmental plan (the specifics of psychosocial rounds, grand rounds, unit inservices, patient care conferences, etc.) by(date)
2. Implement a 6–9 month developmental plan by(date)

Certifications

1. Implement a system that assures that ACLS certification and recertification will be maintained current by policy (with a 3-month variation) by(date)
2. Develop a unit record system that reports current certification status of all staff by(date)

Fiscal Objectives

1. Maintain 100% productivity on a weekly basis for the fiscal year by(date)
2. Maintain overtime within 1% for the fiscal year by(date)
3. Reduce lost charges by 50% for current year from past fiscal year by(date)

*Not in priority order.

Appendix 2-C

A Completed Fiscal Year Plan

Priority	Objectives	Weight(%)
	OPERATIONAL OBJECTIVES	
I.	Orientation	
	A. Centralized Competency-Based Orientation (CCBO)	15
	1. Implement Phase I of a CCBO by August, 1988.	
	2. Present a written plan for Phase II of CCBO by August 31, 1988.	
	B. Staff Development Instructor Orientation	15
	1. Develop program by June 25, 1988.	
	2. Offer program to two new staff by July 8, 1988.	
	3. Evaluate effectiveness of the program by August 31, 1988.	
II.	Educational Curriculum	
	A. Construct and administer a written needs assessment tool to all nursing personnel by June 25, 1988.	10
	B. Tabulate and present priority data in the following categories—common hospital-wide needs, shift needs, and unit needs—by July 11, 1988.	10
	C. Prepare, participate in, and offer management development activities.	5
	Present eight developmental/team activities for Nursing Management by June 30, 1988, e.g., Performance Appraisal, Interviewing, Quarterly Report, Retreat, four follow-up retreats.	
III.	Regulatory Standards Compliance	20
	A. Review, evaluate, and correct departmental deficiencies to assure compliance with JCAH, Title 22, and BRN by July 25, 1988.	

continues

Priority	Objectives	Weight(%)
	FISCAL OBJECTIVES (in priority order)	
I.	Orientation, paid educational leave (PEL) and education budget	15
	A. Develop and submit guidelines for orientation and PEL by February, 1988.	
	B. Develop guidelines for the education budget by June 27, 1988. Submit to Associate Administrator–Nursing by June 28, 1988.	
II.	Marketing Plan	10
	A. Submit a written contemporary marketing plan for the staff development department activities. TOTAL	100

Source: © 1984 Tatiana Isaeff Cordoni

Chapter 3

Role of the Work Environment

The nurse leader of today is continually facing the challenges of an ever-changing world and attempting to manage key change issues. The health care industry is going through a metamorphosis of expanding technology, new clients/consumer orientation, and emerging unfamiliar corporate models in an attempt to maximize services in a time of downsizing and reallocation of resources. As a result of these changes, attitudes, values, and a sense of direction for both ourselves as professionals and the health care organizations in which we enact our professional role are in a state of transition.

Workers' needs, as well as the environment, are changing rapidly. External and internal forces, attitudes, values, and feelings about the contemporary state of health care are pulling the professional in the environment in a thousand different directions. Change, which seems to be relentless, can negatively affect the productivity, satisfaction, and health of health care professionals.

Because leadership is practiced with people working in their work setting, it is essential for nursing leaders to understand the effect of the work and work setting on nurses and their practice. Behavior (B) in any particular situation can be understood as a result of the person (P) interacting with the environment(E): $B = P(E)$ (Lewin, 1951). To achieve the desired behavior—productivity from healthy, satisfied workers—requires a synergistic fit between the nurse and the job in a nourishing work environment. We need to understand the changing needs of nurses and job fit requirements in the changing environment to realize the costs to productivity of a poor job fit.

JOB FIT AND CHANGING WORKER NEEDS

When a good fit exists between people and their jobs, productivity, personal rewards, and satisfaction usually result. In such a situation, management has only to support an already existing healthy system (Hackman &

Oldham, 1980). However, we know that hard work in a job with a poor fit often leads to personal discomfort, individual stress, and many costs to the organization (Hackman & Oldham, 1980).

A nurse leader must address certain considerations about people and their work fit. It is a conservative estimate that 20 percent of all employees are inappropriately matched in their jobs. Out of the 30 million employees in the United States, 6 million thus have a poor fit with their job design or work design (Hackman & Oldham, 1980). What an alarming thought! Many of these 6 million people are underutilized. They may have more skills than the employer seeks or more aspirations than the job can satisfactorily meet. The work may be unfulfilling.

Studies completed in the 1940s and 1950s reported that employees (many of whom had lived through the Depression of the 1930s) considered their chief need to be steady employment. In contrast, studies conducted in the late 1960s showed the need for interesting work to be the highest priority, with job security ranked as seventh out of eight of the most desired aspects of work. Thus, a major shift in values related to work, reward and lifestyle has occurred, with today's worker wanting more intrinsic reward.

Two popular books, *Working* by Studs Terkel (1972) and John Naisbitt's *Megatrends* (1982), discuss employment trends of the 1980s through the year 2000 and the expressed need of workers to find meaning in work and to obtain the needed support to do their jobs well. As workers develop to assume more complex job requirements, their need for support is increased. The support needed includes more knowledge and skill, clarity of goals, and more feedback about performance as they develop and assume more complexity within their role.

Hospitals are the third largest industry in the United States, and yet they often lag behind other industries in dealing with employees' changing needs and productivity. Nursing leaders who learn to deal actively with the changing needs of the employee are more apt to succeed.

People who do not feel valued at work often accept this fate, but withdraw and become unproductive. Sometimes we do not even see this adaptation occurring, especially when changes occur slowly in the organization. Leaders may often need to be detectives, searching for clues, looking for symptoms of lost productivity in the workplace. Poor job fit and lack of reward may then be found.

Approaches to people and work design have changed over the decades as we have learned to improve job fit and work rewards. For instance, we can better match the people to the job through improved selection, placement, or training, thereby avoiding placing overqualified personnel in less challenging positions. Supervisors can be trained to implement change strategies, or we can improve supervisory selection and training. We can change the context in which the employees perform by adding workplace amenities and improving work schedules. We can provide counseling, team building, people-oriented supervision, peer support, mentoring, flex time, and job sharing (Hackman & Oldham, 1980).

Changing the consequences of work by altering the contingencies that determine the benefits and costs to the employee also has positive outcomes (Hackman & Oldham, 1980). For example, positive reinforcement by the supervisor, payment of bonus perks, or promotion as a consequence of some task that has been accomplished may enable the employee to feel valued and rewarded for her actual accomplishments.

OCCUPATIONAL STRESS AND ITS OUTCOMES

By using a stress and coping framework, we can understand the worker within the work environment and begin to build a more nourishing work environment.

Occupational stress is the response of the person to demands experienced in the work place. According to Newman and Beehr (1979, p.1), "job stress refers to a situation wherein job related factors interact with the worker to change (i.e., distrupt or enhance) his or her psychological and/or physiological condition such that the person (i.e., mind-body) is forced to deviate from normal functioning." Occupational stress has consequences for worker health, job satisfaction, and job performance.

Nursing is a high-stress profession (Smith, Colligan, & Hurrel, 1978). The effects of work stress are well documented in research. The stress of a difficult work environment, poor job fit, and insufficient job rewards hinders productivity (Beehr, 1976; Schmidt, 1978; Van Sell, Brief, & Schuler, 1981). Quality and quantity of patient care diminish, job satisfaction decreases (Bedeian, Armenakis, & Curran, 1981; House & Rizzo, 1972; Schuler, 1979), and personal health of the worker is compromised (Rosch, 1979; Selye, 1976).

Figure 3-1 shows the relationships among stressors (personal and work environment), stress and coping, and outcomes. Although stressors have a direct effect on outcomes (e.g., health, job satisfaction, and productivity), coping also influences outcomes. It is not just the perception or experience of stress that matters but the ability to cope that determines the outcome (Lazarus, 1981; see Chapter 12, Stress Management).

Costs to Productivity and the Worker

Today, in both industry and health care settings, a crisis exists in the quality of work life and its relationship to productivity (Hackman & Oldham, 1980). In 1976, 8 million hours were lost to absenteeism. Turnover

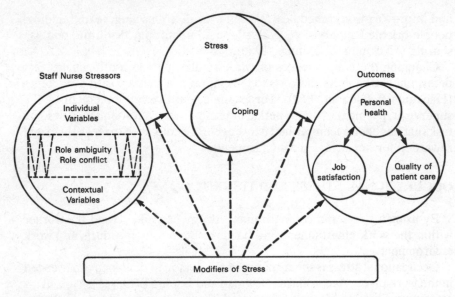

Figure 3-1 Relationship of Stressors, Stress/Coping, and Outcomes. *Source:* From "Stress and Coping in Psychiatric Nursing" by L. Trygstad, 1984.

---

rates, which averaged 1–2 percent per month in 1960, doubled by 1970. More recently, an average of 5–10 percent of General Motors' hourly workers were found to be missing from work without explanation every day (Hackman & Oldham, 1980). The incidence of tardiness, arguments, illnesses, and grievances has increased in industrial settings. Thus, the product cost increases. Is this not also true of the health care industry?

In high-stress occupations, the evidence of turnover, burnout, and physical and emotional illness is overwhelming. The cost of lost productivity due to stress-related factors and the cost of replacing human resources were estimated in 1980 to be $1,300 per employed person per year (Adams, 1981).

In nursing, the high rate of turnover is very expensive. The cost of replacing an experienced nurse ranges from $2,500–12,000 (Fagin, 1982; Schuler, 1980). Patient perception of low quality of care can cost the health care institution its clients. Accidents and nurse errors also have economic costs.

Health Outcomes

Four health-related outcomes of occupational stress are (Margolis et al., 1974):

1. short-term subjective states, e.g., anxiety, tension, anger

2. long-term psychological responses, e.g., depression, malaise, alienation
3. transient physiological responses, e.g., levels of catecholamines, blood pressure
4. physical health, e.g., gastrointestinal disorders, coronary artery disease, asthmatic attacks

High blood pressure, cardiovascular disorders, and peptic ulcers are symptoms or diseases that are often related to stress in organizations (Schuler, 1980). In a study of 51 female psychiatric nurses, higher job stress predicted greater severity of any illness experienced (Davenport, 1983). Other predictors of greater severity of illness are recent life changes and lack of social support.

Job Satisfaction Outcomes

In a review of the literature on job stress, employee health, and organizational effectiveness, Beehr and Newman (1978) reported that job dissatisfaction is a frequent consequence of job stress. There is a consistent correlation between job stress and job dissatisfaction.

Lawler (1973) describes four theories of job satisfaction: (1) *fulfillment theory:* when the individual's needs are met, job satisfaction occurs; (2) *discrepancy theory:* satisfaction occurs when what is wanted is consistent with what does occur or is expected to occur; (3) *equity theory:* satisfaction occurs when the individual perceives a balance between input and output; and (4) *two-factor theory:* intrinsic characteristics (achievement, responsibility, work itself) promote satisfaction, whereas extrinsic characteristics (supervision, salary) elicit dissatisfaction.

Many research studies have identified factors associated with job satisfaction or dissatisfaction. In a longitudinal study of 1,259 RNs, the degree of autonomy was the strongest predictor of job satisfaction (Lawler, 1973). Work satisfaction is enhanced by participation in decision making, social support from one's immediate supervisor and co-workers, a good fit between the job and the worker (Weisman, Alexander, & Chase, 1980), and higher position in the organization (Slocum, Susman, & Sheridan, 1972).

Quality of Nursing Care Outcomes

Quality of nursing care delivered is one aspect of job performance. Decreased quality and/or quantity of work is a consequence of job stress. In a study of 124 nurses employed in hospitals, significant negative correlations were found between occupational role stress (role conflict and role ambiguity) and job satisfaction, perception of own individual performance, and unit effectiveness (Posner & Randolph, 1980).

The importance of stress in nursing work goes beyond economic considerations. Nursing is concerned with person, environment, and health (Fawcett, 1978), the same factors that are important in understanding stress. Understanding the health effects of job stress for the nurse in the nursing work environment can contribute to nursing knowledge. Nurses particularly need this knowledge because we use ourselves as the instrument of our care. The manager's attention to employee stress and health can help the staff become better role models and teachers for patients and improve the care given through the use of their healthy selves. One could logically assume that improved personal health and the delivery of quality nursing care will increase job satisfaction for many nurses.

ASSESSING STRESSORS AND BURNOUT PROMOTERS

The first step in changing anything is becoming aware that it is so. Without awareness, neither the problem nor alternative possibilities can be considered.

Exhibit 3-1 lists stressors and burnout promoters commonly found in nursing. This assessment list was derived from research findings on stress that are relevant to nursing.

Exhibit 3-1 Stressors and Burnout Promoters

INDIVIDUAL STRESSORS
Individual characteristics
Needs and values: achievement, feedback, self-control, certainty, predictability, interpersonal recognition and acceptance, fairness and justice, stimulation, personal space, responsibility, and meaningfulness or purpose
Abilities and experience: familiarity with the situation, past exposure to the stressor, and practice or training dealing with the situation
Personality and coping strategies: type A personality, external locus of control, and learned problem-focused and emotion-focused coping
Socialization experience
Expectations fostered by nursing education are unmet in work situations

STRESSORS FROM ORGANIZATIONAL CHARACTERISTICS
Lack of human resource primacy
Downward communication flow only
Decisions made at the top without input from affected workers
Minimal participation in total organization
Absence of established channels for dealing with problems and complaints
Under- or overpromotion
Low pay

Exhibit 3-1 continued

Insufficient training
Job insecurity

STRESSORS IN THE PHYSICAL ENVIRONMENT
High levels of noise
High levels of light, some types of lighting
High levels of toxins
Lack of space or privacy
Lack of resources
Physical danger

STRESSORS IN THE SOCIAL ENVIRONMENT
Poor relationships with peers/minimal support
Poor relationships with subordinates
Poor relationships with supervisors/minimal support

ROLE STRESS: Variables That Make Role Enactment More Difficult
Role ambiguity: clear information is lacking about expectations, methods for fulfilling
    expectations, and/or the consequences of role performance
Role conflict: incongruent role expectations (contradictory messages from one person,
    two persons have contradictory expectations, two of your roles conflict, your sense
    of self conflicts with your role)
Role overload: too much to do

STRESSORS FROM JOB CHARACTERISTICS
Boundary-spanning requirements
Ongoing interaction with ill persons
Responsibility for well-being of patients without the authority to control that well-
    being
Fast-paced work
Repetitive job tasks
Long hours
Time pressures
Rotating shifts, especially if more frequent than every third week
Insufficient information to make a decision
No one best solution to a problem
Emotionally charged issues

BEHAVIORS THAT PROMOTE BURNOUT
Idealistic *expectations* followed by disillusionment
Conflict between personal and institutional values
Overinvolvement in work: trying to be and do everything, working long hours
Taking responsibility for others, rescuing
Evaluating job performance and connecting self-esteem to gratitude and change from
    clients
Imbalance in the giving and receiving of nurturing
Not allowing process of *separation/change:* avoiding what is happening and not dealing
    with feelings

Source: From "Stress and Coping in Psychiatric Nursing" by L. Trygstad, 1984.

Job stress for nurses employed in hospitals may be caused by individual factors, contextual factors, and/or the interaction of contextual and individual factors (see Figure 3-1). Individual factors include the person's needs, values, abilities, experience, personality, and socialization. Contextual factors include organizational structure, policies and procedures, job characteristics, supervisory and coworker behavior, and the behavior of other personnel. Role conflict and role ambiguity are examples of stressors produced by the interaction of individual and contextual variables. When contextual factors become stressors, the individual nurse may lack the ability to alter them. These contextual factors also influence the individual nurse's ability to cope with other work stressors, such as dealing with difficult clients.

Review the list of stressors and burnout promoters and mark those that you experience. This is your first step toward increased awareness of stress factors in your work setting that you may want to change.

Individual Variables Affecting Occupational Stress

Individual differences are important in understanding stress. Different individuals have different tolerances for levels of stress. What is experienced as an excessive level of stress by one nurse may be the same level of stress that elicits a feeling of well-being in another. In fact, what elicits stress in the same person may vary over time. Individual needs and values, abilities and experience, personality and constitutional makeup, and strategies for coping affect one's perception of the stress experienced in any particular situation (Schuler, 1980). Understanding these specific variables for any individual can help explain the level of stress experienced by her. The nurse leader can use her understanding of self and others as the first step in planned change.

Needs and Values

Needs are defined as physiological and psychological requirements. Values are more subjective. Each of us has different values, and we vary in the extent to which meeting our different values is important to us. In a review of the literature, Schuler (1980) identified these needs and values that affect the perception of stress: achievement, feedback, self-control, certainty, predictability, interpersonal recognition and acceptance, fairness and justice, stimulation, personal space, responsibility, and meaningfulness or purpose. For example, the nurse who has a great need to achieve but is in a situation where achievement is blocked will feel a great deal of stress. The nurse who is very happy with the status quo will not feel stressed in the same situation. Our individual needs and values determine what we perceive as stressful.

Abilities and Experience

Our abilities and experience affect our perception of stress (McGrath, 1970, 1976). Three factors increase arousal of the body to the demands made on it: (1) when the demands are perceived to exceed the individual's ability to meet them, (2) when there is uncertainty about the rewards or costs involved in meeting the demands, and/or (3) when there is a significant difference in rewards or costs according to whether or not the demands are met.

In contrast, familiarity with the situation, past exposure to the stressor, and/or practice or training in dealing with the situation can reduce the perceived threat (McGrath, 1976). Remember the first time you gave an injection? Do you have the same response today when you give an injection? It is not that giving an injection is different today, but rather that your past exposure, practice, and training have made giving an injection less stressful. Enhancing familiarity with a task by practice will likely diminish the stress experienced in the situation.

Personality and Coping Strategies

The degree of role stress perceived by an individual is partly a function of personality (Bedeian, Armenakis, & Curran, 1980; Organ & Greene, 1974). In a study of over 200 respondents in a hospital nursing service Bedeian et al. (1980) concluded that personality influences the amount of role ambiguity and role conflict experienced. They further concluded that (1) an individual's personality disposition elicits particular responses from surrounding individuals, (2) personality factors often mediate between events which happen and the perception of these events which determine experienced levels of role stress, and (3) certain personality dispositions lead to more extensive use of some forms of coping behaviors.

Much of the work with personality effects has compared perception of and responses to stress of Type A and Type B personalities. Type A personalities perceive more stress (Orpen, 1982) and report a greater relationship between workload and anxiety (Bedeian et al., 1980). In a study of occupational stress, Type A behavior, and physical well being involving 57 nurses, Ivancevich, Matteson, and Preston (1982) found that Type A nurses indicate that stressors over which they have the least control cause the most stress. Type A behavior and hostility are independent predictors of coronary heart disease for both men and women (Haynes, Feinleib, & Kannel, 1980).

Individual coping strategies are affected by whether an individual has an internal or external locus of control. Persons with an internal locus of control see the self as having an active choice, whereas individuals with an external locus of control perceive the world as happening to them (Rotter, 1975). Given the same situation, individuals with an internal locus of control report less stress (Kimmons & Greenhaus, 1976; Organ & Greene, 1974). In a related finding, some individuals are described as "stress prone"; that is, they have personal characteristics that predispose them to stress. These individuals are more likely to experience stress of all kinds. Being stress prone may affect both the situations encountered and coping for stress prone individuals (Chiriboga & Cutler, 1980).

To the extent that personality is a factor in role stress, knowledge of personality factors and of the stress inherent in a particular role can guide the matching of person with role. This congruence between role expectations and personality disposition is considered necessary for effective performance (Getzels & Guba, 1955).

Socialization of the Nurse

One source of individual stress in nurses may be professional socialization. Dissatisfaction and turnover in hospital nurses may be attributed to expectations fostered by nursing education that are unmet in work situations (Brief, 1976). For instance, patient teaching and support for the patient's family are taught as essential aspects of professional nursing care. Limited human resources and the increasing number of acute and complex patient illnesses may limit opportunities for the nurse to enact this aspect of her role. The dissatisfaction of providing time-pressured and incomplete nursing care will be stressful and may lead the nurse to resign.

Contextual Variables Affecting Occupational Stress

Characteristics of the organization, the physical and social environment, and the job itself are contextual variables that have been documented as contributing to stress. To understand and intervene in the stress of nursing and nursing work, the important contextual variables affecting stress in nursing must be explored.

Organizational Characteristics

Characteristics of organizations that have been associated with stress reduction include participation in decision making (Likert, 1967), communication flow, human resource primacy, and a higher level in the organization (Bedeian et al., 1981).

Findings from many studies show that employees who participate in the organization and in decision making experience less stress than those who do not (Schuler, 1980). Jackson (1983) tested a causal model of the effects of participation in decision making with 95 nursing and clerical employees in a hospital outpatient department. After 6 months, participation in decision making was shown to reduce role conflict and role ambiguity and increase job satisfaction.

Organizational structure was examined in magnet hospitals—hospitals with low turnover that are considered by nurses to be good places to work and practice nursing (McClure et al., 1983). In these hospitals, nursing organization is decentralized with a participatory management structure and style that facilitate open communication and staff involvement in decision making. Relationships with physicians are described as collaborative, whereas relationships with peers and supervisors are supportive. These hospitals also have a philosophy of caring not only for patients but also for staff, which is reflected in flexible work schedules and staff involvement in planning schedules. In a study of 200 workers, some of whom were psychiatric nurses, Pines and Maslach (1978) reported that staff members who have input into the institution's policies have a more positive view of themselves, their patients, and their work than do those who have no such input.

Physical and Social Environment

Physical aspects of the environment that contribute to stress include high levels of noise, light, and toxins and lack of space and privacy (Levi, 1981). Nurses in intensive care settings are often exposed to the constant noise of machinery and intense lighting. Exposure to toxic drugs and radiation may also be a physical stressor. Nurses seldom have private space in which to work or rest.

The social environment includes relationships with peers, subordinates, and supervisors. Peer and subordinate relationships are negatively affected by stress; work stress also has a negative impact on work group interaction (Bedeian et al., 1981).

A variety of studies in nursing report that nursing work stress is caused by relationships with supervisors (Cassem & Hackett, 1972), physicians (Gribbins & Marshall, 1982), and subordinates and peers (Bailey & Bargagliotti, 1983; Bailey, Steffen, & Grout, 1980). Head nurses have long been identified as sources of stress. Dissatisfaction with their relationships with head nurses has been suggested as a major reason why staff nurses leave their jobs (Diamond & Fox, 1958; Seleh, Lee, & Prien, 1984).

Bailey and Bargagliotti (1983) reviewed seven studies of stress in critical care nursing. All the studies identified interpersonal conflict as a source of stress. The sources of interpersonal conflict varied, as did their ranking. Interpersonal relationships were ranked the highest stressor in a national sample of 566 nurses and second in a regional sample of 1,238 intensive care unit nurses.

One of the authors completed a research study of stress and coping in psychiatric nursing (Trygstad, 1984). Seventy-three percent of the staff nurses in the study said that their greatest source of stress was peer working relationships. Stress derived not only from their peer working relationships, but also from their understanding of and response to the stress of these relationships. As nurses, we know that we need to work together. We control very little individually, and very few goals can be reached individually. In this study, when working together became difficult, the individual nurse usually said to herself, "This is not how it ought to be; there must be something wrong with me." The interpersonal difficulties were not discussed and resolved, but rather became a source of additional stress as the nurse accepted the difficulty as reflecting a personal failure.

Research studies on stress often focus on the nurse's primary tasks—the major patient care activities of a particular unit, such as intensive care or medicine. The assumption is that the primary task is the major determinant of stress. Yet, according to Mohl and coworkers (1982), no empirical research has tested the assumption that the primary task, rather than social system variables, actually determines staff stress level. Their findings from a study of 68 nurses suggest that social system variables, particularly supervisory support and encouragement of mutual support (but not primary task definition), affect nurses' stress levels.

If one assumes that the interpersonal conditions of the work setting are associated with a person's need for acceptance and interpersonal recognition, stress may result when those relationships are unsatisfactory (Schuler, 1980). For example, if an individual perceives that she has an unsatisfactory relationship with another (e.g., there is a low level of trust between the two), she may withdraw from the relationship; if there is some task dependency between the two, she may find task achievement difficult. This withdrawal and lack of achievement can lead to an intensification of the unsatisfactory condition between the individuals and continued low task achievement. Thus, a vicious cycle is created (Schuler, 1980).

Job Characteristics

In a review of stress-related disease incidence according to occupation, Smith et al. (1978) determined that registered nursing is one of 40 occupations with a higher-than-expected incidence of stress-related disorders. Identified stressors that are characteristic of nursing include the ongoing interaction with ill persons, which can lead to a feeling of being emotionally drained, and responsibility for the well-being of patients without the authority to control that well-being. Like other high-stress occupations, nursing has the additional stressors of fast-paced work, repetitive job tasks, and, often, long hours.

A boundary-spanning role is one that serves as a link between two or more "worlds." The head nurse is concerned about the unit as a whole. She must respond to the "worlds" of the nurses, patients, doctors, hospital administration, and society at large. Similarly, the staff nurse must span the worlds of the patient, hospital administration, and physicians. Spanning these worlds and responding to their divergent needs are often stressful.

Hospital-based nurses are among the 25 percent of working Americans involved in shift work, a job condition associated with lowered performance and increased illness and accidents. In a study of nurses in two Canadian hospitals, rotating shift workers were assessed by supervisors as having less job motivation and providing poorer patient care than fixed shift workers (Jamal & Jamal, 1982). Another study of rotating shift workers in many work settings included nurses in the sample (Tasto & Colligan, 1978). It found that 20 percent more workers with rotating shifts than those with fixed shifts reported at least one accident at work in the previous 6 months. Rotating shift workers also reported more fatigue, nervousness, and inadequate sleep than fixed shift workers. It has been suggested that weekly shift rotation may be associated with a 5 to 20 percent shorter life span (Rose, 1984).

To decrease the stress of shift work, rotating to a later shift every third week has been suggested. The benefits of this schedule have been shown to be employee preference and improved health and morale (Czeisler, Moore-Ede, & Coleman, 1981).

Numerous studies have identified characteristics of the job that increase stress. However, because most of these studies used male non-nurse subjects, it is difficult to generalize their findings to nursing. Those characteristics noted below are those likely to be applicable to nursing because they are characteristic of nursing work. Schmidt (1978) reported these stressful job characteristics: time pressures (always present in the shift work in hospital nursing); insufficient information to make a decision and/or no one best solution to a problem (frequent situations for the bedside nurse); competing loyalties (e.g., to patients, other staff, administration, and physicians); and the need to handle emotionally charged issues (e.g., abortion, substance abuse). Other contributors to role stress noted by Van Sell et al. (1981) include perceived environmental uncertainty (a current problem in nursing as patient census diminishes and hospital units close) and lack of autonomy in nursing practice (this has long been identified as a problem in nursing).

After a literature review on occupational stress, Sharit and Salvendy (1982) concluded that uncertainty is the predominant underlying source of occupational stress. Uncertainty may stem from diverse sources, such as task ambiguity, job insecurity, and the lack of feedback about job performance.

A NOURISHING WORK ENVIRONMENT

The phenomenon of stress is clearly complex, with multiple individual and environmental variables affecting the perception, experience, and response to work stress. Although each of the variables associated with stress can present a problem to the worker and the organization, each also presents a possibility for intervention. The goal is to create a nourishing work environment—one that facilitates development of the healthy, satisfied nurse and enables her to deliver quality care.

The authors have incorporated the information on contextual variables into a tool to assess your work environment (Table 3-1). Eleven major components of the workplace are conceptualized along a continuum from non-nourishing or toxic to nourishing. Place a slash mark on the line to reflect your experience with each of the eleven issues.

Goals

We need to know why we are here and what our purpose is. If we are not clear about our goals, how can we know if we have met them?

In a nourishing work environment, the people who work together have clear goals and these goals are shared. In a toxic work environment, goals are obscure. No one really knows what the goals are so no one really knows when or if success has been achieved.

Attitudes, Beliefs, Values

In a supportive work environment attitudes, beliefs, and values are clear and shared. They are talked about, not hidden. In a toxic work environment attitudes, values, and beliefs are not considered and are therefore obscure.

Roles

Roles are an important part of a work environment. If the work environment is a nourishing one, then roles are agreed upon and clear. You expect of yourself what your supervisor expects of you, what people under you expect of you, and what your peers expect of you; everyone has the same role expectations.

In a nonnourishing or toxic work environment, ambiguity in roles and conflict between roles exist. Role ambiguity is present when you are not sure

Table 3-1 Assessment of Supportive Work Environment

Non-nourishing Work Environment	Nourishing Work Environment
Goals	
Obscure	Clear and shared
Attitudes, Beliefs, Values	
Not considered; obscure	Clear and shared
Roles	
Conflicting, ambiguous	Agreed-upon, clear
Decision Making	
Top-down, one-way communication	Input from those affected, two-way communication/consent
Communication	
Passive, aggressive, defensive	Assertive, supportive
Listening	
Alternating monologues	Active listening
Self-Disclosure	
Hide self	Open
Feelings	
Avoided, acted out	Expressed, dealt with
Conflicts	
Avoided attempts to win	Resolved
Task Completion	
One right way	Autonomy
Human Resources	
Staff here for use of organization, treated as material resource	Staff are valued

Source: From "Stress and Coping in Psychiatric Nursing" by L. Trygstad, 1984, *Dissertation Abstracts International, 45,* p. 3775-B.

what anybody expects of you. You do not know what constitutes success and that kills motivation. If you do not know how to define success, why would you bother working to achieve it? Role conflict may derive from the self or from differing role expectations held by staff. A classic example of self role conflict is the devout Catholic nurse who is asked to participate in an abortion. What is expected in her role is contrary to what she expects of herself personally. Role conflicts can come from differing role expectations. What your supervisor expects of you may be different from what three different physicians expect of you, which may be different from what someone you supervise expects from you, and these expectations are almost guaranteed to be different from what the patient expects of you. All of these different people are trying to elicit different behaviors from you. It is essential to be able to prioritize for yourself the importance of these expectations in order to deal with role conflict.

Decision Making

In a nourishing work environment, decisions are made by consensus, rather than by the most outspoken or powerful individuals, and there is input from all of those affected. The people on the front line—the people closest to the job—actually know a great deal about that job. They see what works well or does not work well. A director of nursing alone cannot make good decisions about patient care without considering the input of those actually delivering the care. Businesses have often found that the most cost-saving ideas come from the employees actually doing the work. So good decision making is the result of including staff members involved with the task in the decision.

A toxic work environment operates by "top down" decisions. The person on the top of the pyramid makes decisions, sends a memo, and the employees must abide by the decision.

Communication

Communication in a nourishing environment is assertive and supportive. In a toxic work environment, communication is passive or aggressive, or defensive. Passive and aggressive lie on the same end of the continuum; assertive is on the other. Passive and aggressive communication are very similar in that they are both ineffective in the long run. Over time, assertive communication (see Chapter 5) is much more effective and nourishing for all concerned.

Listening

A nourishing work environment is characterized by active listening, a toxic work environment by alternating monologues. In a non-nourishing setting, generally, one person is polite enough to be quiet while the other one is talking, but the "listener" uses that time to formulate her own response, rather than hearing the speaker.

Self-Disclosure

In a nourishing work environment, we have self-disclosure, and in a toxic one, we hide ourselves. Self-disclosure is not telling your workmates that your grandfather went to prison for robbing a bank back in the last century, it is not talking about your husband's affair, and it is not talking about problems you have with the kids. Self-disclosure is saying what you think and how you feel in this particular situation, right now.

The importance of self-disclosure is that trust is not possible without it. Whenever the authors have asked nurses what they value in a work environment, trust is inevitably mentioned. And trust is very easy to develop. It is developed by saying what you are going to do and then doing it. If you say, "I'll be back in 30 minutes," then be back in 30 minutes. Whether the consequence is positive or negative, whether it involves setting limits or giving rewards, trust develops from this simple principle of following through on what we say we are going to do. If a worker never shares how she would respond in this situation, how she thinks or feels, or what she wants there is no basis for trust. Self-disclosure is a precursor for trust.

Feelings

We all have feelings. Every day of our lives, feelings are evoked. We do not choose these feelings that come up. Our choice lies not in choosing how we feel, but in choosing how we deal with the feelings which occur.

In a nourishing work environment, it is expected that feelings will be evoked by everyday work situations; workers express and deal with them. In a toxic work environment, feelings are hidden and often come to light only in unhealthy ways. Feelings may come out verbally or be enacted in behavior. In an environment where feelings are not allowed to be expressed, feelings are often acted out in passive-aggressive behavior or psychosomatic illness.

Conflict

Conflict, like feelings, is inevitable. In a nourishing work environment workers resolve conflict. In a toxic work environment conflict is avoided whenever possible, and when it does occur each party to it attempts to win. If one person wins, the other loses. If one person wins and someone else loses, the loser may later want to retaliate, which is unhealthy for the organization.

Conflict stems from different response tendencies of individuals. In itself, it is neither positive nor negative. Conflict is a negative only when individuals start to perceive that if others' needs are met, theirs will be unmet. The goal of conflict resolution is to find a win-win solution (see Chapter 6 on conflict resolution).

Task Completion

In a nourishing environment workers are allowed to choose how they do things. They know what is expected of them, what is the goal, and what is the time frame. How they achieve the goal is up to them. The greater the autonomy, the more nourished they feel. In a toxic work environment there is one right way and everyone must do it that way. It does not matter if an employee's way works; he or she has no input.

Human Resources Primacy

In a nourishing work environment, staff are valued as human beings. In a toxic work environment, staff are used like material resources. For instance, if one unit is out of toilet paper and your unit has a box of toilet paper, you send part of the box over to the unit that does not have the toilet paper. We cannot do that with human beings. All nurses are not the same, and someone in one unit is not equivalent to someone in another unit. An operating room nurse cannot effectively be sent to assist on a short-staffed pediatric unit. When we start treating people as material resources, workers feel devalued and therefore take their investment out of the organization. Workers do not want to be invested in an organization that does not treat them as worthwhile human beings.

Use of the Assessment Tool (Table 3-1)

This assessment tool can be used effectively with a work group. After all the members complete the assessment, a composite picture emerges that reflects the entire group. On some items the responses will lie along the entire continuum from very nonnourishing to very nourishing. On other items, responses will cluster. This picture will identify the major problems of the work group.

The next step is goal setting. For example, if you do not think the decision making is very nourishing on your unit, what can you do about that? How can you incorporate consensual decision making into your objectives for this year?

Success in achieving the goals set comes from periodic assessment (evaluation) with the same tool. Over a period of time the changes in the group composite picture will reflect the changes perceived in the work environment.

For example, one group of nurses identified poor relationships with peers and subordinates as the major stressors in their interpersonal work environment. After discussing this stressor as a group, they decided that listening was the first applicable skill for addressing this stressor.

The same group of nurses identified minimal participation in the total organization as the largest stressor in terms of organizational characteristics. After discussing this stressor, they decided that feedback was the most appropriate first step. Did their supervisors know they were interested and willing to participate in the larger organization? This feedback and discussion as to how broader inclusion might be attained were the plans. This same group identified the major stressors related to job characteristics as lack of autonomy and boundary-spanning requirements. Here, they decided conflict resolution skills would be the first logical approach to the problem.

The process of working together to identify stressors and to deal with them is itself a nourishing, supportive activity that is likely to lead to a more nourishing work environment. The more that stressors can be resolved or dealt with in a positive way, the more nourishing the work environment is likely to be.

LEADERSHIP BEHAVIORS TO INCREASE SUPPORT AND DECREASE STRESS

Positive Effects of Support

Supportive supervision is a practical approach for increasing job satisfaction and morale and decreasing stress and burnout. This is well demonstrated and documented through research.

Social support can decrease stress directly. Occupational stress such as role conflict, role ambiguity, job dissatisfaction, and low morale have been shown to be reduced through social support (House & Wells, 1978).

Social support can alter your perception of stress if you are feeling the need to respond to the demands of different doctors, patients, and supervisors. Stress is reduced when your supervisor says, "Let's prioritize these. You aren't responsible for meeting the personal needs of the doctors." Such clarification of what is expected in your role diminishes role conflict and ambiguity. This, in turn, will alter your perception of what is stressful. When someone demands something from you and you are encouraged to consider the demand as not your responsibility, then you do not *feel* as much stress. The importance of the perceived stressor is diminished.

Social support can directly affect personal health. Social ties protect against a wide variety of disease outcomes and death (Berkman & Syme, 1979). In a nine year follow-up study of nearly 7,000 adults, the existence of social connectedness was related to longer and healthier life regardless of health practices. In other words, the isolated person who ate health foods, maintained ideal weight, exercised and meditated daily, abstained from smoking, and consumed minimal alcohol was a person as much at risk or more so than the obese, inactive, cigarette smoking, heavily drinking person with strong social ties. In this study, the socially connected person was more likely to be alive and well after nine years than the person with good health habits but no human connectedness. The four sources of social connectedness or ties examined were marriage, contacts with close friends and relatives, church membership, and informal and formal group associations.

The obvious conclusion to be drawn is age-old wisdom: people need people. Our connectedness with other people has a direct effect on our health.

Social support can also buffer some of the effects of stress on health and functioning. If we put two people in the same situation, exposed to the same amount of stress, but give one person social support and the other a lack of social support, the health effects for the two will likely be dramatically different.

In a landmark study (Nuckolls, Cassel, & Kaplan, 1972), women with high levels of stress and high levels of social support were found to have only one-third as many complications of pregnancy as women with high levels of stress and low levels of social support. Under conditions of high stress, social support buffered the effects of stress on health and functioning.

Workers with high occupational stress and high social support from supervisors may have no change in health status. For workers with high occupational stress and low social support from supervisors, illness symptoms increase dramatically as stress increases (see Figure 3-2).

Most of us encounter stress at work every day. The stress varies in its intensity, but we can generally count on coming to work and finding some stressful situations. One method of intervention is to reduce the stressors experienced. (See Chapter 12.) Here we focus on intervening by developing our ability to provide supportive supervision. We, and those we supervise,

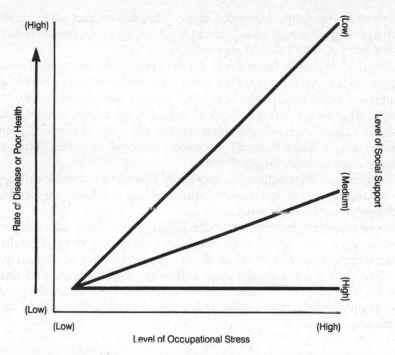

Figure 3-2 The "Conditioning" or "Buffering" (i.e., Interactive) Effect of Social Support on the Relationship Between Occupational Stress and Health. *Source:* From *Reducing Occupational Stress* by A. McLean (Ed.), 1978, Washington, DC: U.S. Department of Health, Education and Welfare, National Institute for Occupational Safety & Health, Publication Number 78-140, 1978.

can survive the stress of work without negative health outcomes with adequate supervisory support.

Since social support and supportive supervision are so important, we need to define them. Supportive supervision does not mean saying everything is fine when such is not the case. Supportive supervision does not mean never setting limits or providing negative consequences. Supportive supervision means making social support a part of the supervisory or leadership role as a practical means for decreasing stress and burnout and increasing job satisfaction and morale.

Social support can be defined by its functions: emotional support, tangible support, and informational support (Schaefer, Coyne, & Lazarus, 1981).

Emotional support is what we usually think of when we talk about social support. Emotional support includes providing reassurance and being able to confide in or rely on another person. This type of support helps us feel that we belong and are cared about.

Informational support includes giving information and advice that can help a person solve a problem. Giving feedback on how a person is doing is also a form of informational support.

Tangible support involves direct aid or services. An example of tangible support is having the supervisor send help when you are short-staffed. Tangible support is often the best kind. Having the supervisor say, "I am really sorry you are having to work so hard," is not nearly as helpful as the tangible support of sending another worker when one is needed. Tangible support may require financial resources, material resources, human resources, and rewards for good work.

Tangible and informational support may also serve as emotional support by helping a person feel cared about. Getting the help you need does indicate that somebody cares.

Social support helps most under conditions of high stress. Social support is always comforting, always feels good, and always works pretty well; but when it really matters is under conditions of high stress. Unfortunately, this is when we usually have the most difficulty finding energy and time to provide social support. It is therefore necessary to work within the group so that people provide social support for each other. Social support cannot come only from leaders.

Giving Support

The manager must possess the necessary skills to provide social support: good intentions are not enough. The ability to give social support can be developed. We will then be able to use ourselves and our role to maximize support when and where it is most needed.

The skills needed to provide emotional support include attention, acknowledgment, empathy, active listening, positive reinforcement, self disclosure, and trust building. Our time and attention are among the most valuable resources we can give to another. More than any words can, giving our time and attention communicates caring and concern for another person.

We can give emotional support by acknowledging the needs, feelings, and efforts of another person. Acknowledgment is the least utilized support skill that we have available. Nurses are doers. If something is wrong, we want to fix it. However, there are many things that we cannot fix. An example is the person who, in spite of all possible medical intervention, is dying. Whether they are dying from cancer, AIDS, or heart disease, their nearness to death is not something we can fix. We can acknowledge their pain, emotional or physical; we can acknowledge to the family that it is difficult; and we can acknowledge to the patient that it is difficult; but we cannot do a thing about the fact that they are dying. Emotional support does not change difficulty or sadness or anxiety, but acknowledgment does communicate our awareness and concern about the other's difficulty, sadness, or anxiety and thus lessens the sense of isolation. Acknowledgment conveys understanding.

Empathy is the ability to see and experience the world through the eyes and position of another. This leads to genuine understanding and is a prcrcquisite to being helpful. Active listening is one way we can develop empathy. Through active listening (a continual, active process of validating that we comprehend what is being said to us), we learn how the other person sees and experiences the world.

We can use ourselves—our time, attention, and acknowledgement—as positive reinforcement for a person in distress. These reinforce the value of the person and the validity of their needs, feelings and perceptions.

Self-disclosure and trust building are ways to use ourselves to provide emotional support. Self-disclosure is disclosing our response to a person and/ or situation. "I too would feel angry in that situation," is an example of self-disclosure. To trust is to rely upon. Others learn to trust us when we say what we will do and then do it. Receiving emotional support depends on the sense that one can rely on another.

Giving informational support depends on having information and the ability to communicate it clearly. To communicate information we must be able to phrase it clearly in a way that can be understood by the other. Then we must check to be sure the message we intended to send was the message received. Informational support includes the ability to clarify, to validate, to provide feedback, and to teach. Examples of informational support include teaching a nurse a new procedure, and setting performance objectives and providing appropriate feedback.

Tangible support includes the provision of financial resources, material resources, human resources, and rewards for good work. The hungry person will feel more supported by the provision of the tangible support of food than by the provision of emotional support such as acknowledgment of hunger. Needed tangible support is an essential component of social support and supportive supervision. The balanced use of emotional, informational, and tangible support allow us to provide supportive supervision.

Examples of situations where supervisory support may be needed include role ambiguity and role conflict. For the nurse who struggles with the ambiguity in her role, the supportive supervisor can provide informational support by clarifying goals and guidelines and providing feedback about functioning. In the same situation, the supervisor can give her time and attention to the struggling nurse and acknowledge the distress in dealing with the inevitable ambiguity in a complex, everchanging system. The tangible support of role modeling and written materials would round out the supportive supervision.

In a situation of role conflict, the supportive supervisor can provide information about priorities and the consequences of alternatives. Emotional support would include acknowledgment of the distress associated with the conflict and tangible support might include mediating conflict resolution.

Accepting Support from Others

Many nurses feel more comfortable giving than receiving and may be uncomfortable asking for, or even accepting when offered, support from others. As human beings as well as nurses, we need to be aware of our own needs for support and any barriers we have to receiving support.

Our own behavior provides clues to our barriers to receiving support. For example, if someone gives you a compliment, do you say "thank you" and feel good? Or are you uncomfortable? Do you discount the compliment or even disagree verbally with the person (e.g., "It was nothing," or "If you look closely you'll see that this is not a nice dress.")? If someone for whom you have no gift gives you a Christmas gift, do you say "thank you" and appreciate it or are you uncomfortable? Some people even keep a wrapped gift in a drawer to be able to reciprocate immediately if they receive an unexpected gift.

Being receptive to support is a necessary part of obtaining support. Another essential component is having supportive persons in our lives. The questionnaire in Exhibit 3-2 will assist you in assessing the support which you receive.

Exhibit 3-2 Assessing Your Social Support

In spaces 1–12 below write the initials of all persons with whom you have tried to discuss something of importance to you in the past two weeks. For person one, consider question one. If you were unable to talk to the person, put a "4" in the first box. If you felt the person helped you to understand better and discover new feelings, put "1" in the fourth box in column 1. Answer all 3 questions for each person.

	1	2	3	4	5	6	7	8	9	10	11	12
1. Were you able to talk with him/ her about how you felt? Did he/ she seem to understand your feelings and situation?												
(4) I couldn't talk.												
(3) I talked but the person didn't understand.												
(2) Seemed to understand. I could express all my feelings.												
(1) Helped me to understand better. I discovered new feelings.												

Exhibit 3-2. continued

	1	2	3	4	5	6	7	8	9	10	11	12
2. Did he/she seem to reject you or to not accept your feelings, to accept you and the way you felt, or even to challenge you to cope better?												
(4) Rejected me.												
(3) Seemed concerned but rejected my feelings.												
(2) Accepted how I felt, gave me encouragement.												
(1) Challenged me to face difficulties and overcome them.												
3. Did he/she seem to be hiding how he/she felt or pretending somehow, or did you feel his/her reaction was completely open and sincere?												
(3) Seemed insincere, just putting on a front.												
(2) Was helpful, but seemed routine, uninvolved.												
(1) Was helpful, really sincerely concerned and involved.												
(4) Was sincere and open, but in a way that made me feel worse.												

Each person now has three numbers corresponding to the three questions. Add these three numbers so that each person (column) has a single score. If the score for the person is 5 or less, circle the person's initials. If the score is 6 or greater, put a square around the initials. The circles indicate persons you experience as supportive and the squares are not supportive. Now subtract the total number of squares from the total number of circles to obtain your support balance. Nonsupportive persons do cancel out other experiences of support. If you have a zero or negative number you undoubtedly feel a lack of support. If you have a positive number you likely feel support. This is also an indicator of persons to whom you can and should turn to for support when it is needed.

Source: From "Social Support in Crisis: Quantity or Quality?" by D. Porritt, 1979, *Social Science & Medicine, 13A*, pp. 715–721. Copyright 1979 by Pergamon Press, Ltd. Adapted by permission.

Just as we cannot get blood from a rock, we cannot get support from a "square". Identifying the supportive persons in our lives and allowing others to give us support are ways we can help meet our own needs for social support.

REFERENCES

Adams, J.D. (1981). Health, stress and the manager's life style. *Group and Organizational Studies, 6* (3), 291–301.

Bailey, J.T., & Bargagliotti, L.A. (1983). Stress and critical care nursing. In W. Holzemer (Ed.), *Review of research in nursing education.* Thorofare, NJ: Charles Slack.

Bailey, J.T., Steffen, S.M., & Grout, J.M. (1980). The stress audit: Identifying the stressors of ICU nursing. *Journal of Nursing Education, 19*(6), 15–25.

Bedeian, A.G., Armenakis, A.A., & Curran, S.M. (1980). Personality correlates of role stress. *Psychological Reports, 46,* 627–632.

Bedeian, A.G., Armenakis, A.A., & Curran, S.M. (1981). The relationship between role stress and job related, interpersonal and organizational factors. *Journal of Social Psychology, 113*(2), 247–260.

Beehr, T.A. (1976). Perceived situational moderators of the relationship between subjective role ambiguity and role strain. *Journal of Applied Psychology, 61,* 35–40.

Beehr, T.A., & Newman, J.E. (1978). Job stress, employee health and organizational effectiveness: A facet analysis, model and literature review. *Personnel Psychology, 31,* 665–699.

Berkman, L.F., & Syme, S.L. (1979). Social networks, host resistance and mortality: A nine year followup study of Almada County residents. *American Journal of Epidemiology, 109* (2), 186–204.

Brief, A.P. (1976). Turnover among hospital nurses: A suggested model. *Journal of Nursing Administration, 6*(8), 55–58.

Caplan, R.D., Cobb, S., French, J.R.P., Harrison, R.B., & Pinneau, S.R. *Job demands and worker health.* (HEW Publication No. 75–160) (NIOSH). Washington, DC: U.S. Government Printing Office.

Cassem, N.H., & Hackett, T.P. (1972). Sources of tension for the CCU nurse. *American Journal of Nursing, 72*(8), 1426–1430.

Chiriboga, D.A., & Cutler, L. (1980). Stress and adaptation: Life span perspectives. In L. Poon (Ed.), *Aging in the 1980's: Psychological issues.* Washington, DC: American Psychological Association.

Czeisler, C.A., Moore-Ede, M.C., & Coleman, R.M. (1981). Rotating shift work schedules that disrupt sleep are improved by applying circadian principles. *Science, 217,* 460–463.

Davenport, M.P. (1983). The health status of psychiatric nurses: Life stress events and social support as predictor variables. *Dissertation Abstracts International, 44*(6).

Diamond, L.K., & Fox, D.J. (1958). Turnover among hospital student nurses. *Nursing Outlook, 6,* 388–391.

Fagin, C.M. (1982). The national shortage of nurses. A nursing perspective. In L. Aiken (Ed.), Nursing in the 1980s. Philadelphia: Lippincott.

Fawcett, J. (1978). The "what" of theory development. In *Theory development: What, why and how.* (pp. 17–33). New York: National League for Nursing.

Getzels, J.W., & Guba, E.G. (1955). Role conflict and personality. *Journal of Personality, 24,* 74–85.

Gribbins, R.E., & Marshall, R.E. (1982). Stress and coping in the NICU staff nurse: Practical implications for change. *Critical Care Medicine, 10*(12), 865–867.

Hackman, R., & Oldham, G. (1980). *Work redesign.* Reading, MA: Addison-Wesley.

Haynes, S.G., Feinleib, M., & Kannel, W.B. (1980). The relationship of psychological factors to coronary heart disease in the Framingham study, Part. III. *American Journal of Epidemiology, 111*(1), 37–58.

House, A.J., & Rizzo, J.R. (1972). Role conflict and ambiguity as critical variables in a model organizational behavior. *Organizational Behavior and Human Performance, 7,* 467–505.

House, J.S., & Wells, J.A. (1978). Occupational stress, social support and health. In A. McLean (Ed.), *Reducing occupational stress,* Washington, D.C.: U.S. Dept. of Health, Education and Welfare (NIOSH) Pub. No. 78–140.

Ivancevich, J.M., Matteson, M.T., & Preston, C. (1982). Occupational stress, type A behavior and physical well-being. *Academy of Management Journal, 25*(2), 373–391.

Jackson, S.E. (1983). Participation in decision making as a strategy for reducing job-related strain. *Journal of Applied Psychology, 68*(1), 3–19.

Jamal, M., & Jamal, S.M. (1982). Work and nonwork experiences of employees on fixed and rotating shifts: An empirical assessment. *Journal of Vocational Behavior, 20,* 282–293.

Kimmons, G., & Greenhaus, J.H. (1976). Relationship between locus of control and reactions of employers to work characteristics. *Psychological Reports, 3,* 815–820.

Lawler, E.E. (1973). *Motivation in work organizations.* Monterey, CA: Brooks/Cole.

Lazarus, R.S. (1981). The stress and coping paradigm. In C. Eisdorfer, D. Cohen, A. Kleinmann, & P. Mazim (Eds.), *Models for clinical psychopathology* (pp. 117–214). New York: S.P. Medical & Scientific Books.

Levi, L. (1981). *Preventing work stress.* Reading, MA: Addison-Wesley.

Lewin, K. (1951). *Field theory in social science.* New York: Harper & Row.

Likert, R. (1967). *The human organization: its management and value.* New York: McGraw-Hill.

Margolis, B.L., Kroes, W.H., & Quinn, R.P. (Eds.) (1974). Job stress: An unlisted occupational hazard. *Journal of Occupational Medicine, 10,* 654–661.

McClure, M.L., Poulin, M.A., Sovie, M.D., & Wandelt, M.A. (1983). *Magnet hospitals, attraction and retention of professional nurses.* Kansas City: American Nurses Association.

McGrath, J.E. (Ed.) (1970). *Social and psychological factors in stress.* New York: Holt, Rinehart and Winston.

McGrath, J.E. (1976). Stress and behavior in organizations. In M.D. Dunette (Ed.), *Handbook of industrial and organizational psychology.* Chicago: Rand McNally.

Mohl, P.C., Denny, N.R., Mote, T.A., & Coldwater, C. (1982). Hospital unit stressors that affect nurses: Primary task versus social factors. *Psychosomatics, 23*(4), 366–374.

Naisbitt, J. (1982). *Megatrends.* New York: Warner Books.

Newman, J.E., & Beehr, T.A. (1979). Personal and organizational strategies for handling job stress: A review of research and opinion. *Personnel Psychology, 32* (1), 1–43.

Nuckolls, K.B., Cassel, J., & Kaplan, B.H. (1972). Psychosocial assets, life crisis and the prognosis of pregnancy. *American Journal of Epidemiology, 95,* 431–441.

Organ, D.W., & Greene, C.N. (1974). Role ambiguity, locus of control and work satisfaction. *Journal of Applied Psychology, 59,* 101–102.

Orpen, C. (1982). Type A personality as a moderator of the effects of role conflict, role ambiguity and role overload on individual strain. *Journal of Human Stress, 8*(2), 8–14.

Pines, A., & Maslach, C. (1978). Characteristics of staff burnout in mental health settings. *Hospital and Community Psychiatry, 29*(4), 233–237.

Posner, B.A., & Randolph, W.A. (1980). Moderators of role stress among hospital personnel. *Journal of Psychology, 105*, 211–224.

Rosch, P.J. (1979). Stress and illness. *Journal of the American Medical Association, 242*(2), 427–428.

Rose, M. (1984). Shiftwork. *American Journal of Nursing, 84*(4), 442–447.

Rotter, J.B. (1975). Some problems and misconceptions related to the construction of internal versus external control of reinforcement. *Journal of Consulting and Clinical Psychology, 43*, 56–67.

Schaefer, C., Coyne, J.C., & Lazarus, R.S. (1981). The health related functions of social support. *Journal of Behavioral Medicine, 4* (4), 381–405.

Schmidt, W.H. (1978). Basic concepts of organizational stress—causes and problems. In R.M. Schwartz (Ed.), *Occupational stress: proceedings of the conference.* (DHEW Publication No. 78-156) (NIOSH). Washington, DC: U.S. Government Printing Office

Schuler, R.S. (1979). A role perception transactional model for organizational communication-outcome relationships. *Organizational Behavior and Human Performance, 23*, 268–291.

Schuler, R.S. (1980). Definition and conceptualization of stress in organizations. *Organizational Behavior and Human Performance, 25*, 184–215.

Seleh, S.D., Lee, R.J., & Prien, E.P. (1984). Why nurses leave their job—an analysis of female turnover. *Personnel Administration, 27*, 25–28.

Selye, H. (1976). *The stress of life.* New York: McGraw-Hill.

Sharit, J., & Salvendy, G. (1982). Occupational stress: Review and reappraisal. *Human Factors, 24*(2), 129–162.

Slocum, Susman, & Sheridan (1972).

Smith, M.J., Colligan, J., & Hurrel, J.J. Jr. (1978). *A review of NIOSH psychological stress research—1977. Occupational stress: Proceedings of the conference on occupational stress* (DHEW Publication No. 78-156) (NIOSH). Washington DC: U.S. Government Printing Office.

Tasto, D.L., & Colligan, M.J. (1978). *Health consequences of shift work.* Menlo Park, CA: Stanford Research Institute.

Terkel, S. (1972). *Working.* New York: Pantheon Books.

Trygstad, L. (1984). Stress and coping in psychiatric nursing. *Dissertation Abstracts International, 45*, 3775-B.

Van Sell, M., Brief, A.P., & Schuler, R.S. (1981). Role conflict and role ambiguity: Integration of literature and directions for future research. *Human Relations, 34*(1), 43–71.

Weisman, C.S., Alexander, C.S., & Chase, G.A. (1980). Job satisfaction among hospital nurses: A longitudinal study. *Health Services Research, 15*, 341–364.

Chapter 4

Clear and Effective Communication—Listening

Communication is the pivotal skill of the nurse leader, and listening makes up at least half of all communications. Yet, even a good listener on a good day hears accurately less than 50 percent of what is said. This prevalent inability to listen accurately makes listening the number one skill to target for improving the communication of the nurse leader.

BARRIERS TO LISTENING

In the communication cycle, one person sends a message and a second person receives it by listening. The receiver then sends a message back. That second message, or feedback, is what makes communication a process or dialogue, rather than a monologue.

One barrier to listening is that many people do not like to listen because doing so interferes with their talking. While the other person is talking, the listener often uses this time to formulate his or her own response, rather than listening to what is being said. We are all our own major barrier to listening.

Before the message sent reaches any listener, it must pass through another major barrier: our own experience, our values, our attitudes, our feelings, and our thoughts (Figure 4-1). This barrier exists for all of us and cannot be eliminated; therefore, we must learn to compensate for it. In the process of passing through this barrier, what is being said is altered by the experience and perceptions of the listener. Often, we assume that we understand what is being said. We then internally validate that we understand the message, rather than checking with the other person to be sure that we have understood what was said.

According to noted therapist Virginia Satir, to assume that one understands is to "make an ass of you and me" (ass-u-me). Usually these assump-

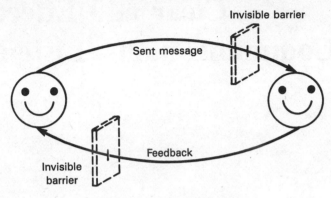

Figure 4-1 Barriers to Listening

tions are neither made consciously nor for the purpose of deliberately distorting communication, and therein lies their danger. We are not aware of assuming that we understand the message of the other person; we simply do so.

For example, one of the authors, who was teaching a group of RN students, prepared to meet with her early evening class. One of the RN students came up to the instructor before class began and said, "My father died recently and my mother didn't want to stay home tonight alone; do you mind that she's here? May she sit through our class with us?" The instructor had had extensive experience working in a hospice and with death and dying and therefore believed that she understood some of the feelings and needs of the recently bereaved. The instructor said, "Of course," and went over to introduce herself to the mother, saying, "You are welcome to be here." The instructor added, "I am very sorry to hear about the recent death of your husband. You must be very sad." In response, the student's mother looked at the instructor, with eyes opened wide and hands on her hips. The mother said, "Sad! That blankety, blank, blank and I were separated for 30 years. What his death means to me is I finally have my house back."

The instructor was astonished. She had never encountered such a reaction from a recently "bereaved" person. Then the instructor realized that she had assumed from her own experience with death and dying that the death of a spouse meant that the survivor was sad. Obviously, this was not true in this particular situation. The student's mother went on to explain that she was simply bored at home alone and thought she would like to see her daughter's class.

This story is a reminder of the ever-present need to practice active listening. We need to validate what is being said by each person, rather than assuming that we understand the situation or the person's need based on our past experience.

ASSESSING YOUR LISTENING SKILLS

No matter how high her listening skill level is, no matter how frequently it is practiced, the nurse leader needs to listen actively to the messages of others if she is to understand what is being said. Perhaps you are skeptical that this applies to you. Perhaps you think your listening skills are better than most and that you are able to hear accurately what is being said to you. Assessing your listening skills can be very instructive. However, doing so can be difficult. We are often unaware of what we do not hear; others may not tell us what we are missing, or we may not choose to listen to feedback.

A recommended way to assess your listening skills is to take the listening test developed by University Associates (see Resources). This audiotaped listening test consists of 30 items. Each statement has one intended meaning. After hearing each statement, which is read by a professional actor, the listener selects one of four choices of the intended meaning of the message. The test developers are satisfied that the intended message was the message delivered.

The correct (intended) answers are given on the audiotaped listening test. The instructor's guide gives the correct answer and also notes the feeling conveyed by each statement. In scoring this test, keep in mind that accurately hearing as little as 75 percent of what is said is considered excellent. Hearing only 50 percent of what is said is considered good. This is a most unusual grading scale and is reflective of normative listening in our culture.

It is useful for professionals practicing their communication skills to take the listening test and not only look at their score as an indication of their listening skill level but also note the feelings that they did not hear accurately. A pattern of listening can generally be found. Most people miss two or three feelings frequently and hear other emotions accurately. A rule of thumb is that we misunderstand feelings with which we ourselves have difficulty.

If you are unable to obtain this useful listening test, you can assess your listening skills more informally. With a group of people, try the age-old game of telephone. One person whispers a message to the next person, who whispers the message to the third person, and so on until the message has been transmitted to all persons in the group. The last person in the group states the message aloud for all to hear. Inevitably, the message delivered at the end differs from the message given by the first person. This occurs because each person repeats what she thinks she heard, which is not necessarily what was said.

Another approach to assessing listening is to watch a televised speech or television drama with a small group. At the end of the speech, have each group member write down the major points or theme of the speech. Group members then compare what they wrote and discuss the differences in what they heard. Or, while watching a drama, have all persons note the feelings being expressed at specified times. At the end of the program, group members compare the feelings noted and discuss the differences in what was heard or received by each listener.

Asking others for feedback about our listening skills can be helpful. Those with whom we work closely can often give useful feedback to us about our listening skills. As you practice active listening you will receive immediate feedback regarding the accuracy of your listening from the perspective of the speaker.

PRACTICE HEARING WHAT OTHERS MEAN TO BE SAYING

As noted earlier, we all have an inborn barrier to hearing accurately: our perception, our experiences, and our own values. Because we can never rid ourselves of this barrier, we must learn to compensate for it on a daily basis. This can best be achieved through the practice of active listening. When we listen actively, it means that we hear a statement but do not make an assumption that we understand what the speaker intends to communicate. Rather, we assume that we do not understand what the other person is communicating.

Active listening requires an active involvement on the part of the listener in reflecting and validating what has been heard. This validation is a process of saying back to the speaker what the listener thinks was said. This validation, this feedback, may occur at one of three levels: content, feelings, or themes. Active listening must occur at all three levels in order for us to fully understand the message of another person.

Active listening at the content level reflects the content of the message. The exact words or a paraphrase of the exact words may be repeated to the speaker to check for accuracy.

Active listening also may occur at the level of feelings. The listener may say, "I understand you are angry about this situation," or "I understand that you are perplexed or uncomfortable with your current position." These feelings may or may not have been labeled by the speaker. It is the listener's understanding that the speaker has these feelings. The feedback, the statement of these feelings, is an attempt at validation that this is indeed what the speaker is experiencing and conveying.

The third level of active listening—at the level of a theme—occurs when a relationship between the communicants has been established and the listener believes she has heard a similar idea expressed several different times. For instance, the nurse may say to the patient, "I'll see you tomorrow. I'm going home now, but I'll be back in the morning." The patient may say, "No you won't." And the nurse may remember and say aloud, "Oh yes, your husband didn't show up as promised this afternoon, your doctor didn't come in this morning as he indicated he would, and yesterday, your daughter didn't come as she promised. You are thinking that nobody is going to show up when they've said they would." This is the attempted validation of the theme of abandonment.

A question often asked with active listening is whether the speaker is offended when his or her thoughts are repeated, particularly when the listener has not heard them accurately. This does not seem to occur. Active listening is a way of conveying interest in and respect for the speaker. What is communicated is that the listener is concerned with hearing accurately what the speaker wants to express.

Active listening also assists the speaker in clarifying his or her own thoughts. Sometimes the listener has heard accurately what the speaker said, but what was said was not what was meant. Through the process of active listening speakers are assisted in thinking and expressing themselves clearly.

Take time now to practice active listening. Ideally this is done in triads, with one person as the speaker, one person as the listener, and one person as the observer. Select a topic that is relevant to the speaker, such as concerns about using active listening, a stressful situation at work, or concerns about an upcoming meeting. For a set length of time (5 to 10 minutes works well), the speaker talks about the topic. The listener listens actively. Then, the listener describes what she has heard at the content, feeling, and thematic levels. The observer then comments on what was seen and heard, with particular emphasis on the listening process. She may offer corrective feedback for the listener. The observer also invites the speaker to comment on how it felt to talk to an active listener (most speakers find the experience of being heard very positive). The listener is then asked how she experienced the role of active listener. Often, the listener feels some discomfort and may have some concern about it sounding "artificial." It is natural to feel awkward when learning a new skill; comfort and ease come with practice. Continue with the triad until all three persons have had the opportunity to be speaker, listener, and observer.

FEEDBACK: TURNING MONOLOGUES INTO COMMUNICATION

The message from the listener to the initial speaker—the feedback loop—is what makes talking to others a process of communication, rather than alternating monologues. There are three major purposes to feedback: (1) acknowledging and clarifying the message that was sent, (2) communicating the response of the listener, and (3) helping the speaker be more effective.

The most useful process for clarifying the sender's message—the first purpose of feedback—is active listening.

Communicating the response of the listener requires self-disclosure and is an essential component in building trust. Trust is developed by saying what one will do and then doing it. Trust requires disclosure of intentions and reactions. Feedback from the listener to the speaker as to how the listener is responding to the speaker's words helps the speaker know what to expect from the listener.

Feedback can help the speaker be more effective when it is behaviorally specific, timely, and in the form of an "I" message.

Feedback that is behaviorally specific describes both the behavior and the listener's response to it; for example, "I felt angry when you called in sick to take care of personal business." Anger is the listener's response, and abusing sick leave was the specific behavior that elicited this response.

Behaviorally specific feedback increases the speaker's awareness. If the speaker knows how the listener responded, then the speaker can choose to continue or alter the behavior that elicited that response.

To be effective, feedback needs to be timely in two ways: appropriate at that time and as close in time to the behavior as is feasible. An example of inappropriate timing is telling a coworker she has bad breath during the process of CPR. Telling her after CPR is completed would be an appropriate time. Another example of poor timing is waiting a year to tell someone you were annoyed with her behavior; it is too late then.

Feedback needs to be given in "I" messages. Research shows that beginning a sentence with the word "you" elicits an increase in the listener's blood pressure (Fryling, 1983). "You" statements often put people on the defensive and are more difficult to hear. Therefore, to increase our chances of being heard accurately, we need to use "I" messages; for example, "I felt angry," rather than "You made me angry."

Inappropriate feedback (e.g., messages that blame, inappropriately timed messages, personal rather than behavioral statements) can be very cutting and hurtful. However, when feedback follows the guidelines given above it can be a significant way to help people achieve personal growth by increasing their awareness of the messages they send and their effect on other people.

COMMUNICATION: UP, DOWN, AND LATERAL

Communication is always difficult, whether it goes up or down or laterally. It is difficult to listen accurately, it is difficult to give clear and useful feedback, and it is difficult to make ourselves understood to others. We can do at least three things to help ourselves get our message across to another person: (1) say what we want to have understood, (2) expect to be misunderstood, and (3) increase our awareness.

We need to say what we see, hear, think, feel, want, or need. Very few people can accurately guess or assume what someone else means to be saying. Interestingly, this is often more problematic in close relationships than in relationships between relative strangers. We often assume or believe that if another person knows us, cares about us, and understands us, he or she will know what we mean to be saying or what we want. A common comment in marital therapy, particularly from the wife, is, "If he loved me, he would . . . ." If the therapist asks, "Have you told him that or have you asked him for that?" the response is all too often, "Oh no, if he loved me, he would know." How this knowing might occur is extremely elusive. Nothing occurs in the marriage ceremony that gives a spouse the ability to read the mind and know the wants and needs of the other spouse, yet this becomes the expectation. This same expectation may be held in the work environment.

We can increase our ability to get a message to another person by simply saying it. However, sometimes we may not want to state what we want nor feel it is appropriate to do so. For example, at a party, a guest came up to the hostess and said, "Oh my, what beautiful flowers: a large bouquet of roses and carnations. Did someone give them to you?" "Yes," replied the hostess, "my husband." "Ah," replied the guest, "How did you get him to bring you such wonderful flowers?" "Why, I simply asked him to bring me some flowers," said the hostess. "Oh no," said the guest, "That ruins it." "Oh," replied the puzzled hostess, "not for me. I have my flowers." The guest disagreed, saying, "If you have to ask for them, then they are not worth anything." Consider which point of view you share. What are your values and attitudes about requesting what you want? Is it worthless if you have asked for it, or are you simply maximizing your chances to obtain what you want?

We can increase our chances of being understood by expecting to be misunderstood. If a good listener has a 50 to 75 percent possibility of hearing you accurately, there is a 25 to 50 percent chance of your being misunderstood. We can help listeners hear us more accurately by using several simple communication techniques. We can ask the listener what he or she heard. We can repeat our message in different ways. Hearing different words in different ways gives the listener additional opportunities to hear what we are saying. We can summarize. We can put our ideas in writing. All of these maximize our possibility of being heard accurately.

We can increase our chances of being understood by increasing our own awareness of what we are communicating. We cannot *not* communicate; any time we are within sight of another person, we are communicating to him or her. However, we may be communicating unclear or conflicting messages without knowing it. This communication may not occur in words, because a majority of all communication is nonverbal. It we are unaware of what we are communicating nonverbally, we cannot alter it to make it more accurate or more congruent with our words. Regular practice in becoming aware of your body and what you are communicating nonverbally is very helpful in learning to get across the message you wish to convey.

When we convey incongruent verbal and nonverbal messages, it is the nonverbal message that is believed. Consider what occurs when a colleague puts her hand on the doorknob, stands half in and half out of the doorway to your office, and says to you, "How are you today? I am really interested in knowing." Her words say one thing and her body says another; which message would you believe? If you are unaware of what your body is communicating, you cannot alter it. By regularly stopping to pay attention to what you are saying with your body, you can alter your body language and therefore alter what is understood by the listener.

On a good day, a good listener may hear 50 percent of what is being said. On a bad day or in a situation that evokes intense feelings, that percentage is reduced. Sometimes it's a wonder that anything is communicated at all. Intense feelings and uncomfortable situations occur frequently in our communication with superiors, those we supervise, and our peers. This difficulty in communication is a source of much stress.

What is easy communication? It is easy to not listen, to talk in monologues, and to give unidirectional communication. The difficulty with "easy" communication is its outcome, which is usually poor. Unidirectional communication is of particular concern because it seems efficient, and its ineffectiveness is not always immediately apparent.

The purpose of this next exercise (Figure 4-2) is to help make apparent the outcomes of one-way and two-way communication. Try this exercise with one or more other persons. Take time to discuss the experience of one-way and two-way communication from each participant's perspective. What was effective? What was ineffective? What feelings were engendered during each process? How can the learning from this experience be applied to the everyday work world?

What is hard communication? It is difficult to achieve two-way communication. It requires patience and practice to develop the skills of active listening and feedback and then to use them in intense situations. Yet, it is even more difficult to deal with the effects of lack of communication. It is also difficult to learn assertiveness skills and to learn to deal with conflict. But again, lack of learning is, in the long run, even more problematic.

The same principles are applicable whether communication is upward, downward, or lateral. For example, whether you are learning to work with a

CHART I. ONE-WAY COMMUNICATION   CHART II. TWO-WAY COMMUNICATION

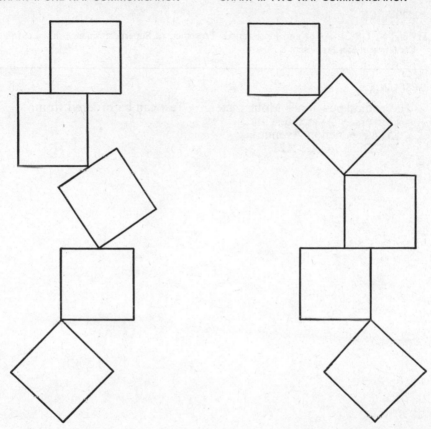

INSTRUCTIONS: Study the figures in Chart I. With your back to the group, you are to instruct the participants how to draw them. Begin with the top square and describe each in succession, taking particular note of the relationship of each to the preceding one. No questions are allowed. Now repeat with Chart II, but this time answer all questions from participants and repeat if necessary.

Figure 4-2 Communication Exercise. *Source:* Reprinted from: J. William Pfeiffer and John E. Jones, (Eds.), *A Handbook of Structured Experiences for Human Relations Training,* Vol. 1, San Diego, CA: University Associates, Inc., 1969. Used with permission.

new boss, orienting a new staff nurse, or helping to orient a fellow head nurse, your ability to send clear, congruent, assertive messages is needed. The effectiveness of your message will be influenced by how well you listen actively and give clear feedback.

REFERENCE

Fryling, V. (1983). Power and imagination. Presented at Superperformance and Learning Conference, San Francisco.

RESOURCE

The audiotaped Jones Mohr Listening Test can be ordered from:
University Associates, Inc.
8517 Production Avenue
San Diego, CA 92121

Chapter 5

Assertive Communication and the Nurse Leader

Today's nurse leader practices in an era of increased demands for productivity and technological expertise. She deals continually with two challenges: getting tasks accomplished and dealing with the people who accomplish those tasks. This chapter discusses the factors and skills affecting and supporting our ability to communicate effectively as leaders.

Communication as a process is often said to be complex, dynamic, and even unpredictable. Taken broadly, it can encompass all of human behavior (Beck, Rawlins, & Williams, 1984). How we develop our communication style and adapt our personalities to the continuous changes in our personal and professional lives is defined but not limited to the following: (1) socialization, (2) self-esteem, (3) self-actualization, (4) value clarification, and (5) assertiveness.

SOCIALIZATION

The early socialization process is an important influence on how we deal with change and conflict, become motivated, achieve, and express ourselves. Our attempts in nursing to emerge as healthy leaders are difficult because we have been socialized both as women and as nurses to be supporters and nurturers and to care for others (Whitman, 1982). Unfortunately, we often eliminate the responsibility of caring for self as we handle the responsibilities of being a helpmate in a male-dominated medical establishment and caring for our families as well.

Our families of origin may have socialized us overtly or covertly with such instructions as these, which we then incorporated into our personalities: don't cry, be feminine, be nice, be quiet, turn the other cheek, always try to make a good impression, be seen and not heard, swallow your pride, don't be self-centered, don't boast, keep your feelings to yourself, you're not good enough, or you'll never make it. These are all examples of family-of-origin socialization messages that can inhibit our later development, growth, and communication. In contrast, other socialization messages—you can do anything you want to do, say how you feel, you'll succeed, women can do it, women can lead, nurses are leaders, it's great to be a woman or it's great to be a man, or taking charge is positive—can be empowering.

Our ability to communicate effectively may further be influenced by patterns we have established of adapting to socialized messages. This adaptation is often expressed through such common defense mechanisms as repression, rationalization, and projection. These defense mechanisms act as automatic responses that help us respond to threatening perceptions so that our self-concept remains secure (Beck et al., 1984).

During our early years of socialization, we begin to define our values, decide who we are, and set our expectations of ourselves and others. It is also in this early socialization time that we begin to learn and use a form of communication that meets our needs. This communication style may, however, be ineffective in the short term and unhealthy in the long term. The effective leader acknowledges the role of socialization in the development of her communication skills.

SELF-ESTEEM

How fully and confidently we are able to lead others is dependent on our self-esteem, on how we feel about ourselves. Through self-understanding and feedback received from others, we experience validation and acceptance.

The leader demonstrating self-esteem believes that she has a right to express and feel, as well as to connect with others. Self-esteem builds upon itself. As we increase our sense of belonging and connectedness to others we often experience high self-esteem, gaining confidence and validation from others. Leaders high in self-esteem join with others and value the contribution they make.

The leader high in self-esteem appreciates her own personal uniqueness and power and integrates peak or life-enhancing experiences. We experience greater belonging and connectedness to others when we:

- appreciate the specialness of ourselves and others
- engage in creative and expressive activities
- are responsible for ourselves
- utilize role models

- form goals
- initiate projects to enhance personal and professional growth
- express needs and feelings
- accept successes and failures
- express self-worth and the worth of others
- treat patients, families, staff, and peers as valued and important

With enhanced self-esteem we are able to set new goals and develop new behaviors. Individuals with high self-esteem tend to be autonomous and display a basic trust in themselves and others (Beck et al., 1984). In effective communication, each person's self-esteem guides the interaction and influences how he or she relates to others. An effective leader seeks to develop self-esteem, self-confidence, and an ability to live and work with others. The authors refer to the importance of self-esteem frequently in this book because it is a key to effective leadership!

SELF-ACTUALIZATION

The self-actualized leader communicates her appreciation of human potential and seeks to lead others beyond the basic requirements of work, thus fostering their creativity, esteem, and respect for themselves and others. Change is constant within our organizations and within our personal and professional lives. To avoid burnout, stress-related illness, and depression, it is essential that the effective leader be able to integrate and appreciate peak experiences.

Peak experiences are any life-enhancing activity, whether simple or complex, that brings satisfaction, challenge, or connection with others. They help us feel more fully alive! The following are examples of peak experiences shared by nursing leaders:

- involvement in creating a new and dynamic health care service (e.g., cardiac health center, childbirth education program, wellness clinic)
- achieving higher education goals
- initiating and implementing creative health proposals
- staffing and coordinating care in busy medical-surgical units
- teaching patients, families, peers, and colleagues
- political action
- assisting in the birth of a child
- helping a family grieve

- supporting the growth of others and appreciating our own personal growth
- laughing with and supporting our colleagues
- solving unique or challenging problems
- witnessing a patient's return to health because of our efforts and commitment to practice

The nurse leader who identifies and accepts the positive outcomes of her work as meaningful and unique despite staff shortages and/or organizational problems is communicating her self-actualization. Seeking creative and innovative solutions, fostering esteem in others, and developing yourself beyond the standard performance criteria are other ways of communicating self-actualized messages.

VALUE CLARIFICATION

The authors know of no other profession undergoing more radical changes in its traditional values than the nursing profession. Historically, nursing has been a humanistic profession, a way of life centered on human relationships and values. There is a need today to call attention to this tradition and to the conflicts within the nursing profession and to face problems confronting us both personally and professionally. Today's nurse leader must build on the values of the past and assimilate new values such as:

- autonomy
- rights to define and control practice
- rights to assert and negotiate for personal and professional needs
- career mobility and development
- attainment of higher education beyond entry level requirements
- political action
- certification in one's specialty
- policy and decision making

As the nurse leader seeks to implement her pivotal role in the health care team, conflicts in values may occur when:

- competition for resources exists in a given work setting
- financial reimbursement for nursing services is questioned
- demands of one's personal life are overwhelming

- an individual nurse leader feels trapped in her role, dissatisfied, "burned out," or overwhelmed by the needs of the organization
- the nurse leader does not possess necessary skills
- a new position requires the nurse leader to give more of herself professionally
- the goals of the nurse leader and the organization are incompatible

The nurse leader may then question how the traditional values of caring, dedication to service, and humanism can be met as she cares for herself and meets the demands of the organization and the profession.

Clarifying our personal values can be the best foundation for creating change and expanding our awareness. We can ask ourselves, "Who am I, what do I value, where am I going, what do I want, and how do I want to achieve it?" These questions are not only important to our professional growth but also to effective nursing leadership. When we understand how these values may influence our behavior, we can begin to change important aspects of this behavior and enhance our ability to communicate.

Values clarification is a process often used to examine one's basic philosophy of life and thereby lead to action. There is often a gap between what we say we value and what we demonstrate in our behavior. Carl Rogers (1951) indicated that healthy personalities express or demonstrate congruent behavior. That is, their values are congruent with their behavior. The clearer we are about our values, the more able we are to choose a response consistent with what we believe. We can change our values just as we change a diagnosis if given new and different data. When we have a clear understanding of our values, then we can choose a method of communicating those values in order to succeed in our role. The relationship between values clarification and decision making is explored further in Chapter 11.

ASSERTIVE SKILLS

We know that nursing leaders need an effective and stress-reducing method to communicate their needs, values, expectations, and feelings in a changing work world. Using healthy, assertive communication is such a method. Assertiveness as a self-help tool was discussed as early as 1958 (Wolpe, 1958).

Assertiveness is neither a genetically determined nor an innate personality trait but rather a learned skill that needs consistent practice, reinforcement, and support. Allowing time to learn and practice it, beginning in small ways, can ensure success.

What are the expected outcomes from the assertive nurse leader? Assertiveness increases both the personal power and the creativity of the leader. Self-understanding and effective methods of dealing with others are the natural outcomes of assertiveness skills development. These skills support and promote satisfying personal and professional lives. As assertiveness is based on self-esteem and respect for self and others, it can reduce tension and stress. Assertive individuals tend to be less anxious and less angry and to use fewer maladaptive coping mechanisms to deal with conflict than do passive and aggressive individuals.

Becoming Assertive: What We Need to Know and Examine

When we are about to change our values and behavior and experience new ways to be, we frequently create a disturbance within our social and work setting. People who are accustomed to our being one way or exhibiting one type of behavior experience that change in us from their own context of understanding. Sometimes our changing alters the relationship. As with any personal change, it is helpful to examine the supports, barriers, myths, and constraints that influence our ability to make the change. In the following exercise (Figure 5-1) you are asked to assess these issues. Later in the chapter, assertiveness is defined, and examples of assertive behavior are given.

Figure 5-1 depicts circles of influence. Take time to list the people who influence you the most in your everyday life. How do these people influence you? Positively, with support, or in a negative, constraining fashion? How do you respond to them—assertively, passively, or aggressively? Have you noted patterns in your behavior? What style do you find yourself using most often to communicate?

Barriers to Assertiveness

There are five barriers to assertiveness:

1. self-dialogue
2. rigid requirements
3. negative labeling
4. myths
5. risking and conscious choice

The barrier posed by self-dialogue—what you actually tell yourself about assertiveness—can be assessed by answering the questions in Exhibit 5-1.

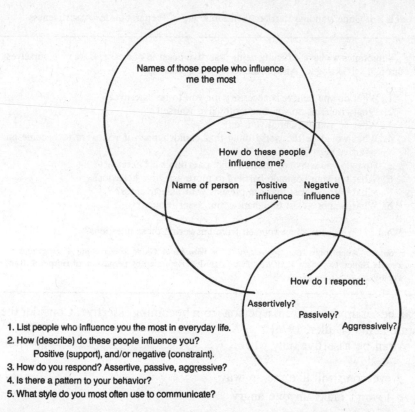

Names of those people who influence me the most

How do these people influence me?

Name of person   Positive   Negative
                   influence   influence

How do I respond:

Assertively?

Passively?

Aggressively?

1. List people who influence you the most in everyday life.
2. How (describe) do these people influence you?
       Positive (support), and/or negative (constraint).
3. How do you respond? Assertive, passive, aggressive?
4. Is there a pattern to your behavior?
5. What style do you most often use to communicate?

Figure 5-1 Circles of Influences. *Source:* Adaptations from *Self-Assertion for Women: A Guide to Becoming Androgynous* by Pamela Butler. Copyright © 1976 by Pamela Butler. Reprinted by permission of Harper & Row Publishers, Inc.

The barrier to assertiveness of rigid requirements denies the concept of androgyny. Jungian theorists believe that within every man and woman is a set of both traditional feminine and masculine traits (Jung, 1966). Because we are a humanistic profession, we tend to exhibit a great many traditionally feminine traits: nurturing, sensitivity, hands-on caring, and the ability to empathize and to feel. We do not give enough credit, however, to traditional masculine traits that we must also exhibit: leadership, assertiveness, supervisory ability, and the ability to manage, control, initiate, and motivate others. We all have known excellent and effective nursing leaders in our work environment who are also nurturing and sensitive women and men. This balance of androgyny is essential for assertiveness because it allows a person to be a leader who is direct and honest, to express feelings, and to deal with conflict while remaining nurturing and loving. Rigid requirements

Exhibit 5-1 Understanding Barriers: Self-Dialogue in Preparation for Assertiveness

Sometimes we have difficulty being assertive because of messages we give ourselves through self-dialogue. Answer the following questions:

1. What do you believe is necessary for you to be assertive?
2. What criticisms do you frequently give yourself?
3. What do you like about yourself?
4. What would be the worse thing that could happen if you were to become an assertive person?
5. How do you convince yourself that assertion isn't necessary?
6. What are your common barriers to more assertive behavior?
7. What barriers exist that can prevent your assertiveness?
8. What supports exist to enhance your assertiveness?

What did you learn about yourself from answering these questions?

Source: Adaptations from *Self-Assertion for Women: A Guide to Becoming Androgynous* by Pamela Butler. Copyright © 1976 by Pamela Butler. Reprinted by permission of Harper & Row, Publishers, Inc.

can be set up that prevent a person from becoming assertive. Consider these statements (Butler, 1976):

I can be assertive only when:

- everyone will like me anyway
- I won't make anyone angry
- I can be unobtrusive
- it is a matter of principle or part of my job
- I know the exact outcome

One can easily see how these beliefs limit opportunities to attempt assertiveness.

We often express habitual self-criticism or claim negative labels that also prevent us from becoming assertive. For example, if someone sees herself as childish or unlady-like, competitive, harsh, egotistical, crazy, bitchy, stupid, or infallible, she denies herself the opportunity to truly share feelings and to be responsible for her own behavior (Butler, 1976). As you define your values regarding honest and healthy communication, you will be able to add more positive self-labels to the repertoire of the things you tell yourself.

In addition to negative images, we often believe myths about assertiveness; for instance, myths that confuse assertion with aggression or consider the assertive person to be self-centered, unfeminine, overly ambitious, or self-serving are major barriers in the leadership role. We tend to believe these myths if they have been supported by painful past experiences. The more opportunities to use assertiveness with positive results, the more apt we are to integrate this skill into our behavior.

The manner in which we allow ourselves to take risks and make conscious choices can also support positive self-talk.

What prevents us from choosing for ourselves? One of the major reasons why we choose not to take action is the notion that we are not entitled to change or to make a choice. We may fear that our choice will be the wrong one; this fear may stem from past failures or our parents' disapproval of our actions during childhood (Grossman, 1978). Messages that promote more negativism and a lack of assertiveness are, "I could never do this," "I am too old to do that," and "this is the way we've always done this." We end up making the past into a current restriction; for example, "The reason I frequently explode at meetings is because my mother could never control her anger." Another barrier to choosing is expressed by such phrases as "they say," or "they're not," or "I am not as good as." Constantly comparing ourselves to others leads us nowhere. The "I could nevers" and the "yes, buts" instill a feeling of defeatism, a sense of potential failure, and an unwillingness to listen actively and openly to new thinking. Negative self-talk affects our relationships with others and our leadership role within our profession.

Conscious choosing is the mark of a healthy leader. It makes possible risk taking and future planning. As a nursing leader, it assists us in controlling our practice and our professional development.

Preparing to be Assertive

In preparing for an assertive encounter, it is helpful to give ourselves positive statements (Butler, 1976), to own the responsibility of expressing our feelings, and to acknowledge that it is acceptable to make a mistake. Prepare for an assertive encounter by telling yourself that:

- "I don't have to be liked or approved of by everyone, nor apologize for what I feel."
- "I value the opportunity to approach a problem-solving event."
- "I have a right to express my feelings."
- "It is acceptable to be nervous."
- "Sometimes we are not going to reach total agreement."
- "I may say things that are not perfect."

After the encounter we need to reward ourselves! It is essential to acknowledge the value of being assertive. Use this form of self-dialogue after an assertive encounter:

- "I'm glad I was honest."
- "I'm glad I said what I needed to say."
- "I'll be more at ease next time."
- "The important thing is that I expressed my feelings."

Defining Assertive Behavior

Review Exhibits 5-2 through 5-4 for definitions and examples of assertive, passive, and aggressive behavior and communication. As you identify patterns and characteristics relevant to your own style, review Table 5-1 for a further understanding of each behavior.

Exhibit 5-2 Definitions of Passive, Assertive, and Aggressive Behavior

---

Nonassertive (Passive) Behavior: A feeling within that discourages standing up for oneself. Only a limited degree of energy is directed toward powerful control of one's life. Sometimes passive behavior is a form of manipulation. Failure to take responsibility for expressing one's own feelings or denial of feelings is also part of passive behavior.

Assertive Behavior: Standing up for one's rights to express one's feelings, reactions, or expectations without alienating the other person. Assertive communication is honest, direct, and appropriate. It is behavior-focused, rather than personal criticism. One feels self-worth and a great sense of wellness when one acts assertively.

Aggressive Behavior: Standing up for one's rights in a way that often humiliates or degrades another person. Sometimes aggressive behavior comes from pent-up anger and frustration. Aggressive behavior often involves holding another person responsible for one's feelings. Aggression gets the person what is desired, but alienates others in the process.

Exhibit 5-3 Characteristics of Passive, Assertive, and Aggressive Communication

---

As you read each description, think of those characteristics that may apply to your personal communication style.

The person with a passive style of communication:

- does not directly express feelings, thoughts, and wishes
- internalizes or withholds feelings
- puts others first
- does more than his or her share of listening
- uses disclaimers
- does what he or she is told even when that is not desired

Exhibit 5-3 continued

- has a soft weak voice
- pauses and hesitates often
- makes others guess what he or she wants to say
- leans against something for support, looks down, or holds self when standing
- has cold and fidgety hands
- tends to look down or away
- may allow others to push him or her around
- stores up resentment and anger
- rarely experiences rejection directly

The person with an aggressive style of communication:

- expresses what he or she thinks or feels at the expense of other's rights or feelings
- uses sarcasm or humorous putdowns
- goes on the attack when he or she doesn't get what is desired
- begins sentences with "you" followed by attack or labeling
- uses absolute terms—never, always, ought to, should
- tends to move with an air of strength and superiority
- can be cold and deadly quiet, flippant, sarcastic, or loud
- has posture that shows aggression—usually the right foot is directed outward in front of the body and hands are on the hips
- points finger and makes a fist
- focuses on being right
- is not usually pushed around by others
- often feels alone

The person with an assertive style of communication:

- makes direct statements regarding his or her feelings, thoughts, and wishes
- stands up for his or her rights while taking into account the rights of others
- listens attentively and lets other people know that he or she has heard them
- is open to negotiation and compromise but not at the expense of his or her rights and dignity
- can give and receive compliments
- can deal effectively with criticism
- conveys an air of assured strength and empathy
- has a relaxed, well-modulated, firm voice
- uses "I" messages
- communicates openness and honesty with his or her eyes
- has balanced and erect posture
- feels well
- experiences self-esteem and worth

Exhibit 5-4 Examples of Assertive, Aggressive, and Passive Behavior

---

You are asked by telephone to be in charge of the Hospital Foundation Campaign for your division. This is a responsibility you have accepted in the past. This year, you no longer wish to accept it. You respond:

PASSIVELY: Say yes, put down the phone feeling pain in your stomach.

ASSERTIVELY: State, "No, I really do not wish to take on the responsibility this year." When the caller pressures you by saying, "Please, we really need you," you respond, "As I said, I really cannot take on this responsibility this year. Thank you for considering me."

AGGRESSIVELY: "Don't you realize people get sick of being asked time and time again to help?"

A friend tends to telephone you each morning as you are preparing breakfast and getting ready for work. You respond:

PASSIVELY: Ask your daughter to ring the doorbell so that you can tell your friend that someone is knocking at the door and you have to go.

ASSERTIVELY: "I have to go now. I really need to start breakfast for the family and meet our morning schedule."

AGGRESSIVELY: "It is 7:45 A.M. You know I have to get breakfast ready. Don't you think of anyone but yourself?"

You arrive at the hotel with reservations. The attendant waits on everyone around you and ignores you. You have to meet someone for a meeting so time is important. You respond:

PASSIVELY: Stand there getting a headache as the attendant waits on everyone else.

ASSERTIVELY: "I would like you to take care of my reservation. I have a meeting to attend immediately, and I believe I was next in line."

AGGRESSIVELY: "Are you ever going to wait on me? Do I have to wait for you to attend to everyone else first?"

You are not pleased with the service rendered for your automobile repair. You respond:

PASSIVELY: Say nothing and leave.

ASSERTIVELY: Contact the manager of the auto dealership and tell him or her that you do not feel that you were given adequate service. You state what you would like to occur.

AGGRESSIVELY: Tell the employees, "You are the dumbest people I have ever seen. I am going to tell everyone in town not to come here."

Your boyfriend does not help you clean up the dishes after you have had mutual friends for dinner. You respond:

PASSIVELY: Make a show of cleaning the dishes, making a lot of noise in the kitchen, and then say goodnight without warmth.

ASSERTIVELY: Tell your boyfriend you really do not want to clean up by yourself and you would like him to do half the dishes.

AGGRESSIVELY: Say with sarcasm, "I just love to wait on our friends. I was born to live in the kitchen."

Source: Adaptation totalling 2 pages from *Self-Assertion: A Guide to Becoming Androgynous.* Copyright © 1976 by Pamela Butler. Reprinted by permission of Harper & Row, Publishers, Inc.

Table 5-1 Assertiveness Grid

Characteristics	Passive-Inhibited	Assertive	Aggressive
Personal understanding	"You're better than me, you're OK" "I am not OK" "You can choose for me" "You are responsible for my feelings, I deny my feelings"	"I respect you, I respect myself" "I am OK and so are you"	"I am in control at your expense." "I am OK, you are not OK"
Communicates	"May I . . ." "Ah . . ." "You know . . ." "Could I . . ." "I can't . . ." "I could never . . ."	"I am . . ." "I like you . . ." "I feel . . ." "When this happens, I feel . . ."	"You're bad . . ." "You should . . ." "You ought to . . ." "It's your fault . . ." "You never . . ."
Acts	Denial of anger Withdrawal Induction of guilt Focus on criticism of self	Openness to others Honest and direct Body feels comfortable Focus on behavior	Anger often acted out physically and reflected in facial muscles Name calling Sarcasm Blaming Focus on criticism of others

Source: V. Baillie.

To assist you in assessing your own levels of assertiveness, take a few minutes to complete Exhibit 5-5, the Assertion Survey.

Problem Areas of Assertive Behavior

After scoring the assertion survey, you may have determined that you already experience certain events with comfort and with assertiveness. However, you may also share in some of the most common problem areas:

- affirming self and others through the expression of positive regard
- dealing with criticism
- saying no, setting limits
- making requests and expressing personal initiative
- expressing anger

Exhibit 5-5 Assertion Survey

Indicate in the right-hand column your level of assertiveness regarding each statement. Scores reflect the following:

1. I feel very uncomfortable
2. I feel moderately comfortable
3. I feel most comfortable

If the situations described do not seem to be part of your lifestyle, try to imagine how you would feel and respond accordingly.

I. BODY AWARENESS

- Looking another person directly in the eyes _____
- Accepting a compliment with full eye contact _____
- Maintaining full eye contact in a difficult encounter _____
- Feeling comfortable throughout your body when angry _____
- Smiling and frowning when you feel like it without fear _____
- Using a firm tone of voice when necessary _____
- Speaking in front of a large audience _____
- Asking questions at meetings, classes, etc. _____
- Holding your head and body erect and in a centered position when under pressure _____
- Knowing how to control your hands when explaining something _____
- Tolerating silence _____
- Speaking slowly _____
- Entering a room when men are present _____
- Entering a room when women are present _____

Exhibit 5-5 continued

II. YOUR THOUGHTS AND EXPECTATIONS

- Enjoying being competent, using your power, refusing to label yourself "aggressive," "castrating," "bitchy," or "bossy"   _____
- Able to request expected service from clerks, in restaurants, etc. when it hasn't been given   _____
- Avoiding saying "I'm sorry" frequently   _____
- Believing "I have a right to express what I feel"   _____
- Liking yourself   _____
- Telling yourself "I'm likable"   _____
- Being glad you expressed yourself, you were honest   _____
- Being comfortable with not apologizing when applicable   _____
- Expecting to be responsible for yourself   _____
- Being able to set limits, say no   _____
- Being able to accept criticism when valid   _____
- Being able to reject criticism that is invalid   _____
- Being able to return borrowed items without apology   _____
- Being able to return defective or unwanted merchandise   _____
- Being able to tell someone that he or she is offending you in some way   _____
- Tolerating not getting the approval you would like from a significant male/female in your life, boss, wife, husband, lover, friend, etc.   _____
- Stating your opinions and ideas to an authority figure—boss, doctor, attorney, clergy, father, etc.   _____
- Disagreeing with an authority figure   _____
- Accepting rejection   _____
- Turning down a request   _____
- Handling patronizing remarks   _____

III. SEXUALITY

- Feeling free to express your sexual needs and feelings   _____
- Initiating sexual activity   _____
- Telling your lover what pleases you   _____

IV. REACTIONS

- Tolerating an argument with another person   _____
- Expressing anger honestly and freely   _____
- Listening to an embarrassing and/or funny story about yourself   _____
- Freedom to joke   _____
- Freedom to laugh   _____

continues

Exhibit 5-5 continued

- Talking with persons about competition with one another   _____
- Openness with people of your sex in regard to feelings of intimacy—can tell a friend when you love her or him with warmth, sincerity, and comfort   _____
- Accepting praise   _____
- Asking for positive feedback and support   _____
- Asking for constructive criticism   _____

SCORE

- 48–72   Unproductive, passive form of communication, limiting use of personal power. Need to learn and use assertion techniques.
- 73–97   Frequently uncomfortable yet attempting some assertion—keep it up!
- 98–122   Frequently assertive—keep trying, you're well on your way!
- 123–144 Assertive! Teach others by sharing your methods.

Source: © 1982 Virginia Baillie.

In a work environment where we must do more with fewer resources, handling these problem areas assertively is critical to effective leadership. Exhibit 5-6 contains examples of assertive statements for each of these areas.

Exhibit 5-6 Examples of Direct Assertive Statements

EXPRESSION OF POSITIVE REGARD

- I really appreciate what you did for me.
- You look very pretty tonight.
- Thank you for appreciating me and for being concerned about me as a human being.
- I really enjoy being with you.
- I think Mary deserves a promotion. Her work is outstanding and goes far beyond her present position.
- I would like to recommend David. He has demonstrated his competency and skill beyond what has been expected. I think he would make a fine member of the new committee.
- You are really funny. I love you.
- I admire your skills as a head nurse.
- I felt great giving my presentation to the physician committee.

LIMIT SETTING: SAYING "NO"

- I understand you would like me to recommend you for the committee, but I really feel I do not know enough about your skills and competencies to do so.

Exhibit 5-6 continued

- I was in line first.
- I would like to pay for my own dinner this evening.
- I do not enjoy hearing jokes that put down other people. It really makes me uncomfortable.
- I appreciate your concern, Mother, but I really have to make my own decision.
- I would appreciate it if you would not smoke.
- If you are going to smoke, please direct the smoke in the opposite direction, away from me.
- I really do not want to take on the responsibility. Please find someone else.
- This is not clear to me. I need more clarification about this policy.
- Thank you for offering help, but I really do not need it right now.
- I have to say "no" to your request.
- Doctor, I will not be yelled at. When you are calmer, I'll be happy to discuss the problem.

DEALING WITH CRITICISM AND ANGER

- I do not agree with you.
- I feel the expectations for this project have not been met.
- I feel resentful when you do that.
- I want you to stop yelling right now.
- I do not like what you are doing.
- I will not listen to criticism when I am being cursed.
- I do not like you spilling coffee all over my desk every morning. Could you please be more careful.
- I feel I am doing all the giving.
- I was furious that you did not support me at the meeting when you promised you would.
- I am very annoyed that you give directions to me through other people.

INITIATION

- I would really love to go out somewhere for dinner and dancing.
- Will you help me clean the house to prepare for company?
- Let's split the check.
- What is your fee?
- My fee for my services is . . .
- I would like to bring up something that is really bothering me; it is a source of concern.
- I would like to have more experience as an intensive care nurse. I am confident I could do the job if given the chance.
- I really need your support right now.

Exhibit 5-7 Helpful Steps in Becoming Assertive and Communicating Positive and Negative Messages

---

1. Be aware of your current communication style.
2. Identify personal barriers to becoming assertive.
3. Become aware of your body posture and tone of voice and how they may change in response to communication.
4. Give yourself ample time to learn by consistent practice.
5. Identify the situations in which you would like to be more effective.
6. Write a personal plan for change. Keep a log of your assertive responses.
7. Use assertion techniques for simple uncomplicated issues before tackling more intense issues.
8. Practice using assertion consistently.

In order to determine how you react to events in the work place and in your personal life, you may wish to keep a log of your communication attempts and interactions. Although it is useful to learn an assertive technique, it is meaningless unless you integrate it with an understanding of your physical, mental, and behavioral reactions. A sample assertion log is provided (Table 5-2). Helpful steps in becoming assertive are listed in Exhibit 5-7.

Affirming Self Through the Expression of Positive Regard

Being able to express positive regard for yourself is most important in developing assertiveness. If you find the expression of positive regard for yourself difficult, this section will be of benefit to you.

The emerging leader can reduce her anxiety and gain confidence by allowing positive images to enter her conscious awareness. Consider the following positive and affirming messages to the self:

- I am confident.
- I am intelligent.
- I can express creative ideas.
- I am an effective nurse and leader.
- I am able to take on challenges.
- I am dependable and conscientious.
- I am fun to be with.
- I am excited about my leadership role.
- I am an excellent nurse.

We often fail, however, to give ourselves these messages and substitute self-criticism and negative responses or messages, comparing ourselves to others:

Table 5-2 Assertion Log

Write down events and your reactions, barriers, and outcomes for 2 weeks. Can you find any patterns? What pattern do you see evolving as you become more assertive?

The Setting: Work situation/event	Physical: Body cues, physical reactions, feelings	Behavioral: What I did or said ard in what manner	Outcomes: What would I like to have said or done?	Barriers: What hindered me from doing what I wanted to?	Supports: What helped me?

- I'm not as good as . . .
- I could never achieve . . .
- I am too old to . . .
- I am not okay.
- I should work harder.
- I am only an "okay" nurse.
- I wouldn't be able to . . .

Self-affirmation is the foundation for becoming assertive. When we hold positive images about ourselves, we can better deal with conflict and stressful interactions that attack our self-worth. To become fully energized to reach our potential and to be able to take risks, we must be able through verbal and internal expression to give positive messages to ourselves. Jung (1966) believed it is essential to develop positive images about ourselves and store them in a mental bank, taking them out when we are in conflict.

It is helpful to consider our fears that arise when we express positive feelings. Positive expressions can range from feelings of warmth, appreciation, and caring to increased levels of intimacy and even love for another (Butler, 1976). Usually we fear expressing positive feelings because we associate them with anxieties. We are afraid that we would be thought of as too pushy, too forceful, boastful, or insincere.

Problem areas in expressing positive self-regard and positive feelings are (1) talking about ourselves, (2) trying to accept a compliment, (3) relating to the opposite sex, (4) expressing initiative, or (5) attempting to set a limit.

The following exercise (Butler, 1976) is helpful to do as an individual when you are attempting to increase feelings of self-esteem. However, it is especially valuable to use with your work group when you are trying to build cohesion and acceptance of one another. In your work group, ask each member to take a few moments to write down a list of her personal positive traits and beliefs. Then ask each person in turn to share for 2 minutes these positive images about themselves. Ask each member to listen to the speaker and then give feedback. A discussion can follow on the barriers to expressing positive images and how it feels when we do it.

Many nurse leaders experience discomfort when verbalizing and owning up to positive statements about themselves. If you felt uncomfortable writing your list or could not think of any positive statements, you may be experiencing low self-esteem and will find it difficult to be assertive.

After you complete the exercise, ask yourself if your positive traits were confined only to one area, or were you able to find various areas in your life that were supportive of positive regard? Once you said something positive about yourself, did you attempt to take it back? Did you feel comfortable hearing feedback from others? Were you specific about your accomplishments? Did it feel good to state what was positive about yourself? Were you able to express areas of your personality that are both traditionally feminine and traditionally masculine? For example, were you able to state that, as a leader, you can be analytical, powerful, ambitious, and organized (traditional masculine traits)? Were you also able to say that, "as a mother or a woman, you are nurturing, gentle, affectionate, compassionate (traditional feminine traits)?

Asserting only one half of ourselves is contrary to our androgynous nature. And yet, many nurses value traditionally feminine components of personality and devalue masculine traits.

Dealing with Criticism

The ability to deal with criticism is the second area of importance in becoming assertive. If we can express what is positive about ourselves, it is then easier to deal with criticism. Positive responses help us feel okay and deal with the reality of criticism. It has been said that hearing one criticism can have more influence on us than hearing 20 positive expressions in the same day.

Often, restrictive thoughts are associated with the way we handle criticism. For instance, if we feel, "In order to be okay, I have to be liked and approved of by everyone," or "To feel good about myself, I must never make a mistake," then we will have difficulty handling criticism (Butler, 1976).

At times we may experience stress from juggling the three processes of thinking, feeling, and listening while attempting to respond to criticism. Because we may be just barely coping, we often cannot take in more input and may feel the impact of the criticism even more. This is often due to our becoming enmeshed in the context of the critic. Especially in stressful situations or if our self esteem is low, we may interpret the criticism as a rejection of the self rather than of the action. It is essential to separate the problem from our own integrity and then respond. In our relationships, each of us is being constantly evaluated in each interaction. To some this evaluation may be felt as criticism.

We can respond to criticism in several negative ways. We can apologize; some of us apologize more than necessary. We may become defensive and offer multiple excuses for what we have done. We may attempt to attack the critic. We may say nothing, internalizing the stress experienced. Or, we may feel bad and return to our home environment feeling physically ill or emotionally distressed.

In contrast to these negative responses, there are five productive and assertive methods to deal with criticism: (1) accept it, (2) disagree with it, (3) set limits with the critic, (4) fog, and (5) delay (Butler, 1976).

The first method—to accept a criticism—is used when we feel the criticism is justified and the critic is someone whom we respect. After examining our behavior or actions, we agree with the critic that she is justified in criticizing what we have done. However, it is important to point out to the critic that, in accepting the criticism, you are not putting yourself down. It is not necessary to give more than one apology. By saying, "I accept your criticism and I will see that this matter is taken care of," or "I will work on resolving the problem," or "I will evaluate what you have said to me," we tell the critic that we feel a sense of personal power and self-acceptance and that we are able to handle criticism. This contrasts sharply with accepting criticism in the negative sense: becoming defensive, apologizing profusely, crying, or saying nothing. These are negative approaches to the critic.

The second method is to disagree with the critic. This is used when we feel that the criticism is either not justified, irrational, or unfair. It is necessary in these situations to follow the disagreement with strong self-affirmation. It is in these situations that positive images about yourself and your specific accomplishments can be used: for instance, "I disagree with your criticism. In fact, I have been working very hard on this project and am quite pleased by the outcome." Or, "I disagree with your criticism; I feel it is unjust. I am a person who is responsible and can demonstrate my accomplishments." Backing up your disagreement with self-affirmation is essential!

The third method is to set limits with the critic. This is especially important if the critic is using profane language, defaming your character, displaying inappropriate behavior, or being more critical than the situation warrants. It is appropriate for the assertive person to say to this type of critic, "Stop! I will not be criticized in this fashion. If you have specific reasons why you are concerned, I will be glad to talk to you." Or, "I will not be yelled at; when you are calmer and wish to discuss this, please contact me."

The fourth method of responding to criticism is fogging. This is especially helpful when criticism is manipulative, petty, or aggravating. Fogging techniques usually reflect an awareness of what has been said, but defuse the criticism. For instance, the person being criticized states something like, "Probably . . . That could be so . . . ," and then immediately changes the subject. In another example, a friend tells you, "You look like you have gained a great deal of weight." You feel that your weight is a personal area and that her remark is somewhat petty criticism. You choose not to discuss it. A fogging technique would be to say, "I guess I have. Tell me, how is your new project coming along?" This sets up a fogbank for the critic, which the critic cannot negotiate effectively. It allows you to make a choice about how much criticism you are willing to accept.

The fifth method is the delay tactic. It is especially useful in leadership positions when we are asked to deal with a great amount of information and respond to it immediately. In using the delay tactic it is essential that we indicate that we have heard the criticism but are unable to give a response at this time and will give a response at some future specified time. For example, the supervisor of a medical center approaches you in the hallway and says, "Do you know that your product report demonstrates you are 4 FTEs above your position control, costing the hospital thousands of dollars?" The supervisor then goes on to state that this is a criticism of your leadership ability. Certainly, at this point you cannot give a definite response to this criticism. The delay tactic allows you to state, "I hear that this is a concern to you. Let me look into it and I will get back to you tomorrow." You then have the responsibility to get back to the critic. Using the delay tactic gives you time to look at the issue, determine the facts, and decide how you wish to respond to the critic.

Setting Limits and Saying "No"

How many times have you wanted to say no? When you set a limit, you are saying, "This is where I draw the line." We often set limits on our time, privacy, energy, money, and expectations of self and others. Limits can be set in both positive and negative situations.

Setting limits often helps preserve communication and valued relationships. We teach others how to treat us by setting limits, thereby contributing not only to the quality of the workplace but also to our own personal lives. Remember that limits are changeable just as feelings are changeable when we have new data.

It is very important in all areas of assertion, but especially when setting limits, that you become aware of your body language, your voice tone, and your facial expression. Maintain eye contact, use appropriate facial expressions that correspond with the matter at hand, and do not withdraw from the encounter. It is also important not to be afraid to be intense or to increase the tone of your voice.

Butler (1976) describes several steps in setting limits. The first step is to make your expectations and limits clear. In other words, ask "What do I really want to change?" Concentrate on a specific behavior. What has happened to upset you? What do you want to see happen?

Then, be aware of the use of partial limits. Often, we want to set a limit and say no to only part of a situation. It is helpful to use what is called the "sandwich approach" in setting limits. First, indicate the positive aspects of the situation. In the second level, the middle of the sandwich, consider the negative aspects, and end with the bottom part of the sandwich, which is a positive statement of outcome. The sandwich approach allows you to set limits on the behavior that causes concern and also points out positive and acceptable behavior. This approach may be used in evaluation as well as when limits are necessary. For example:

> You are conducting an annual performance evaluation for a staff nurse with 1 year's experience. You have noted an area of concern in her performance that calls for partial limit setting.
>
> *First level—positive aspects:* "Ms. Smith, I'd like to share how pleased I am to observe your interest and ability in providing family and patient teaching. Many of your patients have left the hospital better prepared to cope with their illness.
>
> *Second level—problem:* However, I am concerned that I see little documentation of this teaching in the clinical record. This documentation is part of your position's responsibility.
>
> *Third level—positive outcome:* I am sure you will note the importance of this in the future. I will look forward to reading more of your positive teaching concepts.

When setting limits, consider also the four levels of muscle (Butler, 1976):

1. Make a polite request.
2. Strengthen the request.
3. Inform the person that continued unwelcome actions will evoke consequences.
4. Take action; that is, follow up with the consequence.

It is important to use the levels of muscle as though they are on a continuum. Often, people set limits by first making a polite request and then going directly to step 4: taking action and producing consequences.

Be aware of meta levels, the point beyond which you will not go (Butler, 1976). For example, to explain to an aggressive person that the conversation has gone beyond what you can handle, simply state, "This communication is getting beyond me; I'd rather not carry on the discussion at this time. I will get back with you tomorrow and we can talk further."

As in any area of assertion, it is important to start setting limits in simple ways and to practice this skill consistently. You may want to begin with people you seldom see who are not emotionally important to you. With these people, practice setting limits, making requests, and saying no. Use these methods with people close to you or in more sensitive situations when you feel more confident.

Saying no requires that we allow ourselves to have "negative" feelings: the awareness that we are angry or feel upset or simply do not want to do something. Negative feelings also lie along a continuum from "I feel uncomfortable, irritated, frustrated, or peeved" at one end to "I am furious or outraged" at the other end.

We are often taught to suppress these negative feelings. Women tend to express less aggression physically than men, but they are more apt to express aggression verbally. Women may also internalize aggression or negative feelings; the result is physical illness or emotional distress. If we feel esteem and respect for ourselves, we are able to say no because this is congruent with our values.

Making Requests and Expressing Initiative

Expressing initiative is really saying "yes" to what we want and "yes" to what we feel. We are saying, "I would like to see this happen. I want this. I would like to see you help me with this. I am hoping for this." Initiating what we really want and need involves personal respect for self and others. Expressing initiative is also very important when we are establishing our authority and competency in a work setting. We often have more difficulty saying "yes" to ourselves than saying "no." We may not express what we want fast enough or wait for "leftovers."

Taking initiative requires risks, which ultimately enhance our lives. Maslow (1971) pointed to the multiple decisions and risks we face over a lifetime and suggested that we develop the habit of always choosing the growth option. Not only does this improve self-confidence, but it also enhances self-actualization. In a study by Hall (1972), women were found to assert themselves less than men and were less likely to defend their beliefs or support their own ideas. These areas must be improved if we are to effectively take initiative.

Take a paper and pencil and make a list of those things that you want. Look at that list. How many of those requests do you really follow through with achieving? What barriers get in the way of expressing your personal initiative? How often do you volunteer for committee work, for new responsibilities in the work setting, or for additional involvement? The barriers, "I am not as good as" or "I could never really ask for this" often block initiative.

Making requests requires us to know what we want. Out of a sense of respect for ourselves, we allow ourselves to ask for what we want. This does not mean that we always get what we want. Yet, the assertive person feels very good when she realizes that she has not denied what she feels or really needs. Remember, we choose to take responsibility for our feelings.

Expressing Anger

Developing a personal model from which to handle angry feelings is an important component of a healthy personality. An effective approach for dealing with anger is to use the word "I" in the expression of feelings. The word "I" states, "I am aware of what I am experiencing right now, and I wish

Exhibit 5-8 Practical Assertion Techniques

Broken record: This technique allows us to repeat a point without getting sidetracked by irrelevant issues. For example, "Yes, I know, but my point is . . . " "As I said, my point is . . . " "Let me get back to my original point." "As I said, I really cannot take on that responsibility this year, I realize you are concerned . . . "

Negative inquiry: This is an assertive but nondefensive response. It does not criticize the other person, but produces a question that allows the person to examine whether he or she is right or wrong. For instance, you might say, "I don't understand why you think all nurse managers at this hospital are unprepared." "Do you think that we don't know what we are doing?" It suggests the need for re-examination of the criticism.

Assertive agreement: This is used as a response to criticism by admitting that an error indeed has been made. It separates the mistake from your value as a person. For instance, "Yes, I was late for work today. I am usually more responsible and I will see that it does not happen again." So in fact, you are agreeing with the criticism yet backing yourself up with affirmation.

Content to process shift: This technique shifts the focus of the discussion from the topic to an awareness of what is happening between the two people in an interaction. "We are getting off the point now and I am feeling uncomfortable because we are bringing up old history. You appear to be angry with me. Let us talk about what is really happening now." Or, "I really feel we are getting off the track and we are talking about issues that are not relevant to this problem. Let's begin to talk about what is happening here."

Workable compromise: This is a technique used in working with equally assertive people. The other person is someone whom you respect and with whom you know you can work on a compromise. For example, "You and I have worked together for a long time. I trust your judgment and abilities. I know we can work out a compromise to deal with this problem."

Self-disclosure: Self-disclosure is sharing and offering information about yourself—how you think, feel, and react to the expectations of others, to life, and to issues in the workplace. It can be used to help you gain information about how others see you and to help you build trust with other people.

Diffusing: Diffusing is a technique that ignores the content of someone's anger and puts off further discussion until a better time. For instance, "Dr. Smith, I can see you are very upset and angry. I suggest you take a little time to calm down and we will discuss this later today."

Sources: From *The Relaxation and Stress Workbook* (pp. 148–149) by M. Davis, E. Eshelman and M. McKay, 1980, Oakland, Calif.: New Harbinger Publications. Copyright 1980 by New Harbinger Publications; and from *Your Perfect Right* by R. Alberti and M. Emmons, 1974, San Luis Obispo, CA: Impact Press.

to share it with you." "I" statements reflect an intensity of feeling. They do not deny what is experienced, but do allow the critic or the person evoking the anger to listen to what we have to say. They do not cut off communication, but allow the discussion to be continued.

Consider these "I" statements:

- I would like to talk this over and see how we can resolve the problem.
- I don't like to be shouted at; let's talk this out.

- I am interested in hearing how you feel.
- I agree with you, I think I have made an error. Let's look at it together.
- I would like to discuss this with you; can we sit down and talk about it?
- Why do you feel that I never complete my responsibilities?
- I don't agree with you.

Aggressive responses to anger, in contrast, might include, "You don't know what you are talking about, Don't shout at me, Can't you do anything right, You are really stupid, You never do what I ask, You should be better than that, You should be more responsible, You ought not to do that." Aggressive handling of anger often starts with "you."

Another way for the assertive person to deal with anger is to share with another what has happened, for example, to role play the discussion to gain positive resolution. Another method is to anticipate anger and to imagine the way in which you wish to complete the interaction with more positive outcomes. Finding a personal model that works is an effective way to use assertiveness in response to anger.

For additional assertive methods that can be applied to common communication problems, see Exhibit 5-8.

REFERENCES

Alberti, R., & Emmons, M. (1974). *Your perfect right* (rev. ed). San Luis Obispo, CA: Impact Press.

Beck, C., Rawlins, R., & Williams, S. (1984). *Mental health-psychiatric nursing.* St. Louis: C. V. Mosby.

Butler, P. (1976). *Self-assertion for women. A guide to becoming androgynous.* New York: Harper & Row.

Davis, M., Eshelman, E., & McKay, M. (1980). *The relaxation and stress workbook.* Oakland, CA: New Harbinger.

Grossman, R. (1978). *Choosing and changing: A guide to self-reliance.* New York: E. F. Dutton.

Hall, K. (1972). *Sex differences in initiation and influence in decision-making groups of perspective teachers.* Unpublished dissertation, Stanford University.

Jung, C. (1966), *Two essays on analytical psychology.* Princeton, NJ: Princeton University Press.

Maslow, A. (1962). *Toward a psychology of being.* Princeton, NJ: D. Van Nostrand.

Maslow, A. (1971). *The farther reaches of human nature.* New York: Viking.

Rogers, C. (1951). *Client-centered therapy.* Boston: Houghton Mifflin.

Whitman, M. Toward a new psychology for nurses. *Nursing Outlook* (Jan. 1982) 48–52.

Wolpe, J. (1958). *Psychotherapy by reciprocal inhibition.* Stanford, CA: Stanford University Press.

Chapter 6

Dealing with People in Difficult Situations and Resolving Conflict

As leaders we are bound to encounter difficult people and situations that bring us into conflict, stimulate feelings of anger and anxiety, and may even cause us to question our leadership abilities. This chapter discusses the roles of anger and anxiety, difficult behavioral patterns and situations, and steps for conflict resolution.

UNDERSTANDING ANGER

When the common emotions of anger and anxiety influence our interpersonal relationships, our ability to listen and learn, work productivity, capacity to lead, and job satisfaction can be negatively affected. Feelings associated with anger can be viewed on a continuum with mild feelings, such as being peeved, irritated, and annoyed, at one end and absolute outrage at the other end. Feelings of anger change in intensity according to the situation, our personal control, and expression.

Anger is often a warning that we are becoming alienated from the "self" (Beck, Rawlins, & Williams, 1984). When we first become aware of anger's warning signs—feeling threatened, stressed, anxious, and tense—we can then begin to verbalize, to "clear the air," and to reduce tension, thus defusing the anger and its potential build-up. We often have negative associations with the emotion of anger, but in fact, when expressed wisely, this emotion can lead to enhanced relationships, decreased anxiety, and increased creativity. Verbalization of anger gives us the best chance at healthy communication in difficult situations.

If we deny anger and internalize it, we risk psychosomatic illness, depression, and feelings of inadequacy. If we are prone to verbalize the anger aggressively, we risk the alienation of others and feeling a loss of control.

When a person who has learned to internalize and control feelings of frustration, fear, and conflict finally expresses them, it is often through aggression and accompanied by feeling loss of control. Others may feel alienated from this individual and even afraid of them. The emotion of anger has been linked with feeling powerful (Bach and Goldberg, 1974), but this "power" is often a cover-up for frustration, sadness, and/or anxiety. Anger is frequently experienced physically, as well as emotionally.

It is helpful for us to realize that we can use anger, instead of it using us. Exhibit 6-1 presents the process involved in the awareness and expression of anger in three different directions (Beck, Rawlins, and Williams, 1984).

Moreno (1956) describes three stages of anger. The *warm-up stage* is characterized by a building up of events, reactions, and feelings that lets us know we are experiencing the beginnings of anger. For example, the staff nurse who frequently calls in sick at the last minute may at first cause you mild annoyance. However, soon you enter the warm-up phase when feelings

Exhibit 6-1 Anger: Directions and Reactions

INITIAL PROCESS
  Awareness of threat to self-esteem, worth, needs
  Stressful reaction—physical outcome or symptoms
  Emotions: frustration, anxiety, anger

Direction 1: Internalized anger
  • denial of anger
  • over-control
  • often somatic complaints result
  • no expression of anger
  • withdrawal
  • depression
  • illness

Direction 2: Externalized anger through aggression
  • feeling that power is associated with aggression
  • loss of control
  • verbal and physical fighting
  • anger unresolved
  • anger prolonged
  • anger expressed outward in violence, aggression

Direction 3: Verbalization of anger
  • others alerted
  • air cleared
  • feelings clarified
  • tension reduced
  • anger defused
  • feeling of self-worth results

of anger have increased as you think about your feelings, expectations, and reactions to what has happened. You may experience physical symptoms associated with anger.

The *stage of catharsis* follows when you confront the staff nurse with your feelings and clarify your expectations. You may well share how this behavior causes you distress as a leader and describe the consequences if the behavior continues.

Integration occurs in the third stage as both individuals acknowledge what this expression of anger has taught them about one another and how it will affect future performance. In this last stage of integration, we often experience positive regard for ourselves for having confronted our feelings, rather than denying or internalizing them.

We can also experience anger through one or all of five dimensions: physical, emotional, intellectual, social, and spiritual (Beck et al., 1984). See Table 6-1 and note which of these responses to anger you personally experience.

Anger is useful to us when it allows us to discharge creative energy spontaneously and forces us to seek new and positive solutions to human conflict. Without anger as a spontaneous process, we are often left with only anxiety. A decrease in opportunities to express anger often causes an increase in anxiety, which can alter our ability to function and engage in relationships.

Table 6-1 Dimensions of Anger: Common Feelings and Reactions

Physical	Emotional	Intellectual	Social	Spiritual
Stares, glances noting anger	Depression	Fault-finding	Poor self-concept	Absence of meaningful philosophy of life
	Powerlessness	Blaming		
	Annoyance	Sarcasm	"Kill with kindness"	
Tightened jaws	Frustration	Argumentativeness		
Clenched fists	Hurt		Withdrawal	Blocked creativity
Tense posture	Guilt	Repetitive thoughts	Domineering behavior	
Increased blood pressure	Disappointment	Scolding	Intimidation	Contradictory beliefs
	Feelings of inadequacy	Forgetfulness	Over-reactivity	
Tachycardia			Hypersensitivity	
Increase in fatty acids				
Fewer lymphocytes				

Source: Adapted by permission from "Dimensions of Anger" by S. L. Thomas in *Mental Health Psychiatric Nursing* (p. 474) by C. Beck, R. Rawlins, and S. Williams, 1984, St. Louis, MO: The C.V. Mosby Company. Copyright 1984 by The C.V. Mosby Company.

UNDERSTANDING ANXIETY

Few among us have not experienced some form of anxiety. Various images come to mind as we consider the term "anxiety." Performance anxiety can often be a motivator to achievement. For example, in studying to get an "A" on an exam, anxiety may motivate the student. Anxiety may motivate the musician who must perform in front of an audience. Anxiety, however, can act as a major barrier to effective leadership. Nurse leaders sharing in educational sessions have reported that anxiety can and does alter successful role adaptation. One nurse described approaching her new role with fear and apprehension and said that she experienced sleepless nights, self-criticism, and difficulty focusing on work details.

Anxiety can be experienced as a mild reaction to stress or as actual panic. It is often associated with life stress and changes in our personal and professional lives, e.g., divorce, moving, hospitalization, loss of or change in job, increased work demands, a new boss, or new corporate structure (Beck et al., 1984). Individuals experiencing anxiety often report these symptoms:

- tachycardia
- increased respiration
- pacing
- feelings of restlessness and excitation
- helplessness
- sadness
- fear of abandonment
- apprehension
- pessimism
- withdrawal

Anxiety also can be experienced through five dimensions (Table 6-2). Review your personal responses to anxiety.

As we begin to develop healthy methods for communicating our needs, values, self-confidence, commitment, and initiative, we reduce our tendency to experience anxiety in the leadership role. Building self-esteem and adopting realistic expectations are major supports for handling the human emotion of anxiety.

It is helpful to realize that a new role will always bring with it some role stress and anxiety. However, the nurse leader who handles confrontation well, increases staff morale by guiding and mentoring, and elicits active involvement in planned change, functions without undue anxiety and with enhanced self-esteem.

Table 6-2 Dimensions of Anxiety: Common Feelings and Reactions

Physical	Emotional	Intellectual	Social	Spiritual
Sweating	Guilt	Selective inat-tention	Apprehension with a group of people	Alienation
Increased pulse rate	Shame			Indifference
Grief	Impaired short-term recall	Fear of loss of control	No sense of the future
Increased respi-ratory rate	Angor	Focus on detail	Isolation and withdrawal	Fear of death
Resentment	Blocking of words		
Difficulty sleep-ing				
Flushed face		Defensiveness		
Cold extremities				

Source: Adapted by permission from "Dimensions of Anxiety" by M. Chisholm in *Mental Health Psychiatric Nursing* (p. 425) by C. Beck, R. Rawlins, and S. Williams, 1984, St. Louis, MO: The C.V. Mosby Company. Copyright 1984 by The C.V. Mosby Company.

DEALING WITH DIFFICULT PEOPLE IN DIFFICULT SITUATIONS

If you have experienced anger, anxiety, and conflict, chances are that you were dealing with difficult people in difficult situations. There are many types of difficult behavioral patterns. Bramson (1981) describes seven major types of difficult people:

- Type 1: The hostile aggressive
- Type 2: The complainer
- Type 3: The silent and unresponsive
- Type 4: The super agreeable
- Type 5: The negativist
- Type 6: The know-it-all expert
- Type 7: The indecisive

As leaders, we have all worked with and tried to manage the behavior of these types of people. Follow these steps for effectively coping with difficult people (Bramson, 1981):

1. Stop wishing the difficult person were different.
2. Consider the reasons for his or her behavior.
3. Get some distance between you and the difficult person.
4. Formulate a coping plan.
5. Implement that plan, using behavior modification principles and support from others.

6. Monitor the effectiveness of your coping strategy and change it if necessary.

Understanding the reasons why the difficult behavior occurs can enhance the effectiveness of your coping strategy.

Type 1: The Hostile Aggressive*

To cope effectively and intervene with this type of individual, try:

- standing up for yourself and your rights to be assertive
- giving the person time to run down or defuse so you can be heard; remain in place and look directly at the person who is yelling, crying angrily, or exploding—when the hostile, aggressive person begins to lose momentum, assert yourself, using phrases that clearly indicate that you want the behavior to end, such as "Stop!" or "That's enough!"
- not worrying about being polite
- getting the person's attention by standing up, moving your chair, dropping a book, or loudly calling his/her name while maintaining eye contact
- getting the person to sit down
- speaking from your own point of view
- avoiding a head-on fight
- being ready to be friendly

Remember that the hostile aggressive person is responding out of pent-up frustration and hostility. Attempts to lessen and recognize that frustration will help you cope with and intervene with this difficult behavior.

Type 2: The Complainer

Coping and intervening strategies with this difficult behavior call for you to:

- listen attentively
- acknowledge the person

---

* Excerpt from *Coping with Difficult People* by Robert M. Bramson. Copyright © 1981 by Robert M. Bramson. Reprinted by permission of Doubleday, a division of Bantam, Doubleday, Dell Publishing Group, Inc.

- be prepared to interrupt the conversation
- use limiting responses
- don't agree unless you want to
- avoid the accusation-reaccusation sequence
- state facts without apology
- switch to problem solving

Remember, the complainer may actually not be looking for a solution to every problem he or she brings up, but may be seeking your recognition. Stating to this person, "I understand your concern; one thing I admire about you is that you do a fine job despite difficulties or obstacles," can help provide that recognition.

Type 3: The Silent and Unresponsive

With the silent and unresponsive person, coping and intervening methods include:

- open-ended questions
- the friendly, silent stare, allowing time for the person to respond
- not filling the space of silence
- commenting on what's happening
- helping reduce the tension
- setting time limits

When the silent and unresponsive person finally answers, "I don't know," ask yourself if this is a genuine response; what else might the person be saying? Return the statement in a restatement, "You don't know!" If the silent person then opens up, be attentive, let him or her be vague to a point, and give reinforcement for the response.

If the silent person remains silent:

- Avoid concluding your meeting with polite niceties such as "Well, it was good to talk to you," or "Have a nice weekend;" instead, let it be known that the subject is important and will be raised again
- follow through; schedule another meeting time
- proceed on your own if the silent, nonresponsive person will not act; inform them of the consequences of your action

Type 4: The Super Agreeable

Effective coping and intervention strategies for the super agreeable person include:

- Make honesty nonthreatening.
- Be personal when you can.
- Do not allow the person to make unrealistic commitments.
- Be prepared to compromise.
- Listen for humor.

Type 5: The Negativist

The "wet blanket" can best be coped with by these strategies:

- Avoid getting drawn into the negativism.
- Maintain your own realistic optimism.
- Don't argue.
- Don't rush into proposing solutions.
- Ask, "What's the worst that could happen?"
- Use negativism constructively.

Type 6: The Know-It-All Expert

The know-it-all expert can best be coped with by these methods:

- Do your homework and be knowledgeable.
- Listen and acknowledge.
- Question firmly, but don't confront.
- Avoid becoming the counter-expert.

Type 7: The Indecisive

Effective coping strategies with the indecisive person include:

- Clarify the issues.
- Help the person to problem-solve.
- Rank order or prioritize alternatives.

- Link your plan to values of quality and service.
- Give support after the decision is made.
- Keep control.
- Watch for overload.

Difficult Situations

Difficult people are present in the work setting at every level. Finding ways to cope and intervene with their behavior can be a stress reducer to the nurse leader.

Below are described seven situations that involve difficult behavior in staff members. With a partner or work group, discuss the effective coping plan and intervention strategies that you would use in the management of these behaviors. Consider your right to be assertive!

Situation # 1: NO!

Mary Brown, RN, refuses a patient assignment. She demonstrates extreme hostility to the head nurse and accuses her of incompetence in assigning patients.

Situation # 2: NO! I am sick!

Ann Richards, LVN, is floated to another unit. She doesn't want to go, complains of being "ill," and goes home.

Situation # 3: Super Nurse?

This is the third time that you have received a patient complaint regarding care given by Mary Jones, LVN. Ms. Jones has denied any problems related to proper bladder catheterization, but this recent complaint brings renewed concern about her competency in this area. Patient complaints include rough handling, lack of attention to privacy, nurse in a hurry, painful. You have given Ms. Jones an oral reprimand and reviewed the procedure with her. She remains agreeable to addressing this problem, yet her performance does not improve.

Situation # 4: The Impaired Nurse

Karen Janison, RN, Assistant Head Nurse, has arrived for work, and you suspect she has been drinking. In the past few months you have heard rumors that she has an "alcohol problem." Karen's work seems disorganized, and she appears anxious and at times is hostile to staff. This is the first time that you have noted the distinct smell of alcohol.

Situation # 5: In Critical Care

Barbara Anderson, RN, MSN, is a new clinical specialist with advanced skills in critical care. Although you are pleased to have Barbara's skills in your division, you find that she is difficult to communicate with as a team member. Other staff admit to feeling intimidated and consider her a "know-it-all" expert. On two occasions you have overheard her telling staff members that they were "stupid." She is frequently hostile and aggressive during staff meetings. Yet, her clinical work is excellent!

Situation # 6: Drugs for Sale on Hospital Grounds

Mary Saunders, Head Nurse from 6 East, is your closest colleague and trusted associate. In confidence she tells you that Jeff Reed, day aide/orderly on your unit, has been seen selling cocaine. She has been given this information from a reliable staff member who has been with the hospital for many years and is known for her honesty. This staff member indicates that Jeff Reed's dealing in drugs is a widely known fact among the aide staff. Mr. Reed is well liked by everyone and is a very personable individual. Mary's staff member is afraid of retaliation.

Situation # 7: Aren't Staff Meetings Easy?

You have a great deal of material on today's agenda. New staff are to be introduced as well. You realize that Greg and Janet (RNs) appear impatient and offer only sarcastic remarks when you ask for their input. Greg frequently looks at his watch, and Janet states that she has to leave early due to a staffing problem. Greg and Janet are normally among the most supportive and cooperative members. You ask for a discussion of the problem: "What's going on?" Janet tells you she and Greg have heard how unfair you were to Nurse X and what a terrible evaluation she received. They are upset and angry. You know your evaluation of Nurse X was quite accurate, well documented, and supported. Fairness and progressive discipline are essential to you in your dealings with staff. Judging from Greg's and Janet's version, they heard little about the actual outcome of your interaction with Nurse X. You are portrayed as unfair, unrealistic, and "out to get her."

UNDERSTANDING CONFLICT AND CONFLICT RESOLUTION

Conflict can be defined as differing response tendencies. It is not by definition hostile, antagonistic, or otherwise negative. Conflict may take on those qualities, but negative characteristics are not inherent to it. In fact, differing response tendencies are a source of creativity and new ideas. They may also be a source of survival. For instance, if 5 minutes from now a fire breaks out in your unit and you run to telephone the fire department while another person uses the fire extinguisher and a third person closes the windows, these differing responses are likely to enhance everyone's chance of survival. In dealing with difficult situations, differing perspectives and ideas can be brought together to achieve a more workable solution than could be conceived by any one person.

However, differing responses are often perceived as threatening to an individual's goals. For instance, if you want to buy a system to computerize care plans and another nurse wants to furnish a lounge for the staff and only limited funds are available, it is easy for each of you to perceive the other's desire as threatening. If you get what you want, there is likely not to be money for what the other nurse wants. It is through this process of perceiving a threat that conflict is experienced negatively and anger and defensiveness are elicited. For as long as we conceive of the outcome of conflict as "either/ or," conflict will be perceived as negative. As we learn to consider "both/ and," conflict can become a positive, creative, growth-enhancing experience for all concerned. Conflict resolution can be a process through which everybody wins. It is not a process of battle, where there is a winner and a loser, but rather a dialectical process of arriving at an outcome that is satisfactory to all parties concerned.

Nurse leaders can count on different response tendencies existing among staff and even within the same individuals. The ability to use the differences constructively will enhance your ability to influence, motivate, and facilitate staff to meet their potential. Dealing openly and constructively with conflict prevents negatively charged situations from arising and creates a more nourishing work environment.

As you recall, self-esteem guides our interactions. As you consider entering into a conflict resolution situation, review your self-esteem rating for the day. Also, consider the self-esteem of the person with whom you will engage in conflict resolution. You will want to affirm their weak areas and give corrective feedback where they are strong. Your goal is to move toward a win-win situation by enhancing your own self-esteem and that of the person with whom you are resolving conflict through this use of personal power.

Because self-esteem is based on the congruent enactment of values, you may also want to review values—both your own and those of the person with whom you are resolving conflict.

Using Communication Skills to Resolve Conflict: Steps for Conflict Resolution

The process of conflict resolution uses the skills of active listening, feedback, and assertive behavior. Below is an outline of steps that can be used in resolving conflict. Before following these steps, be sure that you really want to achieve an outcome satisfactory to all involved, rather than a situation where you win and someone else loses. Conflict resolution is not a process that will help you win; it is a process that will help every person involved to win.

First, during the "getting ready" stage, consider what in the situation is really upsetting to you. Be specific in identifying the upsetting behaviors. For example, a head nurse was bothered by the behavior of Mary, a staff nurse. Yet, it was only on some days that she felt something in the pit of her stomach and felt ready to kill Mary. There was something in particular that Mary did that upset her, and the head nurse had to identify that behavior. She needed to identify her own feelings and how she was affected by Mary. Maybe she felt angry or frustrated or did not understand her or was bewildered by Mary.

During this stage, talking out your concerns with another person is one of the best ways to clarify what is bothering you and how you feel about it. It is also safer to talk it over with another person before approaching the person with whom you have a conflict.

Once you have identified the problem, ask the involved individual to talk with you and jointly set a date for conflict resolution. The time to resolve conflict is not when it is convenient for only one person but when it is convenient for both. An effective approach is to go to the person and say, "I have something I would like to talk about with you. When can we get together?" Maybe it will be at break, maybe it will be after work, or maybe it will be right then, but the time needs to be jointly decided.

State the problem. Describe one specific behavior at a time. You may have a list of 23, but deal with them one by one. Describe the effect of the behavior on you and the feelings it elicits. Use "I" statements.

Check the communication process. Remember that on a good day, your listener might hear with 50 percent accuracy. In this situation you are talking about a problem, and feelings are involved. Therefore, each person may only hear 25 percent of what is said, so active listening is essential. By having the other person repeat what you said, you are validating that what you said is what the other person heard. Clarify any misunderstandings and expect misunderstanding. Misunderstanding will happen more often than not.

Next, make a request. Consider what change you want from the other person and make a clear statement about it.

Then check the communication process again. Have the other person repeat what you said. You are validating that what you said is what they heard. Clarify any misunderstanding.

Now that you have made a clear request and you have checked to see that the request was understood, it is time to ask, "Will you do it?" Remember that a request is not a demand.

Conflict resolution is a joint process. Now that your problem and request for change in behavior have been heard by the other person, it is time for him or her to respond. There may be whole or partial compliance with your request, or the other person may refuse it. The other person may need time to think about it or to talk it over with another person. He or she is not always able to reply immediately. In fact, an excellent assertive technique is, "I'm not ready to respond to that yet," or "I don't have a response to that yet: I need time to think" (see Chapter 5).

If the solution you proposed is not acceptable, you can ask, "Can we work together to find a solution acceptable to us both?" You may need to define the problem mutually before you can agree on a solution. Perhaps the only point you can agree on initially is the fact that you are uncomfortable with the other person or she is uncomfortable with you. From that point, both of you can go on to define the problem further.

Use the decision-making process (see Chapter 11). Brainstorm alternative solutions and evaluate options to see which are workable and acceptable to both parties. Decide what solution is potentially most successful and be clear about the details of who will do what, where, when, and to what extent. Spell out time and money agreements clearly. Then implement the solution and set a date to evaluate the progress you are making. This is where most people stop the process of conflict resolution. They never reach the point of evaluating such issues as did the solution help, did it work, did we succeed together, or is it working as expected? And do not forget the very last step: acknowledging one another's efforts and congratulating one another for working to achieve a mutually agreeable solution.

Conflict resolution is a skill that is developed with time and practice. As with any skill, it is easier to start with something small and simple. The first time you try this process, it is easier to try something like talking with a coworker about whether or not to open the window, rather than trying to decide a major issue with your family, a friend, or coworkers. In addition, the first time that you try this process, it may be easier to inform the person that you are learning conflict resolution. Two people who have learned this process in class may sit down together with directions in hand and carefully follow each step on the page, to the satisfaction of both.

Unresolved conflict is a major source of stress for nurses at work. In one study of stress and coping in psychiatric nursing, the major source of stress was unit staff conflict (Trygstad, 1984). One out of every three stressors experienced by nurses in this study came from conflict with coworkers over working relationships and staff performance. Fifty percent of the stress experienced by the nurses in this study—that is, every other stressor—derived from communication and conflict between unit staff and with the head nurse. The stress in staff working relationships came from lack of or insufficient communication, not listening to one another, use of defensive responses, ignoring of input, use of indirect or passive-aggressive communication, and the processes of bickering, blame, and criticism, rather than conflict resolution. The stress in staff nurse/head nurse interaction came from lack of input into decisions: a unilateral decision-making process, and the lack of positive reinforcement, information, and communication. The most helpful response from others identified by this group of nurses was listening, and the most detrimental response identified by this group of nurses was not listening.

An essential role of the nurse leader is to resolve conflict. Both role modeling and facilitating the resolution of conflicts among staff are desirable nurse leader behaviors.

REFERENCES

Bach, G., & Goldberg, H. (1974), *Creative aggression*. New York: Doubleday.

Beck, C., Rawlins, R., & Williams, S. (1984), *Mental health-psychiatric nursing*. St. Louis: C.V. Mosby, p. 107.

Bramson, R. (1981). *Coping with difficult people*. New York: Ballantine Books.

Moreno, J. (1956). *Sociometric school and science of mankind*. New York: Beacon House.

Trygstad, L. (1984). Stress and coping in psychiatric nursing. *Dissertation Abstracts International*, *45*, 3775-B.

Chapter 7

Developing Healthy Work Groups

Nurses seldom work alone. We usually work in work groups and frequently work with client groups. Our effectiveness in working with groups is enhanced by our understanding of group process and of the ways in which we can influence group process.

This chapter begins with an exercise (Exhibits 7-1 through 7-4) to help you gain an experiential understanding of group process. It is followed by a discussion of the characteristics and functions of groups and ways to facilitate group process. The chapter concludes with a discussion of teams and team building.

Exhibit 7-1 NASA Exercise Individual Worksheet

INSTRUCTIONS: You are a member of a space crew originally scheduled to rendezvous with a mother ship on the lighted surface of the moon. Due to mechanical difficulties, however, your ship was forced to land at a spot some 200 miles from the rendezvous point. During landing, much of the equipment aboard was damaged, and since survival depends on reaching the mother ship, the most critical items available must be chosen for the 200-mile trip. Below are listed the 15 items left intact and undamaged after landing. Your task is to rank order them in terms of their importance to your crew in allowing them to reach the rendezvous point. Place the number 1 by the most important item, the number 2 by the second most important, and so on, through number 15, the least important. You have 15 minutes to complete this phase of the exercise.

_____ Box of matches
_____ Food concentrate
_____ 50 feet of nylon rope
_____ Parachute silk
_____ Portable heating unit
_____ Two .45-caliber pistols
_____ One case of dehydrated Pet milk
_____ Two 100-pound tanks of oxygen

continues

Exhibit 7-1 continued

_____ Stellar map (of moon's constellation)
_____ Life raft
_____ Magnetic compass
_____ 5 gallons of water
_____ Signal flares
_____ First aid kit containing injection needles
_____ Solar-powered FM receiver-transmitter

Exhibit 7-2 NASA Exercise Group Worksheet

INSTRUCTIONS: This is an exercise in group decision making. Your group is to employ the method of group consensus in reaching its decision. This means that the ranking for each of the 15 survival items must be agreed upon by each group member before it becomes a part of the group decision. Consensus is difficult to reach. Therefore, not every ranking will meet with everyone's complete approval. Try, as a group, to make each ranking one with which all group members can at least partially agree. Here are some guides to use in reaching consensus:

1. Avoid arguing for your own individual judgments. Approach the task on the basis of logic.
2. Avoid changing your mind only in order to reach agreement and avoid conflict. Support only solutions with which you are able to agree somewhat, at least.
3. Avoid "conflict-reducing" techniques, such as majority vote, averaging, or trading in reaching your decision.
4. View differences of opinion as helpful rather than as a hindrance in decision making.

_____ Box of matches
_____ Food concentrate
_____ 50 feet of nylon rope
_____ Parachute silk
_____ Portable heating unit
_____ Two .45-caliber pistols
_____ One case of dehydrated Pet milk
_____ Two 100-pound tanks of oxygen
_____ Stellar map (of moon's constellation)
_____ Life raft
_____ Magnetic compass
_____ 5 gallons of water
_____ Signal flares
_____ First aid kit containing injection needles
_____ Solar-powered FM receiver-transmitter

Exhibit 7-3 NASA Exercise Direction Sheet for Scoring

The group recorder will assume the responsibility for directing the scoring. Individuals will:

1. Score the net difference between their answers and correct answers. For example, if the answer was 9, and the correct answer was 12, the net difference is 3. Three becomes the score for that particular item.
2. Total these scores for an individual score.
3. Next, total all individual scores and divide by the number of participants to arrive at an average individual score.
4. Score the net difference between group worksheet answers and the correct answers.
5. Total these scores for a group score.
6. Compare the average individual score with the group score.

RATINGS
  0-20 Excellent
  20-30 Good
  30-40 Average
  40-50 Fair
over 50 Poor

Source: Reprinted from *NASA Moon Survival Task* by Jay Hall, © 1986. Special permission for reproduction of this material is granted by the author, Jay Hall, Ph.D., and publisher, Teleometrics International. All rights reserved.

Exhibit 7-4 NASA Exercise Answer Sheet

Correct Number		Rationale
15	Box of matches	No oxygen
4	Food concentrate	Can live for some time without food
6	50 feet of nylon rope	For travel over rough terrain
8	Parachute silk	Carrying
13	Portable heating unit	Lighted side of moon is hot
11	Two .45-caliber pistols	Some use for propulsion
12	One case of dehydrated Pet milk	Needs water to work
1	Two 100-pounds tanks of oxygen	No air on moon
3	Stellar map (of moon constellation)	Needed for navigation
9	Life raft	Some value for shelter for carrying
14	Magnetic compass	Moon's magnetic field is different from earth's
2	5 gallons of water	You can't live long without this
10	Signal flares	No oxygen

continues

Exhibit 7-4 continued

_7_	First aid kit containing injection needles	First aid kit might be needed but needles are useless
_5_	Solar-powered FM receiver transmitter	Communication

Most groups doing the NASA exercise find that the group achieved a better score than most or all of the individual participating members. Therefore, one of the conclusions we can draw from this exercise is that *the effectiveness of a group or organization is greatly influenced by the quality of cooperation among its groups and individual members* (Francis & Young, 1979).

The principles of group dynamics demonstrated in the NASA exercise are applicable to nursing practice. The exercise illustrates that whether each member knows a lot or next to nothing about what he or she is doing, a group often can arrive at better decisions than each individual alone. In this exercise, the group had a better chance of survival through group consensus than by individual decision making.

To increase your experiential understanding of group process, take time now to discuss and note what helped and hindered your group as you completed the NASA exercise. Then, compare your experience with the following list of helps and hindrances that was compiled by one group of nurse leaders after completing the NASA exercise.

The supports to group decision making were:

- discussion and collective knowledge
- rational thinking and logic, e.g., "what if" questions and discussion of consequences
- environment perceived as safe and nonthreatening, which led to more individual sharing and risk taking; the group was perceived as safe because of eye contact, validation, feedback, and other nonverbal behavior
- common background of members—there were no experts
- a common and important goal held by all members: survival
- agreed-upon guidelines
- members' willingness to change and to listen to one another
- commitment to the goal and to the group

These elements hindered the group decision-making process:

- lack of knowledge and the perception that this exercise was unfair
- pressure to agree

- perception of unclear goals, expectations, and guidelines
- no set time frame
- anxiety
- perception that this was a fantasy experience, which decreased commitment
- power struggles

Take time now to relate what you have learned to your own nursing practice situation and the groups to which you belong. Consider your list of what helped and what hindered group decision making, as well as the list provided above, in relation to your own work groups.

For example, an environment perceived as safe and nonthreatening was seen as helpful by the group of nursing leaders. Do you also perceive this factor as helpful? How do you perceive the environment of the groups you rated? If you perceive the environment as less safe than is desirable, would more validation or feedback or eye contact be helpful? Relating what helps and what hinders group process to your own work groups allows you to assess them and target areas for improvement. This begins the cyclical process of assessment, problem identification, goal setting, intervention, and evaluation—a process for developing healthy work groups.

CHARACTERISTICS OF A GROUP

A group is two or more persons interacting within a structured environment. Groups come in varying sizes, forms, and effectiveness. However, any group can be described and understood according to the following nine characteristics:

1. purpose and goals
2. structure
3. composition
4. norms
5. atmosphere and cohesiveness
6. sociometric and communication patterns
7. phases
8. leadership
9. individual roles

The first issue is always *purpose*. What are we doing here? How are we going to accomplish the goal? A common purpose is absolutely essential to maintaining a group. Without a common goal and a common purpose, no tasks will be accomplished and the group will dissolve.

The *goals* are the chief determinants of group effectiveness, and these goals must be held in common. Not only must the group as a whole have goals but also every meeting needs a goal that is clear and shared. Without shared goals, the group will not be effective.

Group goals are not the same as the goals of any one member. Persons come to groups (e.g., a staff meeting, a committee meeting) with their own goals. The group works with these individual goals to develop group goals, which are usually slightly different from any one person's goals. The same process of developing group goals was experienced in the NASA exercise. Each person determined a goal (to survive) and priorities, e.g., what to take first. Working together in a group, the priorities of each member changed. The goal was still survival, but the exchange of different ideas led to changes in the individuals' priority ranking. Thus, priorities and goals change as a group evolves. The goals give direction to the group and are the standard for evaluation; without a clear goal there is no way to define success. Group members are dependent on each other to meet the group goal, and that is part of what keeps the group together. Group survival is a powerful motivator.

Structure follows the goals. Groups may be ad hoc or ongoing. They may be leaderless, or they may have an identified leader, an elected leader, or rotating leaders. There will always be power struggles within the group. Even with an appointed formal leader, that person will not necessarily be the most powerful person in the group. Leadership will emerge from the group.

Group *composition* can be heterogenous or homogeneous. One form is not necessarily better than the other. Rather, the group's composition should be appropriate to its goals, and there should be criteria for group membership. It is important to examine the degree of homogeneity and heterogeneity in groups because of the effect of composition on group process.

Norms are the description of acceptable behavior in a particular setting. Norms are different for each group and each different setting. Group norms are developed the same ways that group goals are developed. Individuals bring to the group their own set of norms and then a group culture develops. There is some negotiation (often covert) of what is acceptable.

As people meet in a group, the group becomes increasingly important to the members. Attachment, involvement, and commitment grow. When a group is new, members are often unwilling to comply with "the rules." As the group becomes more important to its members, they are more willing to change their behavior to maintain membership in the group. Individual members will adjust their behavior to meet group norms and gain acceptance and recognition if they want to be in that group. If the group is not important to a member, peer pressure will not have any force because staying in the group is not important.

Atmosphere and cohesiveness develop through working together. An atmosphere that fosters openness, trust, and support will lead to cohesiveness because it allows members to feel safe, e.g., that it is valued to speak up, you do not have to be right, the group will value your opinion and discuss it with you before arriving at a consensus. Each individual learns to share. There is eye contact, validation, and feedback before the group arrives at a decision.

Sociometric patterns are the patterns that reveal who talks to whom and with what frequency. Have you ever been in a group in which there are people who never speak? Have you been in a group in which two or three people dominate most of the conversation? They talk to each other as if the group is a three-person group instead of an eight-person group. What you are observing is a sociometric pattern, tied in with the evolution of power.

The *communication pattern* within a group may be manifest or latent. It may be verbal and open, or it may be nonverbal. Sometimes all the important decisions in a group are made nonverbally. Therefore, it is important to be aware of both manifest and latent levels of communication.

All groups go through *phases*. Whether a group meets one time for one hour or all day, every day for ten months, it will go through these phases: initiation, working, and termination.

During the initiation phase, the purpose and goals are established, leadership emerges, and an atmosphere develops as the question—How are we going to behave together?—is raised and answered. Rapport, trust, and group norms are established. Before the atmosphere is firmly set, the working phase begins. This phase is concerned with problem solving and goal achievement. The task of the group is accomplished in the working phase. Termination occurs when problems have been resolved and action plans have been made. Summary and closure do not always occur. Yet, for a group to feel good about itself and its work, it is important to summarize what was accomplished and to bring closure to the group.

Tuckman and Jensen (1977) have summarized the sequential development of small groups as occurring in five stages: forming, storming, norming, performing, and adjourning (Table 7-1).

Table 7-1 Stages of Group Development

Stages of Group Development	Task Behavior	Relationship Behavior
Forming	Orientation	Testing and dependence
Storming	Emotional response to task demands	Intragroup hostility
Norming	Expression of opinions	Development of group cohesion
Performing	Emergence of solutions	Functional role relatedness
Adjourning	Termination	Disengagement

Source: B.W. Tuckman and M.A. Jensen, *Group and Organization Studies, 2,* pp. 419–427, copyright 1977 by Sage Publications, Inc. Reprinted by permission of Sage Publications, Inc.

Leadership patterns may be authoritarian, democratic, or laissez-faire. In a laissez-faire group, the group often dissolves for lack of leadership and structure. With authoritarian leadership, rebellion may occur that will dissolve the group. A democratic leadership pattern works best in most situations, but is the most time consuming.

Individual roles within the group may be ascribed or achieved and depend on the members' past experience, individual needs, and group needs and characteristics. Some roles are helpful to the group in performing its task, some roles help maintain the group and relationships among members, and some roles hinder the group because they are directed toward meeting personal needs, rather than group needs.

Group members must fulfill certain roles for completing the group's tasks and for building and maintaining the group process. Following are lists and descriptions of these roles (Nylen, Mitchell, & Stout, 1967).

Task roles, functions required in selecting and carrying out a group task, include:

- *Initiating activity:* proposing solutions by suggesting new ideas, new definitions of a problem, a new attack on the problem, or new organization of material.
- *Seeking information:* asking for clarification of suggestions, requesting additional information or facts.
- *Seeking opinion:* looking for an expression of feeling about something from the members, seeking clarification of values, suggestions, or ideas.
- *Giving information:* offering facts or generalizations, relating one's own experience to the group problem to illustrate points.
- *Giving opinion:* stating an opinion or belief concerning a suggestion or one of several suggestions, particularly concerning its value rather than its factual basis.
- *Elaborating:* clarifying, giving examples or developing meanings, trying to envision how a proposal might work if adopted.
- *Coordinating:* showing relationships among various subgroups or members.
- *Summarizing:* pulling together related ideas or suggestions, restating suggestions after the group has discussed them.

Group building and maintenance roles, functions required in strengthening and maintaining group life and activities, include:

- *Encouraging:* being friendly, warm, responsive to others, praising others and their ideas, agreeing with and accepting contributions of others.

- *Gatekeeping:* trying to make it possible for another member to make a contribution to the group by saying, "We haven't heard anything from Jim yet," or suggesting limited talking time for everyone so that all will have a chance to be heard.
- *Standard setting:* expressing standards for the group to use in choosing its content or procedures or in evaluating its decisions, reminding the group to avoid decisions which conflict with group standards.
- *Following:* going along with decisions of the group, thoughtfully accepting ideas of others, serving as audience during group discussion.
- *Expressing group feelings:* summarizing what group feeling is sensed to be, describing reactions of the group to ideas or solutions.

Group task and maintenance roles, which fall into both of the above categories, include:

- *Evaluating:* submitting group decisions or accomplishments to comparison with group standards, measuring accomplishments against goals.
- *Diagnosing:* determining sources of difficulties and appropriate steps to take next, analyzing the main blocks to progress.
- *Testing for consensus:* tentatively asking for group opinions in order to find out whether the group is nearing consensus on a decision, sending up trial balloons to test group opinions.
- *Mediating:* harmonizing, conciliating differences in points of view, making compromise solutions.
- *Relieving tension:* draining off negative feeling by jesting or "pouring oil on troubled waters," putting a tense situation in a broader context.

Working with the group with which you completed the NASA exercise, identify the roles enacted by each member during the exercise. Were all roles enacted or were some missing? Discuss whether the roles enacted during the NASA exercise were typical or unusual. What roles did you enact? Are these the roles you usually enact? Now that you have identified the needed roles, how can you facilitate the development of these needed roles by others and by yourself?

DEALING WITH PROBLEMS IN GROUPS

Problems With Individual Role Behavior

The problem group member is usually a person who experiences a problem. It is not that she is intentionally difficult, but rather that she has already experienced a problem and her attempts to remedy the problem create more problems, rather than diminishing them. Understanding the goal or the need of the person acting dysfunctionally makes it possible to negotiate a change.

All members need to feel included, heard, and valued. A felt lack of these is often the root of dysfunctional behavior. For example, the person who keeps sharing her personal experiences probably has a great need to be heard. You might negotiate with her that once during each session she can share something personal that is also relevant to the group and she can receive feedback that her comments are relevant and interesting. Chances are that she does have something relevant and interesting to say, which gets lost when the volume of her comments becomes problematic.

Negative group members need corrective feedback and limits. The person who is always negative, always destructive, needs to ask herself, "Why am I here? Do I do something of value to contribute to this group? What is my role?" The negative behavior also must be addressed. It is not simply a matter of rejecting a negative person from the group, although that person may arrive at the conclusion that she does not belong in the group. Rather, it is hoped that through feedback the negative person may change her behavior.

Another problem for many groups is posed by the quiet member. We learn from the study of psychology that all behavior has meaning. If we do not know the meaning of some behavior, we usually assign a meaning to it, but often we do not validate this meaning with the person.

Often, we assign negative meanings to quietness; we perceive ourselves as working hard while the quiet person does not work at all. We perceive ourselves as taking risks and exposing our ideas while they remain safe in their quietness. Often, we do not express these feelings in words. However, feelings not expressed in words are expressed in behavior (e.g., withdrawal from the quiet person) and/or physiologically (e.g., leaving group members with headaches or upset stomachs). It is healthier for all concerned to encourage participation from all members and to deal openly with nonparticipation problems in the group.

In general, when an individual assumes a dysfunctional role within the group, it is the responsibility of the leader and all members to give feedback to that person. If the behavior does not change, the conflict resolution process will be needed. Clarifying expectations and setting limits are particularly helpful when dysfunctional behavior occurs. As a group, nurses tend to want to be the "good guys." We tend to abdicate our roles of giving negative feedback and setting limits whether we are in a group member position or a group leader position. However, these difficult tasks are essential to the success of the group. Problem behavior will only change with feedback, limit setting, and consequences. Only as a last resort is it good process to ask a member to leave the group.

A function of the group is to help members become better-functioning group members. This occurs through identifying problems as they occur, verbalizing them and discussing the process within the group, providing feedback, setting limits, and providing consequences for behavior.

Problems in Group Process

"Getting stuck" with group process is best dealt with by verbalizing what is happening and discussing it within the group. Felt problems with group process can often be helpfully redefined as the "normal" evolutionary group process. For instance, testing of the group and individuals in the group occurs during the initial stage. This process seems to be necessary for trust and openness to develop. It is helpful to view testing as a process to be acknowledged and facilitated, rather than a problem to be eliminated.

Control is another issue that must be resolved within any ongoing group. Struggles occur both for formal and particularly for informal control. The outcome of these struggles cannot be predetermined, and they can be stopped only by authoritarian behavior, which usually yields short-term gain and long-term loss. The group itself becomes stronger and more functional if control issues are acknowledged and discussed as they arise.

FACILITATING EFFECTIVE GROUPS

As a member, you can facilitate task-group effectiveness in the following ways (McKay, Davis, & Fanning, 1983):

- Determine the purpose of the group.
- Know your own mind.
- Listen.
- Contribute.
- Keep your cool.

As a leader, you can do the following to increase the effectiveness of task groups:

- State the group purposes.
- Elicit contributions from group members.
- Determine a group consensus.
- Keep order.
- Maintain group morale.
- Choose the appropriate leadership style.

Groups are most effective when they have these characteristics:

- Goals are clear, shared, and seen as important by all members, who are committed to them.
- Diagnosis of group problems is careful and systematic; solutions flow from the diagnosis and address basic causes of the group problems.
- Decisions are made through consensus. Different ideas are integrated into the solution, and there is a high degree of commitment to it.
- Participation is broad; all members are active and involved in contributing to group efforts.
- Listening is active and attentive; clarification or elaboration of ideas is sought.
- Feelings are expressed and are considered important "data" for group effectiveness. Empathy and consideration are shown to members.
- Influence is shared, with many people having input; individual perspective is valued and influence is widely distributed.
- The leadership role changes as different leadership needs become important.
- Conflict is openly expressed and acknowledged; members willingly confront differences and actively seek a mutually satisfactory resolution.
- Trust is high among members who are willing to take risks and reveal sensitive information. There is no fear of reprisal when negative reactions are expressed, and such candor is encouraged.
- Creativity and growth occur because innovation and experimentation are encouraged, new ideas and approaches are actively tried. The group seeks new and better ways to operate or resolve problems, and the group is flexible.

TEAMS AND TEAM BUILDING

A group merely renamed a "team" is not a team. Whereas a good work group is an organized group of people working together to achieve a goal, a team is not only good at tasks, but it is also good at group process. Francis and Young (1979, p. 8) define a team as "an energetic group of people who are committed to achieving common objectives, who work well together, and enjoy doing so, and who produce high quality results."

The costs of team building are high. Team building takes resources: time, energy, and commitment. Developing the team takes conscious effort and continuing nurturing. Those who participate must be willing to take risks, to open their minds to new experiences and ideas, and to let go of old ways of thinking and doing. Old issues must be worked through, and new relationships must be built. New skills may be needed for this process.

Inevitably, a mature, effective team is one that has been deliberately developed. Group problems have been identified and worked through, roles clarified, and relationships strengthened. Francis and Young (1979) compare a good team to a good marriage. Neither one is effortless, neither one just happens.

The advantages of a team are obvious. In a team, members complement each other in such a way that they are able to achieve results that they could not achieve individually. Their satisfaction with both the process and the high-quality results of the teamwork is evident. A team is not a team without good results. Something comes out of a team that is not possible from a group.

Successful teams show progress in all of the following areas (Francis & Young, 1979):

- *Appropriate leadership:* The team manager has the skills and intention to develop a team approach and allocates time to team-building activities. Management in the team is seen as a shared function. Individuals other than the manager are given the opportunity to exercise leadership when their skills are appropriate to the needs of the team.

- *Suitable membership:* Team members are individually qualified and capable of contributing the appropriate "mix" of skills and characteristics.

- *Commitment to the team:* Team members feel a sense of individual commitment to the aims and purposes of the team. They are willing to devote personal energy to building the team and supporting other team members. When working outside the team boundaries, the members feel a sense of belonging to and representing the team.

- *Constructive climate:* The team has developed a climate in which people feel relaxed, able to be direct and open, and prepared to take risks.

- *Concern to achieve:* The team is clear about its objectives, which are felt to be worthwhile. It sets targets for performance that demand effort but are achievable. Energy is mainly devoted to the achievement of results, and team performance is reviewed frequently to see where improvements can be made.

- *Clear corporate role:* The team has contributed to corporate planning and has a distinct and productive role within the overall organization.

- *Effective work methods:* The team has developed lively, systematic, and effective ways to solve problems together.

- *Well-organized team procedures:* Roles are clearly defined, communication patterns are well developed, and administrative procedures support a team approach.

- *Critique without rancor:* Team and individual errors and weaknesses are examined, without personal attack, to enable the group to learn from its experience.
- *Well-developed individuals:* The skills of team members are deliberately developed, and the team can cope with strong contributions from individual members.
- *Creative strength:* The team has the capacity to create new ideas through the interactions of its members. Innovative risk taking is rewarded, and the team supports new ideas from individual members or from outside. Good ideas are followed through into action.
- *Positive intergroup relations:* Relationships with other teams have been systematically developed to provide personal contact and identify where working together may yield the maximum payoff. There are regular contact and review of joint or collective priorities with other teams. Individuals are encouraged to contact and work with members of other teams.

The work group that is interested in becoming a team is referred to the manual, *Improving Work Groups,* by Francis and Young (1979). It addresses the rationale for team building, provides an assessment tool, and includes experiential exercises for developing those areas assessed as being in need of development.

Because nurses consistently work in and with groups, an understanding of group dynamics is essential to your role as leader. The norms of your unit group will affect the implementation of primary care or other changes in working patterns. The purpose of the staff meeting will affect how you exercise your leadership in it. The composition of the group will affect how you prepare for an inservice education session. The sociometric patterns of an extended family will influence your discharge planning with that family. Understanding these dynamics will help you avoid pitfalls and maximize benefits in working with these groups.

REFERENCES

Francis, D., & Young, D. (1979), *Improving work groups.* La Jolla, CA: University Associates.

McKay, M., Davis, M., & Fanning, P. (1983). *Messages: the communication book.* Oakland, CA: New Harbinger.

Nylen, J., Mitchell, J.R., & Stout, A. (1967). *Handbook for staff development and human relations training.* NTL/Learning Resources.

Tuckman, B.W., & Jensen, M.A. (1977). Stages of small group development revisited. *Group and Organization Studies, 2*(4), 419–427.

Chapter 8

Developing Others: Interpersonal Challenges and Techniques

An empirical tenet of nursing leadership is that the leader achieves clinical and managerial goals through the activities of others, primarily the staff of the nursing unit. The quality of care is directly related to the capabilities and performance of the staff. To ensure quality of care, it behooves the nurse manager to expend energy in staff development activities (Fournies, 1978). As the nurse leader systematically interacts with each staff member, she inspires, motivates, and directs each to achieve her career goals. This chapter outlines the professional nurse leader's pivotal role in staff development.

The dramatic technological changes affecting health care institutions will lead to additional professional responsibilities for the nurse leader (Joiner & Van Servellen, 1984). As health care facilities are downsized, diversify, and maximize their scarce resources in order to develop a competitive edge, you as the nurse manager must place greater emphasis on staff development to prepare for these changes. As patients require more intense and technically complex care, it is critical that the staff capabilities be developed to provide such care. And as the nursing shortage intensifies, each nurse becomes more valuable, less expendable. Nursing leaders must emphasize staff development and career enhancement to promote retention. They cannot afford to miss opportunities to develop employees (Brown, 1985).

Developing others is a dynamic process between the nurse manager and her staff; it requires that the nurse leader have sensitivity and effective interpersonal skills. It demands a reciprocal measure of employee commitment and must be supported by an effective program that is designed and implemented by the nurse manager (Fournies, 1978). The individual staff member brings to the process her own personal history, values, and attitudes, as well as her work experience and capabilities. As the nurse manager, you bring to the process well-defined standards of practice and the interpretation of unit, departmental, and organizational goals.

137

DECENTRALIZED STAFF DEVELOPMENT PROGRAM

In many nursing divisions, the task of staff development has been primarily delegated to a specific education/staff development department. The functional components of such a department include:

- a periodic needs assessment activity
- an orientation (centralized and decentralized) program
- an inservice and continuing education program
- a patient and community education program

However, as nursing units become more specialized, it is increasingly difficult for the staff development department to provide specific educational programs for individual staff members. Therefore, the authors recommend that staff development activities be shared between the nurse manager and the staff development department (Douglass, 1984).

Under such an arrangement, the staff development department retains primary responsibility for centralized orientation and community education while the nurse manager is responsible for decentralized orientation and patient education (Tobin, Wise & Hull, 1979). Although assessment of educational needs is conducted jointly by the nurse manager and the staff development department, the nurse manager has primary responsibility for targeting which inservice and continuing education programs are needed by her staff. The nurse manager continues to rely on the staff-development department staff for material and human resources to help her plan, conduct, and evaluate programs she designs for the unit staff (Marriner, 1984).

Staff development can provide you with personal job enrichment and self-actualization (Douglass & Bevis, 1983). Nurse educators have long shared the rewards of the learner's enhanced self-esteem during an effective staff development process. Nurse managers who provide unit-based or decentralized staff development can also enjoy these rewards. A well-designed decentralized development program can be career enhancing for both you and the staff. As an employee's performance evolves to reflect unit-based standards of practice, her personal job fulfillment will increase. The nurse manager who journeys into the role of staff developer can directly and positively affect the well-being of patients, the careers of nursing professionals, and the caliber of care within the institution.

An *ineffective* unit-based staff development program may foretell significant managerial problems (Tobin et al., 1979). The underdevelopment of current staff may contribute to low morale and high turnover rates, and, most unfortunate of all, stifle any improvement in the levels of competency in the resident staff (Douglass & Bevis, 1983). Therefore, in order to maintain staff viability, the processes of nurturing and developing others must be ongoing.

If the staff members have a positive attitude and are motivated to engage in career-enhancement activities, you will easily secure staff commitment to participate in development activities. If the staff have low self-confidence and lack trust in the process, you will need to begin by motivating them to be committed to the process.

The first step in creating a staff development program is to evaluate the staff members' readiness for development activities (Douglass & Bevis, 1983). During individual conferences or as a part of a unit meeting, determine how the staff members view the following aspects of self-directed staff development:

- What skill or performance areas are they aware that they need to develop?
- Where are the opportunities available for acquiring these new skills?
- How do they assess their own growth?
- Do they agree that the acquisition of new capabilities enhances their self-fulfillment?
- Do they experience a heightened level of self-esteem and self-confidence as they evolve in their professional roles?
- Do they perceive the process of growth as an enjoyable lifelong challenge?

Once attitudes are assessed, you can begin to motivate the staff to participate in the decentralized developmental program.

ROLE FUNCTIONS OF THE NURSE MANAGER AS STAFF DEVELOPER

As nurse manager, you perform several key role functions in implementing the decentralized developmental program. Your interactions with the staff ensure that they acquire the skills to perform their roles effectively (Stevens, 1985) as you encourage behavior that promotes both quality performance and personal satisfaction. As staff developer, you perform the following five key role functions: (1) set staff development goals, (2) enhance and encourage decision making, (3) provide education and training opportunities, (4) monitor staff growth and development through the evaluation process, and (5) serve as a mentor to staff by facilitating career advancement and development (Pareek & Rao, 1984).

First, you *set staff development goals* for the unit, for groups, and for the individual staff members. Involve the entire staff in goal setting by adopting a six-step planning strategy for goal development:

1. Analyze the present staff development needs and forecast future needs.
2. Explore and develop learning opportunities.
3. Establish broad-based, measurable, and obtainable goals based on projected and expected developmental opportunities.
4. Develop specific time-referenced action plans that measure progress toward the goal.
5. Develop and ensure that resources are available for goal attainment.
6. Communicate time frames for achieving goals to the staff, resource personnel, and to your superordinate.

Second, you *enhance and encourage decision making* by involving groups and individuals in decision making when staff participation is appropriate. To facilitate individual involvement in decision making, take the following actions:

- instruct the staff in the use of various decision-making models
- adopt a model for decision making and problem solving
- delegate decisions to appropriate individuals, identifying each staff member's accountability and level of responsibility in decision making
- encourage staff to consider and develop several options before implementing solutions
- give feedback on the outcome of the decision

Third, you *provide education and training opportunities*. Begin this activity by delineating the qualifications, knowledge, skills, and abilities required for the various unit positions. You inform the staff of the expected performance standards. Determine to what degree each staff member meets these standards and communicate this information to the staff and educational resource personnel. You then encourage staff to maximize learning opportunities available on the unit and sponsor staff for developmental experiences. The next step is to determine the new level of employee performance based on their participation in the developmental experiences and how they incorporate new knowledge into the work setting. Finally, take the following actions to activate an annual education plan that ensures continued mastery of contemporary knowledge in the unit's area of specialty practice:

- institute discussion arenas to delineate group learning needs
- appoint and support an active unit education committee
- identify general unit educational needs on an ongoing basis
- tabulate and record this data
- designate specific unit developmental days during which the staff members learn new concepts and plan future experiences.

Fourth, you *monitor staff growth and development through the evaluation process* by identifying, clarifying, and demonstrating performance standards; periodically reviewing job descriptions with each staff member; and evaluating each staff member according to her current knowledge, skills, and ability level against expected standards of performance. Teaching self-evaluation techniques to the staff is another part of your staff development role. Schedule feedback sessions on a regular basis to coach for improved performance. During these sessions, do the following:

- help each staff member recognize her strengths and areas to be improved through periodic feedback
- acknowledge staff for their successes and achievements
- encourage staff to set challenging individual and group goals
- encourage peer review through preceptorships and a clinical ladder

Generate a climate of mutuality, openness, and trust that encourages staff to take risks and improve their performance by providing regular feedback to staff on the outcome of their decisions.

The final role function of the nurse leader is to be a *mentor* by facilitating the involvement of staff in career advancement and development activities. "A mentor gives support. A manager/mentor relationship is an apprentice/teacher one. Mentors tell you what you need to know and show you how to do it" (Sullivan & Decker, 1985, p. 53). You act as a mentor as you:

- share your personal vision/philosophy and career development plan with the staff (see Appendix 8-A for an example of a personal philosophy statement)
- help the staff develop their own philosophy statement
- develop collaboratively a unit philosophy
- identify career opportunities in the organization for staff members and gain access to the necessary resources to facilitate staff entry
- encourage staff to assume new role tasks and functions that are challenging and creative

- encourage staff to develop their potential by providing opportunities to perform in their area of interest
- help staff explore different career options and give feedback to staff about their potential
- acknowledge the contributions of staff as an indicator of their professional growth
- reward teamwork, collaboration, and group achievement

COMPONENTS OF A DECENTRALIZED STAFF DEVELOPMENT PROGRAM

A decentralized staff development program has these components:

- As part of the evaluation process, the nurse manager organizes the development of unit-based *performance standards.*
- As a mentor, the nurse manager collaboratively develops a *unit philosophy.*
- As a decision maker, the nurse manager *selects new employees.*
- As a result of hiring new staff, the nurse manager provides a *compentency-based orientation.*

Figure 8-1 depicts the circular process of staff development with feedback loops after each component. The staff development program is modified according to the feedback received.

Setting Performance Standards

General performance standards provide and ensure organizational continuity of care. They become a measurable tool for the nursing leadership to use in evaluating quality of care. Each specialty unit requires individual and unique performance standards to reflect community standards for state-of-the-art clinical practice (Bernhard & Walsh, 1981). Each standard must be approved by authoritative signature within the nursing division and be dated before it is introduced as a standard. Each must be reviewed periodically and modified to reflect changes in technology, protocol, and legal requirements.

By definition, nursing performance standards are written statements that prescribe the level of practice required to maintain legally mandated, quality patient care. Each standard must contain a component that quantifies and defines the degree of compliance (either minimal or optimal) required of the

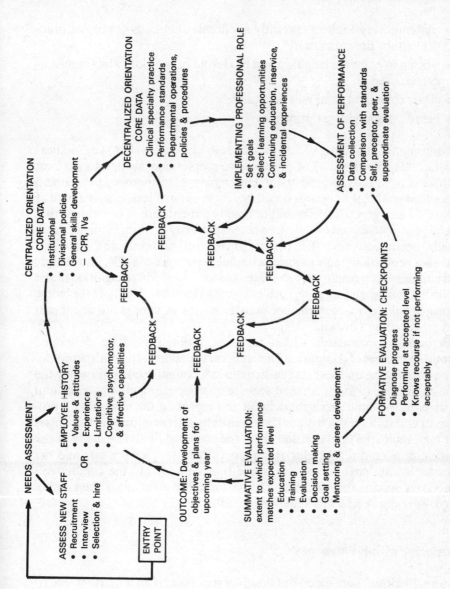

Figure 8-1 The Process of Staff Development. *Source:* T.I. Cordoni. © 1986.

performance (Marriner, 1984). To be appropriate and effective, performance standards must be:

- contemporary—reflect currently applicable standards of nursing practice within the community
- written in common language and be devoid of any potential for misunderstanding
- clear, consistent, and non-negotiable
- based on sound legal principles

Performance standards should include reliable, observable "key" indicators that identify the level of professional preparation needed to perform such standards. They cue and orient new employees to approved policies and procedures within the organization. They serve as an objective assessment of individual and group achievement of quality patient care. They ensure that qualified, oriented, and experienced nurses *correctly* perform complex, technically specific activities. Such performance standards reinforce the concept that each professional role requires a unique repertoire of skills, knowledge, and abilities. As a result, performance standards provide recognition of the individual nurse and of group achievements (Stevens, 1985). If the nurse manager fails to set performance standards, consequences are significant and far-reaching (Brown, 1985).

Performance standards within an organization should be developed through a process of consensus. The authors recommend that unit representatives, including unit leaders, participate in a committee appointed by the nursing division to formulate and activate appropriate standards. Each unit representative should contribute input and report on the committee's progress to unit staff for discussion. If consensus by all committee participants is not achievable, the final decision about the standard should be made by the nursing division director. Her awareness of pertinent legal issues and her broader institutional perspective would thus be added to the committee's process in making that decision. The performance standard is then authorized. It is reassessed and renewed annually.

Developing a Unit Philosophy

A well-written, unit-specific philosophy statement is an important leadership tool. The power of a philosophy statement is that it synthesizes and crystallizes the beliefs and values of an individual unit about patients, nursing, and nursing practice. The philosophy statement is not intended to imply the rightness or wrongness of variations in clinical practice. It is intended to reflect accurately how all members of the unit value the art and science of nursing (Stevens, 1985). Its periodic revision is an effective time to incorporate changes in nursing practice that have occurred or are planned.

Before developing a unit philosophy statement, the members of the unit should agree on what is meant by a philosophy. A philosophy is a set of values and beliefs that influence the practice of nursing. A philosophy statement is a statement of beliefs that direct the individuals of a particular group in the achievement of their purpose. It is also a visionary and inspiring summary of nursing, professionalism, and patient care within the specific organization (Stone et al., 1984).

Because a philosophy accurately reflects the current values and beliefs of a group or individual, it is a powerful promoter of mastery and excellence in providing patient care. It enhances the commitment of current staff to the unit. It further serves to orient and inculcate new members into the unit. A well-written unit philosophy provides direction to achieving the organization's goals. As a recruiting tool, it can enable the hiring of nurses with congruent philosophies, thus increasing work harmony and team building while minimizing schisms in clinical practice. See Appendix 8-A for a philosophy statement on supervision and Appendix 8-B for a unit philosophy statement.

Content of the Unit Philosophy

Any committee or group developing a philosophy statement should review a variety of materials before starting to write it. During these brainstorming sessions, consider the following components for inclusion in your statement:

- a specific nursing theory, either in its entirety or a portion of it (Stevens, 1985) (see Appendix 8-C for excerpts from various nursing theorists)
- how nursing is practiced on the unit (e.g., team, primary, total nursing care) and why that system is valued
- the relationship between nurse and patient and the relationship between the nurse and other health care professionals
- how unit decision making is accomplished; include the nursing management values, e.g., participative management, situational leadership
- existing values that relate to patient rights and their relationship to nursing practice
- existing values that relate to employee rights and concepts of professional growth and development

Process Used in Developing a Unit Philosophy

All interactive behavior stems from values and beliefs about self and others (Kast & Rosenweig, 1985). We interpret and modify our behavior based on our cultural and environmental experiences. Each of us has nursing practice values and beliefs. Developing a unit philosophy requires healthy and vigorous debate of each person's practice values. Organizing, supporting, and completing such a discussion is an essential responsibility of the nurse leader. To ensure completion of this task, follow this process:

- Initiate a work group, set progress checks, and help the group negotiate blockages; ensure that the group develops clear goals and is made up of capable, committed, and philosophically divergent members.
- Delineate each member's responsibilities; identify resources and set target dates for completion.
- Encourage staff to brainstorm ideas and discuss them freely; minimize the use of labels of right and wrong, good or bad.
- Encourage all staff to give verbal or written feedback to the philosophy work group.
- Encourage staff to negotiate their ideas.
- Encourage use of examples as a means of communicating values specifically and concisely.
- Accept only a philosophy statement that all participants agree with and support.
- To facilitate compatibility, ensure that the divisional and organizational philosophies and goals are reviewed before beginning the group process.
- Use the philosophy statement to direct future goals and unit planning activities.
- Update the philosophy annually, or more often, based on unit and organizational changes.
- Publicize the philosophy to patients, unit staff, and interdisciplinary staff.

Selecting New Employees

The two most powerful opportunities to develop others occur during the selection of new employees and during their subsequent orientation. Organizations traditionally invest a tremendous amount of time, energy, and resources in inservices and in providing continuing education activities to their employees. Although these activities are developmental in nature, they allow only incremental changes to occur within the unit. The nurse leader has a greater opportunity during the hiring and orientation of new employees to mold the future of the nursing unit.

Selecting new employees is one of the most challenging and crucial aspects of the nurse manager's role (Decker & Hailstone, 1985). In times of escalating costs, organizational downsizing, and nursing recruitment shortages, selecting a professional match is critical for the patient, the staff, you, the organization, and, of course, the nurse applicant. By seeking employees who are philosophically congruent and experientially prepared to enhance the unit, team building is strengthened. Professional mismatches can drain energy, motivation, and creativity from the work environment at an accelerated speed. Hiring mistakes can be very costly.

An essential element to ensure the hiring of successful new staff is a structured interview tool (Decker and Hailstone, 1985; Felton & Lamb, 1984). The employment interview is the time for a mutual exchange of information between the interviewer and the applicant. The interviewer is trying to make some judgments as to the applicant's qualifications, level of performance, and professional match with the work environment (Massie & Douglas, 1981). The goal of the interview is to develop an accurate data base from which to evaluate the applicant. An effective interview has well-thought-out objectives and includes questions with criteria-referenced, weighted answers that elicit information about the applicant as to her:

- knowledge, skills, abilities, and achievements
- professional strengths and areas to be strengthened
- role conception and level of performance
- leadership attributes and vision of future professional practice
- motivational characteristics that enhance individual performance and team effectiveness
- experience: clinical, teaching, and leadership

This information can predict if the applicant has the knowledge and motivation to assume successfully the role being sought.

Interview Framework and Process

The format of an interview may vary from being brief, concise, and informal to one that is lengthy, formal, and repetitive in nature. The authors recommend an interview process in which a group of five to six people has the opportunity to interview the applicant systematically (Vestal, 1987). The group should be made up of representatives from staff, resource personnel (e.g., clinical nurse specialists, educators, quality assurance staff), and unit management. The interview should occur in a quiet, unhurried environment, free of operational interruptions. The group process ensures that all members hear each question asked and the applicant's response.

A specific time frame and structure for the interview must be developed. It is particularly important to standardize the interview when there is more than one applicant for the same position. In this way, all candidates are given equal time and opportunity to answer the same questions because the same tool is used in each interview. The questions are criteria-referenced and weighted, with the "best" answers agreed to before the interview begins. Applicants can be objectively evaluated and quantifiably rated in such a structured interview. This objectivity promotes commitment to and support of the successful candidate from all interviewers.

Fifteen minutes should be allocated for the review of the applicant's file immediately before the interview. The file should include the applicant's resume, philosophy statement, letters of reference, and other supportive documents, as appropriate. Fifty minutes is allocated for the structured interview of the applicant. Five minutes of the hour is reserved for the applicant to ask the group questions. Fifteen minutes is spent, after the interview, writing down comments and evaluating the applicant's qualifications according to predetermined standards. This activity is done individually and without discussion. After each interviewer has rated the applicant, all scores are totaled, weighted, and averaged. The successful candidate should emerge from this rating process. If there is a significant variance in the ratings of the interviewers, the group should review the rating criteria to ensure that each interviewer has interpreted the criteria in the same way.

Because members of the interview committee have a significant role to play in shaping the future of the nursing unit, they must be committed to three basic principles:

1. Be familiar with each applicant's file.
2. Be objective, listen actively and rate responses, and represent all staff members.
3. Support the group decision.

Each interview team should have a person designated as the "facilitator." The facilitator plays an important process role by ensuring that the applicant has the opportunity to present her best profile. The facilitator introduces the applicant to each of the interviewers. She ensures that the applicant has a comfortable place to sit, eye contact with each interviewer, and a glass of water. The facilitator orients the applicant and the group to the interview process in the beginning of the interview. She serves as the time keeper and intervenes to guide the process in case something uncomfortable or unpredictable happens.

Content of the Interview

Most nurse managers have developed interview instruments over the years. Despite the use of these tools, every nurse manager has selected staff members, who, for one reason or another, have not met expected performance criteria. When this occurs, we ask ourselves how we could have ascertained that critical piece of data that would have predicted this mismatch. The authors propose some core questions as good predictors of successful candidates. There are four major categories of core questions: (1) clinical mastery, (2) teaching/learning experiences, (3) role conception and motivation, and (4) team effectiveness. See Appendix 8-D for an example of a structured interview tool that was developed for a perinatal community nurse specialist role. The tool can be easily tailored to any practice specialty. When you review Appendix 8-D, note that the interview questions are in sequence and that preferred answers (e.g., weighted criteria) are provided in the boxed area. By agreeing in advance on the written criteria, each interviewer can listen for the applicant to provide the appropriate answer, or not. Questions 1 through 4 and 10 through 18 are applicable to all nursing positions. To create your own tool, you need only develop role-specific questions (e.g., questions 5 through 9 are role specific). Appendix 8-E includes questions that assess basic medical/surgical/clinical competency to assist you in developing a staff nurse interview tool. Specialty units would need to add specific questions that relate to their clinical specialty.

Each interview tool should include a summative rating sheet (see Appendix 8-F). The rating sheet has space for notetaking during the interview. By completing the rating tool during the interview, the interviewers have readily available and sufficient data to evaluate the candidate (Stone et al., 1984). All applicants are asked the same questions, in the same sequence, and within the guidelines described above. The interview rating sheet is divided into the same four core categories as the interview tool. Each category has weighted criteria that illustrate it. Each interviewer uses this rating sheet for each applicant interviewed. The number of the question from the interview tool appears next to the criterion with which it correlates.

Providing a Competency-Based Centralized and Decentralized Orientation

An orientation is a formal mechanism to introduce new employees to their respective roles, to current performance standards, and to the organizational environment in which they will practice. The goal of an orientation is to ensure that the new employee is competent to meet at least the minimum performance standards required of her new role (Stone et al., 1984). The competent new employee gains the capacity to perform at a level that meets specific unit-based performance standards. Collaboration among staff, management, and the educational resource staff is used to develop role-specific performance standards.

Both centralized (the nursing division) and decentralized (unit-based or role-specific) competency-based orientations are complementary and build on each other. A centralized orientation is a general orientation to the professional role, the policies and procedures, the documentation system, various procedures (e.g., intravenous (IV) therapy, cardiopulmonary resuscitation (CPR), patient care planning), and the organizational resources of the nursing division. A decentralized orientation focuses on either unit-specific performance expectations and/or clinical/administrative role-specific performance activities.

A competency-based orientation promotes independent learning and is often self-paced. Learning is self-directed, and expectations of the orientee are stated clearly in writing. All activities focus on the learner and the learner's performance. Learning activities are based on real-world situations. Objectives are written for each activity and are outcome oriented. Post-tests are given for each learning activity to assess the level of performance according to preestablished standards, to give feedback, and to provide corrective action as necessary.

A competency-based orientation is a valuable management tool and has many advantages over traditional lecture-type orientations. It evolves from the clinical setting and is developed by unit practitioners to reflect real clinical situations. It becomes the entry-into-practice standard for minimally competent performance. It places an emphasis on clinical activity, clinical learning, and performance evaluation. Competency-based orientations provide immediate, personalized feedback regarding performance. It meets the unique learning needs of nurses as adult learners (Douglas & Bevis, 1983) by promoting learning and motivating the nurse to perform well. All new staff members are oriented within a consistent framework.

In contrast, the traditional orientation process used in many nursing environments is an informational barrage. Content is primarily delivered in a lecture format that is identical for all learners whether they are experienced and skilled or inexperienced and unskilled. Outcome measurements or posttests are rarely employed to assess clinical competency for such skills as medication dosage, CPR, and IVs. Often, the nurse's actual level of performance is not known until well into the probationary period or after, when there are limited resources for reorientation or skill development activities. It is of critical importance to maximize and target learning during orientation, as it is so costly.

Before developing a competency-based orientation, evaluate your current orientation program to determine its degree of effectiveness. The evaluation should include the following questions:

- Are staff of 3–5 years tenure aware of what is currently being covered in the orientation of new employees?
- Is there a consensus about the interpretation and understanding of policies among the staff?
- How proficient are resident staff in what is being taught to new staff?
- Are you aware of what is being taught to new staff in the centralized orientation?
- How capable and effective are the educational resource personnel in providing the orientation?
- Are preceptors well oriented to their role? Do they stay abreast of current unit policies? Is their dispersal of information consistent for each new employee?
- What content is covered for each employee?
- How is the orientation diversified for nurses with varying degrees of experience?
- Is there a smooth transition from orientee to staff member?
- How effective is the orientation?

These are provocative questions. The response to the above series of inquiries will identify the strengths and weaknesses in the current orientation process. Based on the outcome of this evaluation, you can target areas to be improved.

Part of decentralized competency-based orientation that was developed and implemented in an orthopedic acute care setting is found in Appendix 8-G. It is a 10-day orientation spread over a 6-week period. Learning time is integrated into actual patient care experiences. This integration enhances mastery of learned skills. The orientee is not expected to be competent to perform skills or behaviors on the unit until after they are covered in the orientation.

A unique feature of a competency-based orientation is that each day of the orientation has the same format but contains different content. Each day starts with a written competency statement that is time referenced. The statement is followed by criteria that describe performance expectations that the learner will achieve and when they will achieve them. Once the criteria are met, the learner is assured that she meets the competency statement. Finally, a list of learning activities is provided to show the orientee how she can achieve these criteria and meet the competency behavior. The learning activities further specify activities that are to be performed independently or with her preceptor. The post-test or evaluation occurs immediately after the learning. If the orientee has successfully met the performance criteria, she is competent in that behavior and is able to assume that aspect of her role on the nursing unit.

REFERENCES

Bernhard, L.A., & Walsh, M. (1981). *Leadership: The key to professionalization of nursing*. New York: McGraw-Hill.

Brown, W.S. (1985). *13 fatal errors managers make and how you can avoid them*. New York: Berkley.

Decker, D., & Hailstone, S. (1985). Recruiting and selecting staff. In E.J. Sullivan & P.J. Decker (Eds.), *Effective management in nursing* (pp. 245–278). Menlo Park, CA: Addison-Wesley.

Douglass, L.M. (1984). *The effective nurse: Leader and manager*. (2nd ed.). St. Louis: C.V. Mosby.

Douglass, L.M. & Bevis, M. (1983). *Nursing management and leadership in action* (4th ed.). St. Louis: C.V. Mosby.

Felton, B., & Lamb, S.R. (1984). A model for systematic selection interviewing. In Stone et al. (Eds.), *Management for Nurses: A multidisciplinary approach* (pp. 210–216). Menlo Park, CA: Addison-Wesley.

Fournies, F. (1978). *Coaching for improved work performance*. New York: Van Nostrand Reinhold.

Joiner, J. & Van Servellen, G. (1984). *Job enrichment in nursing: A guide to improving morale, productivity, and retention*. Rockville, MD: Aspen Publishers, Inc.

Kast, F. & Rosenzweig, J. (1985). *Organization & management: A systems and contingency approach* (4th ed.). New York: McGraw-Hill.

Marriner, A. (1984). *Guide to nursing management* (2nd ed.). St. Louis: C. V. Mosby.

Massie, J.L., & Douglas, J. (1981). *Managing: A contemporary introduction* (3rd ed.). Englewood Cliffs, NJ: Prentice-Hall.

Pareek, V., & Rao, T.V. (1984). Line managers and human resource development. In J.W. Pfeiffer & L.D. Goodstein (Eds.), *1984 Annual: Developing human resources* (pp. 161–167). San Diego: University Associates.

Stevens, B. (1985). *The nurse as executive* (3rd ed.). Rockville, MD: Aspen Publishers, Inc.

Stone, S., Firsch, S., Jordan, S., Berger, M., & Elhart, D., Eds. (1984). *Management for nurses: A multidisciplinary approach* (3rd ed.). St. Louis: C.V. Mosby.

Sullivan, E.J., & Decker, P.J. (1985). *Effective management in nursing*. Menlo Park, CA: Addison-Wesley.

Tobin, T., Wise P.Y., & Hull, P. (1979). *The process of staff development: Components of change* (2nd ed.). St. Louis: C.V. Mosby.

Vestal, K. (1987). *Management concepts for the new nurse*. Philadelphia: J.B. Lippincott.

Appendix 8-A

Philosophy of Supervision

Nancy Snyder, RN, MS

My philosophy of supervision is grounded in my philosophy of nursing. I believe nursing is both an art and a science; the art combines caring, communication, and supportive behaviors with knowledge of human physiology, medical science, and nursing practice. A critical role of the nurse is that of teacher; through knowledge, the patient gains independence and can direct his/her own health care. I believe nursing is a humanistic, holistic, and advocative relationship with patients and their support systems. Patient-centered, collaborative relationships between nurses and the other members of the health team are essential for the delivery of quality care. I believe only nursing can define its practice within an organization.

I believe nurses are human beings with multidimensional lives first and nurses second. I believe nursing is a career and not an avocation. I believe it takes a commitment to individual worth and a willingness to risk and expend energy to be a nurse.

Nurses are also employees. Each employee has value and is at work to contribute his/her best. Nurses have employee needs, personal needs, and professional needs, and there must be harmony between these needs for "good" work to occur. The nurse and the organizational leadership should collaborate to assure such harmony.

My philosophy of supervision includes certain beliefs about supervisory role characteristics. Perhaps, through these beliefs, you can gain additional information about my philosophy of supervision.

The supervisor is not a line manager. The line manager is the head nurse who has appointed a designated manager for the PM shift; usually the Assistant Head Nurse. The supervisor's primary role is to provide leadership on the PM shift, not to manage a group of nursing units. She does not develop the unit philosophy or unit objectives, but must be aware of them, support them, and facilitate their implementation with the PM staff. There

153

must be excellent communication between the line managers and the supervisor.

The supervisor represents the values and philosophy of the entire nursing management team and often the hospital administration on the PM shift. She provides continuity of leadership in the absence of the other members of the nursing management team. When global departmental or hospital-wide issues or problems occur, the supervisor will need to assume a management role. In particular, the centralized allocation of staff resources for the night shift, disaster and fire emergencies, and risk management situations would require supervisory management. The supervisor must have thorough knowledge of the resources and limits of the organization.

The supervisor provides leadership in facilitating unit managers and other staff in accessing resources both inter- and intradepartmentally. She interprets policies and procedures of the organization for staff and acts as a liaison representing nursing needs to other departments.

Appendix 8-B

Unit Philosophy

Nursing is a sensitive, caring, and helping profession. Our profession requires integrity, accountability, responsibility, and commitment to high nursing practice values for each and every patient. As the staff, we value professional growth and development. We believe that it is a personal responsibility to maintain competency in nursing practice. We are self-directed, independent, and interdependent practitioners. We believe Primary Nursing is the most beneficial patient care delivery system because it maximizes opportunities for the patient, the caregiver, and the health care team. Our professional goal is to coordinate the care for each patient to facilitate the promotion, maintenance, and restoration processes that help the individual achieve an optimal level of wellness. This optimal level of wellness occurs through patient and family teaching.

Appendix 8-C

Excerpts from Nursing Theorists

What to you believe to be the nature of nursing
(nursing acts)?

1. • Patient advocate

   • Empathy role

   • Helps patient/family understand   } **Riehl**

   • Uses resources

2. • Strong assessment capabilities

   • Nurse uses herself as the   } **Systems in Change**
     catalyst to interact with others

3. • Science of humanity (study of nature/
     direction of human development)

   • Seeks to promote symphonic interaction
     between humans and their environment

   • Nursing assessment looks at the individual
     as a whole

   • Nursing is a critical part of the   } **Martha Rogers**
     patient's environment

   • Nursing acts are directed toward
     individual's maximum level of health

   • Nursing assessment is not just an
     assessment of illness or disease

4. • Assists in helping others toward self-sufficiency

   • Gives direct assistance to a person unable to meet own self care needs   } **Dorothy Orem**

   • Emphasis on self care

Who is the patient (client)?

1. • Person anywhere along the life continuum

   • Someone who is respected

   • Someone who requires assistance because there has been some alteration in his biological system, social system (role change, culture) or personal system (self concept, body image, sexuality, etc.)   } **Systems in Change**

2. • Someone who possesses individual integrity

   • Man's life is unidirectional

   • Growth and development can be reached by different pathways

   • Man is thinking, sentient being

   • Man is an open system which is continually changing to move toward a higher level   } **Martha Rogers**

3. • Person is an adaptive system receiving internal and external stimuli   } **Callista Roy**

4. • Man is an integrated whole

   • Patient is an individual who is in need of assistance in meeting his health care demands because of lack of knowledge, skills, motivation or orientation.   } **Dorothy Orem**

What do you believe to be the relationship between nursing acts and patient?

1. • Advocacy role   } **Riehl**

2. • Nurse intervenes in presence of illness or threat of illness   } **Dorothy Johnson**

3. • Nurse helps patient regain, maintain, achieve integrity

   • Nurse plays an integral part with patient in planning and decision making actions

4. • Active and informed participation of client

   • Creativity and imagination are essential

   • Nursing is working with the patient, not to or for the patient

   • Goal directed process

   • Man has the capacity to participate knowingly in change

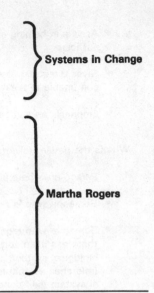

Systems in Change

Martha Rogers

REFERENCES

Orem, D.E. (1980). *Nursing: Concepts of practice* (2nd ed.). New York: McGraw-Hill

Riehl, J., & Roy, C. (1980). *Conceptual models for nursing practice.* New York: Appleton-Century-Croft

Rogers, M.E. (1970). *An introduction to the theoretical basis of nursing.* Philadelphia: F.A. Davis

Roy, C. (1976). *Introduction to nursing: An adaptation model.* Englewood Cliffs, NJ: Prentice-Hall

Appendix 8-D

Perinatal Community Nurse Specialist Interview Questions

1. Tell me about your most recent position, the role, and the boundaries of your responsibilities.
2. Could you highlight your philosophy of learning and describe how it interrelates with the concept of Staff Development?

> Promote excellence in patient care; achieve successful outcomes by assessing, planning, implementing, and evaluating organized programs; aspire to create an environment that values learning and professional growth; develop an atmosphere that maximizes each nurse's ability to provide contemporary and comprehensive care. Learners are adults who are self-directed and capable of mastery learning; professionals assume primary responsibility for maintaining competency in carrying out role expectations and developing potentials; professionalism and patient care are enhanced when nurses achieve goals successfully; SD people are the trend setters and role models; we share a commitment of responsibility for improving nursing practice and health care delivery through the application of theory-based research; patient (client) is the reason why we are here.

3. What professional attributes are you the proudest of and that you see as your professional strengths?

> Someone who works well with others, professional, master teacher, knows how to develop and implement viable systems, contemporary, visionary.

4. A. Could you describe your concept of the Perinatal Community Nurse Specialist role?

> Program development, Program Maintenance, Advice Nurse, Marketing. High interface with community, nurse managers, CNS, staff, doctors, etc. Establishes and orchestrates contemporary curriculum, competent teachers, accesses resources. Part of many different teams as a member; has leadership role in community education team.

159

    B. How would you predict that it could enhance this environment?

    C. What past experience have you had that makes you feel especially qualified for this position?

5. Would you describe your past teaching experience and responsibilities and highlight different kinds of teaching strategies used?

Traditionals of lecture, seminars, workshops, skills lab, process group, AV aides. Nontraditionals of modules (written & video), guided design, computer assisted instruction.

---

6. An acute care hospital is actively marketing its family-centered maternity service. Its present volume is 150 births per month including 10 births per month in the Alternate Birth Center.

    A. As a Perinatal Community Nurse Specialist, what would you include in a core curriculum for a contemporary family during the childbearing year?

- Early pregnancy
- General prenatal
- Prenatal exercise (water)
- Childbirth preparation
- Cesarean preparation/support
- Postpartum support (Mothers/Fathers)

- Sibling preparation/changing family relationships
- ABC orientation
- Postpartum exercise
- Infant exercise/swim
- Infant massage
- Newborn care and feeding
- Parent support groups

    B. In our present system, we have approximately 20 educational offerings per month with many different instructors sharing the program responsibility. What would be your strategic and tactical plan to assess the existing community program?

Evaluate program data as well as people data. Do an introductory meeting with all claimant groups to introduce self and see what "is"; develop relationships; review curricula; audit classes; assess/evaluate work and tracking systems (computerization); get feedback from nursing staff, instructors, clients, physicians, etc.

---

7. Much discussion has transpired between teachers and learners as to what are the most facilitative means for learners to learn and be successful.

A. Could you identify two teaching behaviors that you would consider effective during evaluation? Two that are ineffective during evaluation?

Effective: Positive feedback, honest, constructive criticism, clearly defined expectations.
Ineffective: Insufficient feedback, only negative feedback, lack of expectations.

B. Could you identify two priority behaviors that you would consider effective during instructive/assistive interactions? Two that are ineffective?

Effective: Availability, provide individual feedback time, not oversupervising, willing to help, answer questions freely, knowledgeable. Help see alternatives.
Ineffective: Not available, unrealistic expectations, not recognizing individual differences.

---

8. As a Perinatal Community Nurse Specialist, you have the management responsibility for supervising and evaluating all community/maternity instructors in their community role. Today you received a telephone complaint about one of your childbirth instructors from an unhappy consumer. The client stated, "Attending this Lamaze class is a waste of my time and energy! I'm not learning anything!"

   How would you handle this?

   (manager/leadership responsibility, conflict resolution)

---

1. Listen, actively (feelings versus ventilation versus differing expectations).
2. Clarify what was being said, in what sequence and context.
3. Clarify client's expectations of the class.
4. Acknowledge that there are in fact unmet or conflicting expectations.
5. Ask if feedback was given to the instructor and, if so, what instructor said.
6. Assess exactly what client is asking for (money back, another class, resolve this, etc.).
7. Maintain positive neutrality, thank them for the feedback; however, state that you will need to follow-up with the instructor, assure that you will get back to them.
8. Follow-up with instructor by identifying situation and asking her perspective, clarifying the issue of unmet expectation, help instructor problem solve options to resolve. Follow up by most appropriate source. (If it is the instructor who doesn't meet the expectation, clarify and provide developmental progression to meet the expectation successfully).
9. Continue follow-up with instructor and client.

9. You are the Maternity Advice Nurse responsible for answering consumer/client phone calls, including those for information about your hospital's maternity service, physician referrals, and counseling situations. A client calls and says, "My doctor who has privileges at your hospital has scheduled me for a repeat cesarean. I want to try a vaginal delivery this time since last time was so awful. Can you give me the name of a doctor who will let me do this?" It's important to know that your hospital has a vaginal birth after cesarean protocol. How would you approach this?

(clinical mastery, advice nurse role)

- Just do a referral (wrong answer).
- Goal is to clarify the actual intent of the request, meet consumer need, and handle a very difficult physician relations issue. Need to balance these issues.
- Assess if person discussed request with physician.
- Review criteria protocol with caller to see if she meets the VBAC criteria (she may not be candidate). If not a candidate, support existing physician. If a candidate, would give referral choices for second opinion.

---

10. Could you briefly describe what kind of worker you are and list some of your work habits?

Quality of work, do things right, hard worker, complete projects, enact responsibility of role, work well with others.

---

11. What type of situations on the job frustrate you? How do you manage to handle them?
12. As a member of a team, what personal and professional behaviors do you possess that will enhance/complement team effectiveness?

Hard worker, do your share of work, like working with others, honest, open, can facilitate process.

---

13. Do you have a creative project that you are proud of?
14. What type of orientation do you project that you would need to assume this job?

Needs to be realistic; oriented to hospital, nursing dept., staff development, maternity service rate, community program, physicians, key people. Collect data base and assessment of existing system and interrelationships of roles.

15. In evaluating all the candidates, tell us why you think we should pick you?
16. Anything else you would like to share with us that we have not asked you?
17. When would you be available for work? Any restrictions?
18. In the 5 minutes remaining, what questions do you have for us?

Source: T.I. Cordoni, 1986.

Appendix 8-E

Assessing Clinical Competence: Nursing Core Questions

QUESTION	ANSWER
1. Mr. Kay (72 years old) underwent a small bowel resection four days ago. He continues on IV nutritional support, N/G suction, and low flow O_2 (3 L/min) for postop atelectasis. His most recent ABGs report is:	

pH	7.48	HCO_3	31
pO_2	60	B.E.	+6
pCO_2	32	SaO_2	95%

a. What are the *normal* ranges for ABGs?

   a. pH 7.35–7.45 (7.4)
      pO_2 80–100 mm Hg
      pCO_2 38–42 mm Hg (40)
      HCO_3 22–26 mEq/L
      SaO_2 95–100%

b. What does the pH in this case indicate? (i.e., the acid-base status of the patient)

   b. Alkalosis

c. Is there an acid-base abnormality here? If so, what is it?

   c. Yes—mixed problem of metabolic and respiratory alkalosis.

     ● metabolic component ($\uparrow HCO_3$)

     ● respiratory component ($\downarrow CO_2$)

164

QUESTION	ANSWER
d. What factors might be contributing to the abnormal value(s), or why do you think abnormalities are present in this patient?	d. Factors contributing to metabolic alkalosis: NG suction (loss of acid, K+, Cl^-). Factors contributing to respiratory alkalosis: Hyperventilation 2˚ to atelectasis/low pO_2.
e. Comment on Mr. Kay's oxygenation status.	e. Moderate hypoxemia (<60 mm Hg) • For a man of this age, a pO_2 of 70–75 mm Hg would be acceptable. • Don't forget, this pO_2 is on a 3 L/min flow = 32% O_2 delivered.
f. What are the normal compensatory mechanisms that come into play with a metabolic alkalosis? With a respiratory alkalosis?	f. CO_2 retention to balance off excess base (therefore, $pCO_2 \uparrow$). This is an immediate process. There is an $\uparrow$ excretion of HCO_3 by the kidney in an effort to balance off the low pCO_2 (therefore, $HCO_3 \downarrow$). This process takes 2–3 days to occur.
g. Is there any compensation going on in this case?	g. Difficult to determine due to the mixed nature of the problem, but it appears as though there is some respiratory compensation present. You would expect the pH to be higher with both systems involved.
2. Mrs. Peabody (82 years old) with a history of ASHD, CHF and diabetes is 3 days post total hip surgery. She begins to c/o dyspnea, fatigue, and heart	a. Results of a chest exam— listen for rales, rhonchi, wheezes, etc. b. Results of a C/V exam— can you hear an S_3? Is

QUESTION	ANSWER
palpatations. Her urine output has decreased over the last two shifts and her HR is elevated to 110 bpm. You also notice she has a moist-sounding, persistent cough. You are about to notify the attending physician. What additional information might you anticipate he will ask for?	there JVD? Are there any signs of peripheral edema? c. Is there a recent weight? How does it compare to the last weight? d. Tally up the I & O to this point. Look at the pattern over the last 24–48 hours. e. Look for recent lab data reflecting volume status, i.e., Hct, NA+ (?$\downarrow$), CXR reports ($\uparrow$ congestion).
3. Describe the steps you go through in assessing A-V shunt patency.	a. Palpate the external loop of the shunt. It should feel warm. You can also feel pulsation in the tubing and over the vessels just proximal to the access sites. b. Observe the color in the tubing. It should be uniformly red in appearance. Any dark bluish or black strands/separations of fluid may indicate clotting of the shunt. c. Check for bruit over the shunt (with the bell of the stethoscope or Doppler).
4. You are having a problem with denuded skin around your patient's colostomy. The adhesive to the pouch is apparently not sticking at all points of contact and leaking has occurred. How would you approach this problem?	a. Consult with the ostomy nurse. b. Obtain a skin barrier (stomahesive). This will aid the healing of denuded skin and keep the pouch on. c. Wash, rinse, and dry the skin well before application of the stomahesive.

QUESTION	ANSWER
	d. Apply pouch directly to stomahesive.
5. You receive an order to place Mr. Green on a 40% mask with humidification to aid him in coughing up his thick secretions. Describe how you would set up this O_2 delivery system.	a. Fill nebulizer unit with sterile NS. b. Set dial at 40%. c. Provide high flow at least 8–10 L/min in order to obtain the desired % of O_2 via mask.
6. a. Describe the desired position for a postcraniotomy patient. Explain your answer.	a. HOB elevated 15–30°; this facilitates venous outflow. Head in alignment with the trunk; this avoids compression of the internal jugular vein into which the dural sinuses drain. Avoid extreme head or hip flexion as this may put increased tension on the cord, impairing CSF circulation.
b. What nursing procedures/ stimuli can increase intracranial pressure?	b. Suctioning of patient Malpositioning of patient Coughing patient Putting patient on bedpan Emotional stimuli (noise, conversation, etc.) Stimuli that cause posturing (decerebrate/decorticate); muscle contraction increases blood pressure.
7. A central subclavian line has just been traumatically inserted by the physician for hyperalimentation therapy (three attempted sticks before success!) a. Where should the catheter tip lie?	a. In the superior vena cava, just proximal to the right atrium.

QUESTION	ANSWER
b. What nursing assessments would you make after such an insertion?	b. Observe closely for signs/symptoms of pneumothorax (the apices of the lungs are vulnerable in this supraclavicular region): dyspnea, anxiety, ↑ HR, ↑ R/R, ↓ BS, ↓ tactile and vocal fremitus). Observe for bleeding—hematoma formation at neck, change in vitals reflecting volume loss (↑ HR), respiratory distress 2˙ to airway compromise. Call for CXR results to check for pneumothorax and catheter tip placement.

8. Mrs. Grape is 60 years old. She is 2 days postop cholecystectomy and has become increasingly agitated and somewhat confused over the shift. Blood gases are ordered after the physician examines her. The results on room air are:

pH   7.30 pO_2 50 mm Hg
pCO_2 60 mm Hg HCO_3 24 mEq/L

a. What does the pH indicate?	a. Acidosis
b. What is the primary problem(s) here?	b. Respiratory acidosis. Severe hypoxemia.
c. Are any compensatory mechanisms going on?	c. No. HCO_3 is normal. Process is acute.
d. What factors may be contributing to this patient's normal ABGs?	d. Possible postop atelectasis. Infectious process.

Source: Linda Linehan, RN, MS, 1986.

Appendix 8-F

Interview Rating Sheet

APPLICANT NAME: _____ POSITION: _Perinatal Community Nurse Specialist_

INTERVIEWER: _____ DATE: _____

	POSSIBLE SCORE	ACTUAL SCORE	COMMENTS
SECTION I: Clinical Mastery			
A. Recent Clinical Experience	7		
QUESTION: B. Clinical Skills (Q:9)	5		
	12	____	

		POSSIBLE SCORE	ACTUAL SCORE	COMMENTS
SECTION II:	**Teaching/Leadership Experience**			
(Q:5)	A. Previous formal teaching experience (nursing, Staff Development, education)	5		
(Q:2)	B. Philosophy of education/learning and interrelationship with Staff Development	9		
	C. Enjoys teaching/nursing	9		
(Q:7)	D. Effective versus ineffective teaching behaviors	3		
(Q:5,6)	E. Knowledge of curriculum development and ability to use different teaching strategies	9		
(Q:6,8)	F. Leadership/managerial ability for program planning and instructor responsibility	9		
		44		
SECTION III:	**CNS Role Concept**			
(Q:4)	A. Philosophy of CNS Role	7		
	B. Past experience as CNS	2		
(Q:4,14)	C. Knowledge of role concept desired and realistic expectations of role responsibilities and orientation necessary	7		
(Q:4)	D. Verbalizes role as mentor to professionally bolstering nursing role as instructors/leaders for community	4		
		20		

SECTION IV: Motivation/Team Effectiveness

	A. Motivation; positive attitude (toward self and others)	8
(Q:10,12)	B. Enhance team effectiveness (work habits supportive)	8
(Q:8,11)	C. Conflict resolution	6
(Q:13)	D. Creative projects/innovative ideas	2
		24

SECTION V: Bonus Section

A. Outstanding achievements in clinical specialty

B. Publication/articles

C. Management experience

TOTAL SCORE: _____   RECOMMENDATIONS: _____

COMMENTS:

TC

Source: T.I. Cordoni (1986).

Appendix 8-G

Decentralized Competency-Based Orientation

Welcome to 2 North

We are one of three orthopedic units specializing in total joint replacements and microsurgery. Nursing is one component of the orthopedic team, which includes physicians, physical/occupational therapists, orthopedic technicians, and UC orthopedic residents. We are happy to have you and look forward to working with you in your professional development as an orthopedic nurse.

The following is a detailed competency-based decentralized orientation plan. Each day of your orientation is clearly outlined with competency statements, criteria, and learning activities to help you meet these objectives. We encourage you to look over this packet and discuss any questions or concerns you may have with your Head Nurse and/or Preceptor.

Again, welcome and have a wonderful orientation!

Overview of 10-Day Decentralized Competency Orientation: Competency Statements

Professional Role Entry: By the end of Day 1, the orientee will be able to verbalize the professional role and responsibilities of an Orthopedic Registered Nurse on 2 North.

New Orientee's Integration into the Professional Role of the Orthopedic Nurse: By the end of Day 2, the orientee will be able to provide direct and indirect nursing care that meets the physical, emotional, and psychosocial needs of the orthopedic patient on 2 North.

Source: Leslie Costa, Kathryn Hesser, and Mary Howard © 1986.

172

Classroom Instruction: By the end of Day 3, the orientee will be able to integrate medical/surgical skills with the specialized skills of an orthopedic nurse on 2 North.

Role Interrelationships: By the end of Day 4, the orientee will be able to perform general systems responsibilities associated with the ward clerk role.

Specialty Skills, Role Development and Integration: By the end of Day 5, the orientee will be able to explain and demonstrate selected orthopedic diagnostic and surgical procedures.

Specialty Skills, Role Development and Integration: By the end of Day 6, the orientee will be able to provide all essential aspects of nursing care for a patient undergoing total hip replacement.

Specialty Skills, Role Development and Integration: By the end of Day 7, the orientee will be able to provide specialized nursing care for the patient with a lumbar laminectomy and/or fusion.

Specialty Skills, Role Development and Integration: By the end of Day 8, the orientee will be able to provide specialized nursing care for the patient undergoing microsurgery.

Specialty Skills, Role Development and Integration: By the end of Day 9, the orientee will be able to provide specialized aspects of nursing care for the patient undergoing knee arthroscopy, arthrotomy, or total knee replacement.

Leadership Role Development: By the end of Day 10, the orientee will be able to evaluate and modify comprehensive nursing care using the nursing process for self, patients, staff, and the unit/organizational culture.

ORIENTATION DAY 1 (first day on unit): PROFESSIONAL ROLE ENTRY

Competency Statement:

By the end of Day 1 the orientee will be able to verbalize the professional role and responsibilities of an Orthopedic Registered Nurse on 2 North.

Criteria:

By the end of Day 1, the orientee will be able to:

1. Set guidelines for performance appraisal with the Head Nurse and Preceptor.

2. Establish direct communication lines with the Head Nurse and Preceptor by being open to feedback.
   a. How does orientee prefer to receive feedback?
   b. When does orientee prefer to receive feedback?
   c. Clarify information as needed.
3. Assess learning needs with the Head Nurse and Preceptor.
   a. Review clinical skills checklist.
   b. Review Nursing Experience Summary.
   c. Establish realistic goals for orientation including:
      1. How does orientee prefer to learn?
      2. When is the best learning time?
4. Describe the role, philosophy, and expectations of the Head Nurse.
   Role of the Head Nurse
   a. Manages the nursing unit assuring the provision of high quality
      nursing care and responsiveness to the needs of patients, staff,
      physicians, families, and visitors while maintaining efficient and
      effective use of resources.
   b. Introduces new staff members to unit staff and preceptor.
   c. Arranges work schedule for new employee.
   d. Prepares performance appraisal with input from preceptor and
      orientee at the end of 40 and 80 days.
   Head Nurse Expectations of New Orientee
   a. Assumes responsibility for self and effectively utilizes orientation
      time.
   b. Assumes responsibility of being a part of the solution of issues,
      rather than part of the problem.
   c. Provides basic nursing care that reflects safe nursing practice and
      sound judgment for 2–3 patients during the first week.
   d. Is open and honest in communication.
   e. Willingly accepts feedback.
   f. Is motivated.
   g. Projects an attitude that reflects professional nursing values, such
      as commitment to nursing and punctual and consistent adherence
      to work schedule.
   h. Participates in nursing care planning activities for all patients and
      documents accordingly.
   i. Goes to lunch and breaks on time.
   j. Demonstrates a positive and enthusiastic attitude toward work both
      as an individual and team member.
   k. Participates in unit staff meetings.
   l. Plans, organizes, and completes work in a manner that contributes
      to an efficient and harmonious work environment.

m. Accepts changes in assignment in the interest of patient care.
n. Participates in unit educational activities.
o. Supports and understands the philosophies of the unit, nursing department, and organization.
p. Orients on the day shift for 6 weeks, then goes to assigned shift—communicates with head nurse and preceptor if additional orientation time on the day shift is needed.
q. Provides basic care for 4–5 patients in a safe, organized, and professional manner by the end of 6 weeks.
r. Provides nursing care consistent with standards of care by the end of 6 weeks, for the following orthopedic patients:

- Fractured hip
- General hand surgery
- Knee arthroscopy
- Lumbar laminectomy and fusion
- Patients in pelvic, cervical, and bucks traction
- Total hip replacement
- Total knee replacement

5. Define the role and expectations of the preceptor.
Role Concept
   The preceptor is an experienced Nurse Practitioner who has a specific responsibility to sponsor a new RN employee. The preceptor can help facilitate and support RN role transition and role development. He/she facilitates professional success within the setting. The preceptor introduces new employees to all members of the health team. The preceptor familiarizes the new employee with the physical environment by touring the unit with the orientee.
Preceptor Expectations of the Orientee
a. Provides basic nursing care that reflects safe nursing practice and sound professional judgments for assigned patients.
b. Seeks clarification for the unknown.
c. Communicates openly and honestly.
d. Provides nursing care for full caseload of patients (4–5) by the end of 6 weeks in a safe, organized, and professional manner.
e. Demonstrates knowledge of standards of care by the end of 6 weeks for the following orthopedic patients:

- Fractured hip
- General hand surgery
- Knee arthroscopy
- Total hip replacement

- Total knee replacement
- Patients in pelvic, cervical, and bucks traction

6. Outline learner responsibilities of the orientee to the Head Nurse and Preceptor.
   a. Takes responsibility for own learning.
   b. Completes assigned learning activities.
   c. Attends classes (if applicable).
   d. Participates actively in learning activities.
   e. Completes, returns, and reviews with Head Nurse and preceptor the nursing skills summary and skills checklist.
   f. Seeks direction actively when needed.
7. Discuss the patient care delivery system on 2 North.
   We are currently performing total patient care. In this system each team member delivers all care within the scope of her practice as outlined in her job description. Registered Nurses are assigned to cover medications and IVs as needed for staff whose responsibilities do not include these. Each staff member is responsible for keeping current on all new physician orders and implementing them in a timely fashion.
   2 North is evolving into Primary Nursing. We expect to be delivering patient care in this manner by August. A committee is working on developing this system to meet our unit's specific needs. Input is encouraged by all staff members.
8. Observe the role of the nurse in total patient care by buddying with the preceptor on the first day of decentralized orientation.
   a. Observes patient care.
   b. Clarifies roles and responsibilities.
   c. Becomes familiar with shift routines.
9. Familiarize self with physician staff.
   Physician reference page   (On this page were placed the photographs and names of the orthopedic physicians practicing on the unit level. This helped new staff associate names with faces.)

Learning Activities

1. Meet with Head Nurse and Preceptor for ½ hour each to discuss roles and expectations.
2. Read Head Nurse position charter (Directive 7-20) (15 minutes).
3. Read unit philosophy (15 minutes).
4. Read unit primary nursing manual (30 minutes).
5. Read position charter for Orthopedic Resource Nurse (Objective 7-17) (15 minutes).
6. Familiarize self with unit by completing scavenger hunt (1 hour).

ORIENTATION DAY 2 (second day on unit): NEW ORIENTEES' INTEGRATION INTO THE PROFESSIONAL ROLE OF THE ORTHOPEDIC NURSE ON 2 NORTH

Competency Statement

By the end of Day 2, the orientee will be able to provide direct and indirect nursing care that meets the physical, emotional and psychosocial needs of the orthopedic patient on 2 North.

Criteria

By the end of Day 2, the orientee will be able to:

1. Provide basic patient care, as defined below, for two to three patients under the supervision of the preceptor.
   a. Provides bedside nursing care that meets physical, emotional and psychosocial needs of the patient in accordance with established standards, regulations, and policies.
   b. Administers medication accurately to assigned patients and is knowledgeable of proper dosage, action, expected effects, and untoward reactions.
   c. Administers treatments properly to patients and is knowledgeable of the correct techniques and desired effects.
   d. Starts and administers intravenous infusions and drugs and blood transfusions after proper instruction and in keeping with hospital policy. (Did you forget? see centralized orientation module)
   e. Provides patient care and makes nursing judgments that reflect safe nursing practices.
   f. Maintains awareness of the conditions of assigned patients and informs Head Nurse of all pertinent information.
   g. Maintains accurate records of nursing care provided, including observations of patient behavior, condition, and responses to medications and treatments, and follow-through on physician's orders. (Refresher needed? obtain PONR module from Staff Development and see Preceptor.)
   h. Performs various related tasks as assigned.
   i. Assists staff members (i.e., LVNs, nursing attendants, and nursing students) with the development of the nursing skill necessary for the provision of comprehensive physical, emotional and psychosocial nursing care.
2. Review Standards of Care for assigned patients (Standards of Care Manual) and integrate standards into care provided.

3. Write individualized nursing care plans designed to meet the needs of the patient based on nursing diagnosis and appropriate standard of care for assigned patients by the end of the second day.
   a. Develops short- and long-term goals.
   b. Communicates plan of care to all appropriate individuals.
   c. Assesses priority of care based on patient's activity and/or preference.
   d. Modifies nursing care plan as required by changing patient needs.
4. Create a professional relationship with the physicians by participating actively in patient rounds on assigned patients.
   a. Assist physician in exams and treatments as needed on assigned patients.
5. Perform comprehensive system assessment by the end of the second day on one assigned patient under supervision of preceptor.
   Performing a head-to-toe assessment is like learning to walk. At first you may stumble or it may take a while to do, but once you learn the basics, the rewards are tremendous. So take your time at first. Use these first 6 weeks to create your own organization for doing head-to-toe assessment using the specific guidelines that follow. What you learn about your patient and the trusting relationship you begin to foster with that patient will be your reward!

Assessment Guidelines

Interviewing the patient
   a. Create a suitable environment.
      1. patient comfortable?
      2. low noise level
      3. nurse sitting to maintain close eye contact
   b. Identify patient's chief complaint.
      1. when did it start?
      2. what are the symptoms?
      3. continuous or aggravated by activity?
      4. how has it limited activity level?
      5. what has the patient done at home to alleviate symptoms?
   c. Identify any chronic health issues by briefly touching on the following and noting any routine meds.
      1. respiratory—any history of shortness of breath, allergies, asthma, COPD; frequent colds, upper respiratory infections
      2. cardiac—chest pain, high blood pressure
      3. diabetes
      4. ulcers—active

     5. frequent or painful urination

     6. regularity of BM—any diarrhea past 24˚

  d. Observe patient closely while interviewing.

     1. Note mental acuity—able to remember past as well as present, does patient repeat answers, is patient alert? Observe for facial symmetry while patient answers questions. These observations are all part of your neurological assessment, which can be noted while you are interviewing!

     2. Does patient have difficulty hearing?

  e. Complete the rest of your neurological assessment and continue to assess from head to toe.

    A. *Neurological Assessment*

      1. Determine level of consciousness

      2. Determine orientation (name, location, time)

      3. Check pupils

        a. both pupils simultaneously; equality, size, regularity

        b. direct pupillary light reflexes

      4. Motor functioning

        a. facial symmetry

        b. hand grips (cross fingers!)

        c. leg lifts

    B. *Abdominal Assessment*

      1. Proper progression: inspection, auscultation, percussion, palpation

      2. Inspection

        a. shape and size

        b. contour

        c. skin

      3. Auscultation

        a. warm stethoscope

        b. listen: four quadrants; epigastrium

        c. verbalize to preceptor what is heard

      4. Percussion—proper technique

        a. all four quadrants

        b. check for distended bladder

      5. Palpation

        a. ask patient to identify painful areas; examine those *last*

        b. lightly palpate all four quadrants

    C. *Musculoskeletal Assessment*

      Using the techniques of inspection, palpation, and ROM (range of motion), assess the following bones/joints/muscles: (noting any swelling, deformity, redness, bogginess, crepitation)

1. Head and neck
2. Hands and wrists
3. Elbows
4. Shoulders
5. Feet and ankles
6. Knees
7. Hips
8. Spine

D. *Respiratory Assessment*
1. Proper progression: inspection, palpation, percussion, auscultation
2. Inspection
   a. extremities: nailbeds; skin color
   b. masses, scars, trachea position
   c. respirations: rate, depth, rhythm, equal expansion; use of accessory muscles (shoulders; intercostal retraction)
3. Palpation
   a. tenderness; abnormalities
4. Auscultation
   a. listen to inspiration/expiration in each location:
      1. LUL
      2. RUL
      3. RML
      4. RLL
      5. LLL
   b. progress from side to side, and top to bottom of lung fields
   c. observe patient for hyperventilation; allow rest periods
   d. describe breath sounds in the five locations, identifying presence of any of the following abnormal breath sounds:
      1. rales
      2. rhonchi
      3. tubular or bronchial sounds

E. *Cardiovascular Assessment*
1. Auscultation
   a. heart rate and rhythm
      1. count apical rate
      2. identify rhythm: regular?
2. Palpation
   a. palpate pulses (bilaterally)
      1. radial
      2. pedal
      3. assess   equality, strength
6. Provide comprehensive report to oncoming shift.

Receiving Report

All members of the nursing staff listen to report in the 2 North conference room. Report starts at 7:00 A.M., 3:00 P.M., and 11:00 P.M. Each person is responsible for knowing her patient assignment and listening for information on those patients, as well as taking report on the entire team.

Giving Report

Day shift report is taped in the conference room between 2:00 P.M. and 2:45 P.M. All RNs are required to tape their own report. The following are some guidelines to help you tape a complete end of shift report.

    a. State your name and all the patient room numbers you will be covering in your report.

    b. Begin your individualized patient report with:
       1. room number
       2. patient name
       3. age
       4. diagnosis
       5. physician's name

    c. Give concise, pertinent information on patient status or change in status.

    d. Include the following:
       1. scheduled diagnostic procedures and lab work
       2. IVs, including needed site changes
       3. issues that need follow-through
       4. vital signs and I&O when indicated

    e. Report verbally any pertinent orders or changes in patient status that occur after taping to the oncoming shift.

Learning Activities

1. Provide total patient care for assigned patients.
2. Read Standards of Care for assigned patients.
3. Review nursing directives related to assigned patient care if needed.
4. Discuss with preceptor progress at end of second day.
5. Establish realistic goals for remaining 8 days at orientation.
6. Review "A Guide to Physical Examination" by Bates if needed (available in Staff Development office or library).
7. Perform comprehensive system assessment on one assigned patient with supervision of preceptor (1 hour).
8. Provide comprehensive report to oncoming shift on patient assigned.

Chapter 9

Motivation and Performance

Motivation implies the presence of a forceful incentive that leads an individual to take a determined action. In job performance, motivation can be derived either from a positive external influence or from personal ambition or be the product of self-engendered pride in work accomplished. Whatever its source, motivation to achieve is the great catalyst for advancement on the career ladder.

Highly motivated employees are vested in working toward goals that are important to them (Stevens, 1978). As a consequence, job satisfaction increases (Joiner & Van Servellen, 1984), the work environment improves, productivity escalates, and rates of absenteeism and turnover diminish. However, motivation alone cannot sustain or improve performance; new knowledge and skills required by continually advancing nursing technology must also be developed to ensure competent professional practice and facilitate job enrichment (Bothwell, 1983). Job enrichment is a strategy where the manager looks at the role of the nurse and identifies ways to enhance the role within the existing organization. Therefore, this process provides the nurse manager and the organization with a prescriptive guide to improve staff morale, job satisfaction, productivity, and quality in services which enrich the job, the organization, and the quality of care provided. Figure 9-1 illustrates the relationships among motivation, job performance, and performance evaluation.

Some employees demonstrate role competency, but lack enthusiasm for developing new skills, and as a result they seek out the same experiences over and over (McFarland, Leonard, & Morris, 1984). This tendency can diminish motivation and relegate them to eventual incompetence as their role evolves beyond their current skill level. The nurse manager must identify these staff members through coaching, counseling, and the evaluation process (Fournies, 1978). She must also stimulate them to keep abreast of these

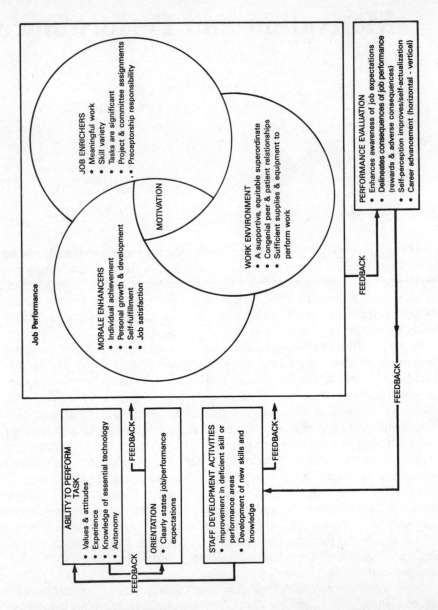

Figure 9-1. Relationship of Motivation, Job Performance, and Performance Evaluation. *Sources:* From "A New Strategy for Job Enrichment" by J.R. Hackman et al., 1975, *California Management Review, 17*, pp. 57–71. Copyright 1975 by University of California at Berkley; and from "The Wise Old Turk" by F. Herzberg, 1974, *Harvard Business Review, 52,* pp. 70–80. Copyright 1974 by Harvard University.

role performance changes. External detractors may be preventing the employee from pursuing more rewarding job-related experiences. Counseling, support, and understanding by the nurse leader may restore employee self-confidence and result in renewed job enthusiasm and motivation to learn new roles.

Employees are more productive when they clearly know what they are supposed to do, what authority they have, and what their relationships, responsibilities, and accountabilities are to other individuals in the organization. Employees also need frequent, periodic, and timely feedback about the following (Skousen, 1960):

- what constitutes a job well done, in terms of results
- what they are doing exceptionally well
- where they are falling short
- what they can do to improve

The nurse manager should convey values that reflect the following:

- there are appropriate rewards for exceptional work
- the work they are doing and the ideas they are thinking of are of value
- she, as supervisor, has a deep interest in them and sincerely desires their individual success and progress

The nurse leader conveys some of these values on a daily basis. However, the nurse manager must maximize each opportunity throughout the year to give formative feedback (Stevens, 1985). Such a consistent method confirms that the nurse manager is committed to helping the employee improve performance. This consistency strengthens mutual respect and the professional relationship. Therefore, the performance evaluation interview is an ideal time to highlight achievements, discuss expectations, and make plans for the coming year.

Each of us is motivated to perform well by certain internal values, physical conditions, and by different work situations. What will motivate one person may not motivate another. The nurse leader who is aware of the factors that motivate the individual staff members to perform well can enhance these factors and promote employee satisfaction and quality of care (Douglass & Bevis, 1983).

This awareness begins with the premise that each of us, as individuals, has a need for achievement and self-actualization (Massie & Douglass, 1981). Other factors may prove to be motivators for employees as well:

- a perception that the job requires skills and abilities that are valued and possessed
- a perception that rewards are conditional on good performance
- timely performance appraisal and feedback on unit issues
- the opportunity to participate in decisions
- a nurse leader who is congenial, approachable, equitable, and straight-forward
- policies and procedures that are well defined and clear, thereby decreasing ambiguity about what constitutes competency and mastery performance
- a positive work environment both physically and socially
- the belief that conditions of the job (e.g., salary, benefits, developmental opportunities, breaks, meals, discipline, handling of grievances, discrimination) are adequate, fair, and equitable
- the perception that one's role provides job satisfaction

The presence of rewards or consequences for one's actions is an important factor in an employee's motivation toward positive performance. If the staff nurse does not exhibit the expected behavior, you must first determine if there are:

- positive consequences when the behavior occurs
- negative consequences when the behavior occurs
- no consequences whether or not the behavior occurs

There also must be agreement between you and the staff that the behavior is possible.

Employee motivation to complete specific tasks depends on the relationship between the activity and its expected outcome, and between the activity and any consequences. Accomplishment of smaller tasks, or components of a larger objective, stimulates and motivates one to greater effort to achieve further goals.

A program to stimulate employee motivation can be developed for individuals or for the unit. The advantage of such a program is that it creates a positive, valued environment for employees and provides you with a tool to encourage positive performance (Douglass & Bevis, 1983). First, assess the status of those factors that motivate each member of the staff. Ascertain the type of activities or projects staff members would prefer to be involved in. For example, a staff member who enjoys working with new orientees may be more interested in and committed to evaluating and modifying the existing orientation plan than another staff member, who enjoys doing the research to draft a new standardized procedure. The nurse manager can keep a reference sheet that lists what each staff member considers as motivating for them. This list can be updated annually and used as a resource list when new projects are incorporated into the unit plan. Once the data base/assessment is complete, the next task is to develop a program to increase employee motivation:

- investigate, through feedback from the staff, unit policies and procedures that are satisfactory or unsatisfactory
- investigate which activities are positively motivating to the staff by designing a questionnaire that will elicit candid comments, conducting personal interviews with the entire staff, and discussing the issues at regular staff meetings or arranging a special meeting for their discussion
- analyze and distribute all accumulated data; seek further validation from the staff as to its completeness and accuracy
- through a series of special meetings, review and discuss all issues and problems that have surfaced
- list all solutions elicited during these meetings and in one-to-one conversations with the staff
- implement the suggested and approved changes

As nurse manager, you retain the final authority on the decisions reached. Because group participation and consensus building were part of the process, group compliance and support for the solution should be forthcoming. Change initiated using participatory decision making often results in improved employee attitudes, morale, and productivity.

The relationship between the employee's ability to meet her needs satisfactorily and her morale, job performance, and productivity is complex (Olson, 1986). Unfortunately, satisfying needs does not always motivate the employee to better performance. Every nurse manager will encounter situations in which an employee is not satisfactorily meeting performance standards (King, 1984). In extreme situations, job security may be jeopardized. If warranted, verbal counseling is given and a written notation describing the situation is entered in the performance record. The verbal counseling covers agreed-upon actions that the employee must demonstrate immediately and sustain or be subject to suspension, demotion, or termination.

Fortunately, few employees are unable to improve. Compassionate counseling will often improve the performance of those employees not meeting work standards. The transformation of the employee who is encouraged to reach her potential is a positive, rewarding experience for most nurse leaders.

PURPOSE OF THE PERFORMANCE EVALUATION

The purpose of a performance evaluation is to assist the employee to rate her performance against basic nursing standards that are criteria-referenced (King, 1984). As part of the evaluation process the employee, with the nurse leader, sets annual goals (Stevens, 1978). These goals facilitate development into more progressive and masterful levels of performance (Douglass, 1984).

In addition to the annual written evaluation and the scheduled interview that accompanies it, you should have frequent exchanges with all employees to ensure timely feedback. Such exchanges can be a motivator for the employee to contribute to the unit with distinction.

Even the best designed evaluation format is subjective. Preconceived biases and notions are inevitable. Therefore, you should develop an evaluation process that relies on scientific, objective, quantitative, and qualitative data as much as possible to overcome bias and judgmental conclusions.

One outcome of the performance evaluation is documentation that the employee's performance meets the standards and competence criteria. By assessing the employee's levels of knowledge and skills and comparing them to expected levels of competence, the evaluator and employee develop consensus about the work standards and objectives. The above observations are then converted to an action plan that will strengthen the employee's capabilities and develop her additional competencies.

The performance evaluation also provides you with the opportunity to acknowledge attitudes and behaviors that positively or adversely affect performance. If necessary, corrective action plans to improve adverse behaviors are agreed upon at this time. In the evaluation, you can recognize and acknowledge accomplishments through salary adjustments, merit awards, or promotion.

The evaluation can also motivate the employee to seek career enhancement opportunities in two ways: (1) by identifying educational opportunities that will maximize, strengthen, and augment the employee's experience and (2) by giving the evaluator an opportunity to encourage, guide, and support such activities.

The performance evaluation also provides an opportunity for direct communication between evaluator and employee. This one-to-one exchange can clarify issues, solve problems, and strengthen the relationship between them.

The evaluation establishes a permanent record of employee performance, including the employee's salary history. It documents the criteria for the employee's role placement and actions taken to alter employee status, e.g., promotion, demotion, transfer, or termination. Finally, it can create a pool of professional resources within the institution.

When the performance evaluation is taken seriously by both the staff member and the nurse manager, individual staff's strengths and achievements are updated and acknowledged. Nurse managers can then sponsor their expert resident staff as a resource to other nursing units, other departments, and organizational committees and task forces. When human resources are effectively used, employee motivation and performance increase.

THE ROLE OF THE EVALUATOR IN PERFORMANCE APPRAISAL—HOW AND WHAT TO EVALUATE

Before beginning to evaluate an employee, review a current job description for the applicable position. Because it contains specific, identifiable, behavior-referenced criteria, it is the tool by which the employee should be evaluated. The employee should be given a copy of the position description to review and an evaluation tool when she is hired and again several weeks before the evaluation (Kruger, 1987).

Performance appraisals are based on observed, recorded behaviors as evaluated against the written criterion-referenced expected performance behaviors (Bernhard & Walsh, 1981). The documentation should consist of behaviorally descriptive and anecdotal notes, rather than interpretative comments. The language should appropriately describe an event, not an employee's subjective trait.

An adequate sample of behavioral observations about each aspect of the employee's job should be compiled. Obtaining a series of observations made on different days and at different times helps ensure a representative sample of observations.

Gathering data can be difficult if the nurse manager does not have a systematic method of data collection. One method to ensure an adequate sample of observations is to select one behavior each day and note the achievement level of this behavior for all staff on that day. Repeat the process until all staff and all behaviors are observed (Olson, 1986).

There are several sources of data available to form the basis of an objective evaluation:

- anecdotal notes from observations and coaching
- audits of charts, care plans, and attendance records
- patient interviews
- input from peers selected by both the evaluator and the employee

- incident reports
- employee's self-evaluation

Notable positive or negative episodes should be recorded in anecdotal notes. However, overall appraisals should not be merely a generalization of those isolated events. Focusing on one event, either positive or negative, can distort the true performance of an employee. In addition to generalization, several other distortions commonly occur in performance appraisals (Stevens, 1985):

- *Halo effect:* The staff member is known to be proficient in some areas so she is assumed to be proficient in all areas.
- *Recency effect:* Recent behavior is counted more heavily than other behaviors occurring during the appraisal period.
- *Problem distortion:* A problem or negative behavior is noted while expected and acceptable behaviors are ignored.
- *Sunflower effect:* The team as a whole is proficient; therefore, it is assumed that all members must be excellent.
- *Central tendency effect:* Everyone is average.
- *Rater temperament effect:* Some evaluators are more severe in their appraisals, whereas others are more lenient.
- *Guessing tendency:* The rater guesses at the employee's performance, rather than acknowledging that a particular behavior has not been observed.

PREPARATION FOR THE PERFORMANCE EVALUATION INTERVIEW

You should develop a method to track evaluation due dates to ensure their timely administration. Tag the anniversary date on the personnel file of each employee as one method of tracking. Mark the due date and the "begin to prepare" date on your annual calendar at the beginning of each year. Schedule the interview several weeks in advance of the annual review date. Inform the employee of the purpose of the interview and discuss any specific problems or administrative actions that may come up during the review; send her a copy of the standard evaluation form. Annual performance evaluations, conducted objectively, with clearly stated outcome goals and no surprises, should be constructive experiences for the employee and the nurse manager, not episodes of stress.

Ask the employee to prepare for the interview by doing the following:

- ranking her performance on key functions of the job description
- completing a self-evaluation that includes strengths, limitations, current actions to correct deficiencies, type of assistance required from the evaluator, and annual goals for the next year
- obtaining written input from two of her peers, preferably someone who works on the same shift and someone who works on a different shift
- submitting any additional supportive data that will highlight performance, such as community performance and committee performance

PERFORMANCE EVALUATION INTERVIEW PROCESS

Take the following actions to ensure a positive interview process:

- Schedule the appointment to ensure there are no unavoidable interruptions. Allow adequate time for the interview, and state the time frame at the beginning of the interview.
- Provide a private, comfortable setting for the interview.
- Allow time for the employee to analyze your written evaluation. Give the employee a copy of their evaluation the day before the interview. The employee should submit a self-evaluation to you 24 hours in advance of the interview using the same form, performance criteria, and offering any additional documentation.
- Encourage a written response on the institutional evaluation form for the employee. Most evaluation forms have a "comments" section. Allowing the employee to write comments of agreement or disagreement reinforces the bidirectional nature of the evaluation process.
- Encourage free discussion in order to mutually identify problems and goals. Respect the employee's opinions and her right to express them.
- Identify processes by which goals can be achieved and problems solved.
- Assist and counsel with humanity and compassion, as indicated.
- Inform the employee of recognition, as indicated. Reward achievement with an appropriate salary adjustment, merit award, or promotion. State the consequences of unacceptable performance.
- Summarize the interview in a succinct note for the personnel record.
- Establish a mutually agreed-upon time for reassessment of progress.

SKILLS REQUIRED DURING THE PERFORMANCE EVALUATION INTERVIEW

As nurse manager, you must use all your interpersonal skills during the performance evaluation. It can be an emotionally charged experience and your ability to use these skills effectively can determine the outcome of an interview (Bothwell, 1985). These skills include:

- active listening
- feedback
- clarification
- conflict resolution: confrontation and negotiation
- problem solving
- decision making
- goal setting
- contracting

Summative Feedback

It is essential that a receptive climate be created for the performance evaluation interview. Use your verbal and nonverbal skills to reflect your attention, interest, and willingness to listen. Use your active listening, feedback, and clarification skills to assist and to plan developmental objectives and activities for the next evaluation time period.

You must establish the expectation and facilitate the process of two-way communication (Stevens, 1985). One method to ensure two-way communication is to prepare questions to ask the employee about her key work performance and job functions.

Unfortunately, some employees have underdeveloped communication skills for use during an appraisal interview. After all, how realistic is it for one to achieve or maintain competency in an evaluation interview by doing such an activity only once a year? During the interview employees often anticipate that the worst will occur. This anxiety is hardly an ideal situation for open communication. Therefore, your role during the evaluation process is to be overtly supportive of the employee. A nurse manager shows support by being human, working with the employee as a professional colleague, being clear and prescriptive, and openly valuing what the employee contributes to the setting.

Once a supportive climate is established, identify, discuss, and resolve any variances between the evaluator's and the employee's interpretations and attitudes concerning the job (Kirkpatrick, 1982). An open discussion in which these issues are acknowledged can be a consensus-building strategy. If agreement is not reached, the evaluation is an opportunity for the evaluator to make the expectations clear and to ensure that an action plan is developed.

The employee's self-evaluation and peer review data should be included in the evaluation. Discuss any similarities or differences between these and the evaluator's appraisal. Acknowledge areas where progress has been made, and identify any priority problem areas. Mutual identification of areas to be strengthened is the goal of this discussion. Ideally, a consensus can be reached; however, the interview is not to be subverted to a bargaining session. If the employee cannot or will not identify areas to be strengthened, the evaluator may have to assert that, despite the employee's lack of agreement, those particular behaviors are deficient and must be changed.

In the final part of the interview, needed behavior changes and areas for skill development or career enhancement activities are identified mutually. These changes and activities should be expressed in the form of written measurable objectives.

In order to make behavioral changes, the employee must understand what behaviors are desired and which must be corrected. During this final phase of the interview the employee must:

- understand how she is going to change to the desired behavior and agree to do so
- understand the consequences of changing or not, identify desired behaviors, and participate in setting goals to change behavior
- develop an action plan on how the change will be accomplished, either at the interview or within one week of the interview
- establish a time frame in which the change will be accomplished
- ensure that the goal is measurable, achievable, and clear to both the evaluator and the employee
- understand that the nurse leader and other resource personnel are available to provide assistance as needed
- participate in setting ongoing checkpoints to receive feedback on how the employee is accomplishing specific goals

If the employee's behavior is satisfactory, encourage the employee to select skills to be enhanced or new knowledge to be learned. The employee who is a self-motivated achiever and requires only limited guidance and direction from an authority figure will enjoy pursuing such a goal. At the end of the interview, summarize the current status of the employee's efforts and goals.

The substance of the discussions should also be summarized in a follow-up written notation. Include a concise description of the problems, goals, and the date of anticipated achievement of the goals in this summary. Ensure that valued rewards are tied to goal achievement. Both you and the employee should receive a complete copy of the written evaluation. The original is retained in the department files.

Before ending the interview, ask for feedback regarding your own performance. Often, nurse managers tremble when they hear such a suggestion. However, if our goal is to develop and strengthen professional and interpersonal relationships, how can we omit such a critical step? The format can be very simple. Ask the employee to highlight one thing that you do particularly well and to recommend one thing that might help her enact her role more effectively. Facilitating such an open dialogue models professional behavior and helps you be more effective in your role (Douglass & Bevis, 1983).

REFERENCES

Bernhard, L.A., & Walsh, M. (1981). *Leadership: The key to the professionalization of nursing.* New York: McGraw Hill.

Bothwell, L. (1983). *The art of leadership.* Englewood Cliffs, NJ: Prentice-Hall.

Douglass, L.M. (1984). *The effective nurse: Leader and manager* (2nd ed.). St. Louis: C.V. Mosby.

Douglass L.M., & Bevis, E. (1983). *Nursing management and leadership in action* (4th ed.). St. Louis: C.V. Mosby.

Fournies, F. (1978). *Coaching for improved work performance.* New York: Van Nostrand Reinhold.

Joiner, C., & Van Servellen, G. (1984). *Job enrichment in nursing: A guide to improving morale, productivity, and retention.* Rockville, MD: Aspen Publishers, Inc.

King, P. (1984). *Performance planning and appraisal.* New York: McGraw-Hill.

Kirkpatrick, D.L. (1982). *How to improve performance through appraisal and coaching.* New York: AMACOM.

Kruger, N. (1987). Making the most of expertise. In K.W. Vestal (Ed.), *Management concepts for the new nurse* (pp. 107–125). Philadelphia: J.B. Lippincott.

Massie, J.L., & Douglass, J. (1981). *Managing: A contemporary introduction.* Englewood Cliffs, NJ: Prentice-Hall.

McFarland, G.K., Leonard H.S., & Morris, M.M. (1984). *Nursing leadership and management: Contemporary strategies.* New York: John Wiley.

Olson, R.F. (1986). *Performance appraisal: A guide to greater productivity.* New York: John Wiley.

Skousen, M.B. (1960). Increasing individual productivity through motivation controls. In *Meeting the Productivity Challenge.* New York: American Management Association. Management Report #40, pp. 76-84.

Stevens, B. (1985). *The nurse as executive* (3rd ed.). Rockville, MD: Aspen Publishers, Inc.

Stevens, W.F. (1978). *Management and leadership in nursing.* New York: McGraw-Hill.

Chapter 10

Employer-Employee Relations

by Mileva Saulo, RN, EdD

NURSE MANAGER ROLE

This chapter introduces the nurse manager to guidelines for fulfilling her legal role under the National Labor Relations Act. It includes information and guidelines relevant to the collective bargaining process, common contract provisions, administration of the contract, grievances, discipline, discharge, negotiation, and strikes. The guidelines are applicable whether or not employees are covered by a collective bargaining agreement.

As the manager on your unit, you hold a pivotal role in creating an environment that provides quality care for patients and opportunities for growth and development of staff. A constructive and positive attitude toward employee relations makes good management sense. People respond to leadership. Your attitude is critical to the ability of staff to meet both their own professional goals and the goals of the organization.

When you became a nurse manager and made the transition from staff nurse to nurse manager, two roles were fused. You became the manager of patient care, as well as of the resources necessary to provide that care. Patient care and employee and employer needs must be balanced if you are to perform your role as an employer representative. For example, your actions as a supervisor in grievance handling, employee discipline, and employee termination must protect the dignity and rights of the employee, as well as those of management. Thus, you integrate all phases of the manager role. The perspective from which the functions are performed becomes the unifying theme.

If you are contemplating taking a management position in an agency in which the workforce is organized, before accepting that position, consider the following (Fralic, 1977):

- What is your personal philosophy regarding health care professionals and collective bargaining? Can you accept collective bargaining as a legitimate activity for professional nurses?

- What is your educational preparation for the role? If more is needed, are you willing to put in the time and energy?
- Are you objective? Will you be able to see both the labor and management views in an issue or grievance?
- Do you recognize the restraints and could you function irrespective of, and within, a written collective bargaining agreement?
- Are you willing to implement the contract on a continuing basis, including grievance responses?

Today, employees are interested in being involved in the decisions that affect them. They need reasons for and an understanding of the changes in policies and procedures that affect them, and when given an opportunity to do so, they will participate in and be creative about improving their workplace.

Employee behavior is motivated; all people act to satisfy needs. Unmet employee needs lead to frustration. One response to circumstances and conditions that leave needs unmet is to seek collective bargaining and unionization as mechanisms for change in the workplace. Rakich, Longest, and O'Donovan (1977) use Maslow's hierarchy of needs and Herzberg's motivators and maintenance factors to describe why employees choose labor organizations (Figure 10-1). They further suggest that employees join unions

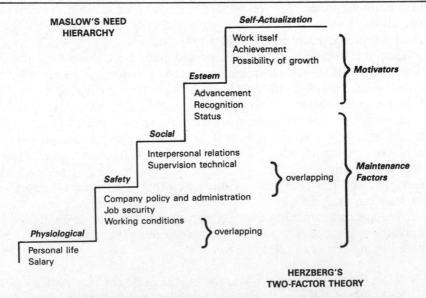

Figure 10-1 Employee Needs and Motivators. *Source:* From *Management Theory: Process and Practice* (p. 326) by R.M. Hodgetts, 1985, Philadelphia, PA: W.B. Saunders Company. Copyright © 1985 by W.B. Saunders Company. Reprinted by permission.

Exhibit 10-1 Why Employees Join Unions

CONDITIONS OF EMPLOYMENT
Concern for such matters as
1. Pay and consistency among pay grades
2. Fringe benefits, such as hospitalization insurance, holidays, vacation time, bereavement time
3. Physical and nonphysical working conditions, such as work breaks, clean-up time, safety conditions, parking, and security
4. Hours of employment
5. The scheduling of employees and the assignment of specific work activities

DEMOCRACY IN THE WORK SETTING
Concern with unfair, unwarranted, or inconsistent administrative actions often restrained by the establishment of procedures for
1. Layoffs, typically based on a seniority basis
2. Promotions, typically based on a combination of seniority and qualifications
3. Dismissal of employees
4. Disciplining of employees

CONTENT OF EMPLOYMENT
Concern for the atmosphere of employment, such as
1. Desire to be treated as a human being
2. The ability to have some control over one's job and the factors that affect it
3. Being kept informed and listened to through the establishment of communication channels—often accomplished with a grievance procedure
4. Desire to apply pressure to force supervision to be humanistic toward employees

Source: From *Management Theory: Process and Practice* (p. 326) by R.M. Hodgetts, 1985, Philadelphia, PA: W.B. Saunders Company. Copyright 1985 by W.B. Saunders Company. Reprinted by permission.

because of (1) conditions of employment, (2) democracy in the work setting, and (3) content of employment (Exhibit 10-1).

The items under conditions of employment and democracy in the work setting correspond to the physiological and safety needs described by Maslow and the maintenance factors described by Herzberg. The social, esteem, and self-actualization needs and motivators fall under the category of content of employment. Maintenance factors are not important as motivators unless they are absent. It was not surprising, then, that when nurses first started to organize many of the early issues raised were concerned with compensation, job security, and working conditions.

Longest's research (1974) indicates the following ranking of motivational factors for RNs in a hospital setting:

1. achievement
2. interpersonal relations
3. work itself

4. policy and administration
5. responsibility
6. supervision—technical
7. salary
8. working conditions
9. recognition
10. advancement

NURSE LEADERS' OPINIONS DIFFER

There has been, and continues to be, controversy over collective bargaining and collective activity as mechanisms for professional nurses to seek effective input regarding the terms and conditions of their employment. Some nurse leaders see collective bargaining as an effective mechanism for nurses to join together and avoid the employer's divide and conquer techniques to (1) redistribute the power base in the health service organization and (2) serve as a process for joint decision making on professional issues (Cleland, 1975; Jacox, 1980). Others (Rotkovitch, 1980) contend that unionization results in a loss of professionalism, diminishes nursing's public and self-image, and ultimately leads to the deteriorization of professional practice.

Limited research has been conducted regarding the differences between unorganized and organized nurses. However, one report indicated that nurses who are involved in collective bargaining have a higher sense of job satisfaction than those who are not involved in bargaining (Hunter et al., 1986).

To organize or not to organize is not the issue. Rather, considering the challenges that face contemporary health care, our energies should be addressed to developing the environment necessary for high-quality patient care and job satisfaction for nurses. Guidelines for due process are applicable whether or not employees are covered by a collective bargaining agreement. Your attitude and leadership ability will be critical in creating an environment for quality patient care and staff satisfaction.

NATIONAL LABOR RELATIONS ACT—SOURCE OF AUTHORITY

The relationships among employees, employers, and the union in an organized work setting is governed by labor law. For private employers, it is governed by the National Labor Relations Act (NLRA or the Act). The Act is the basis for what "thou shalt" and "shalt not" do with respect to labor management relations; it provides the ground rules. The description of the Act that follows is not intended to make you a quasilawyer nor is it a substitute for the expertise of your agency's personnel director and/or labor counsel. Rather, it provides a broad overview of the Act as it affects your day-to-day relationships with the persons you supervise.

The Act provides a framework in which peaceful labor relations can take place. There is nothing in it to compel or force either party to agree to any contract proposal put forward during negotiations. However, it does demand that the parties bargain in good faith "for the purpose of negotiating the terms and conditions of their employment or other mutual aid or protection" and that they attempt to reach agreement. Any agreement reached by this process is binding upon all parties. (NOTE: Those of you employed by public (district, city, county, state, or federal) agencies, are not covered by the NLRA but may be governed by labor law or statutes regulating civil service employees, union recognition, etc. Although many public entities that are organized operate under what seem to be similar guidelines to the NLRA, do not assume that what is said of the Act is directly applicable to your situation if you are in a public agency.)

Structure of the Act

The Act is divided into many sections. Those that have relevance to your role as a nurse manager are as follows:

- Section 7: defines the protected rights of employees
- Section 8: prohibits the commission of certain unfair labor practices by employers and unions
- Section 9: establishes the rules governing the determination of appropriate bargaining units and the conduct of elections
- Section 10: describes the enforcement and remedial provisions used by the National Labor Relations Board (NLRB) to enforce the Act
- Section 19: describes the exemptions for individuals on the basis of religious convictions
- Section 213: outlines procedures for the conciliation of disputes in the health care industry

COLLECTIVE BARGAINING PROCESS

The collective bargaining process is divided into four distinct phases: (1) organizing, (2) recognition, (3) negotiating, and (4) administration of the agreement.

The written contract is a result of the negotiations between the labor organization and the employer and, as such, sets forth their mutual agreement as to wages, hours, and other terms and conditions of employment. Note that this is a relationship between the union and the employer and not a relationship between individuals and the employer. Henry (1984) suggests that caution should be exercised in the interpretation of the word "contract." This document as entered into by the union and the employer is not an employment contract in the same sense as a commercial contract. That is, it is not a contract of employment. Rather, it is an agreement that both parties have made and agreed to abide by. Disputes regarding the contract's interpretation may be settled through a grievance procedure if one is included in the contract.

Collective bargaining agreements vary from institution to institution because the priorities of the employees and employers vary from setting to setting. In an organized facility, employees are bound to the agreement in their own workplace, as well as to their employer's policies and procedures. Staff in an unorganized facility are guided by the policies and procedures written by the employer.

Some collective bargaining agreements begin with a statement of purpose. These clauses can be used to establish the basis upon which the collective bargaining relationship will operate.

Collective bargaining is based on bilateral, rather than unilateral, action. This mutual agreement about the terms and conditions of work may not be limited to the specific terms listed in the contract. Circumstances may arise during the life of the Agreement that were not discussed during the contract negotiations. For example, in the mid-1970s during a physician malpractice insurance crisis, hospitals in the San Francisco Bay Area, faced with a dramatic reduction in census, found it necessary to lay off nurses. There were no provisions in the contract for layoffs. Since this is a matter which affects the terms and conditions of work, it is a subject reserved for bargaining. Because this matter arose during the term of the Agreement and not at the bargaining table during contract negotiations, the bargaining obligation was met once the parties met to discuss the matter.

If an impasse occurs in such a situation the employer's proposal may be unilaterally implemented. In several instances, rather than negotiating layoffs by seniority as is typically done, the parties were able to agree upon a work-share arrangement whereby nurses reduced their hours, maintained benefits, and did not lose their jobs. Therefore, before making changes that affect the individual's terms and conditions of work, check with your supervisor and/or appropriate labor relations staff to determine if the contract prohibits such action.

Management retains the right to manage in all areas not specified by the contract. This is important to you as a nurse manager because you are management in your nursing unit and are therefore bound by the contractual relationship.

COMMON CONTRACT PROVISIONS

Although most contracts have a great deal in common, no one contract should be viewed as typical. When reading any contract, follow these suggestions (Henry, 1984):

- Read and reread those sections that affect the employees under your supervision.
- Note limitations, restrictions, or qualifying language.
- Never assume that the language as presented is superfluous or unimportant.
- If you are unclear about an interpretation, ASK FOR HELP.
- Verify your understanding of a contract provision with someone in authority, e.g., your supervisor or personnel/labor relations director.

Subjects in contracts fall into two major categories:

1. The contractual relationship between the union and the employer; for example, recognition, dispute resolution, and no strike-no lockout.
2. The relationship between the employees and their employer and even between employees themselves; for example, (a) compensation, including wages, credit for previous experience, tenure increases, shift differentials, call-back and standby pay, relief in higher classification; (b) hours, which define straight time, overtime, rest periods, rest between shifts, weekends off, posting of work schedules, and shift rotation; and (c) fringe benefits, such as sick leave, vacations, holidays, health benefits, retirement, life insurance, leaves of absence for education, maternity/paternity, funerals.

In addition, RN contracts may include provisions that address professional issues involving the quality of patient care and the right of professional nurses to have input into those matters that affect nursing practice. California has taken the leadership role in the inclusion of such items as:

- professional performance committees
- input into staffing
- clinical nurse classifications
- assignments and training in special care units

ADMINISTRATION OF THE CONTRACT

As management in the nursing unit and as the person responsible for contract enforcement and interpretation, you should follow these principles when you review and interpret provisions of the contract (Henry, 1984):

- *Residual rights theory*—What management has not given away, it retains. The contract cannot cover all policies, rules, and procedures concerning the day-to-day activities of employers and employees. Because the contract does not cover all issues, the concept of "residual rights" exists to aid in contract interpretation. This concept may not be agreed upon by the union.
- *Clear contract language versus past practice:* Clear and unequivocal contract language cannot be ignored nor given a new interpretation by the arbitrator. In situations where contract language is unclear, ambiguous, or incomplete, arbitrators can go beyond the literal wording in the contract.
- *Past practice:* This relates to a consistent and long history of handling similar questions in one particular way.
- *Prior arbitration awards:* Arbitrators are not bound by the awards of previous arbitrators in similar situations. However, arbitrators frequently apply common principles to common fact situations.
- *Grievance settlements as contract law:* How management and the union have settled similar grievances.

Getting Acquainted with the Contract

To become familiar with the reading of contract language, it is helpful to ask questions, find the appropriate contract clause that governs the situation, and review your answers. Try the following exercise (Exhibit 10-2) in your work group.

How do your responses to the questions in Exhibit 10-2 compare to those of other groups of nurse managers?

Question 1: Yes. If the nurse is required to work through the lunch period she is entitled to be paid for working the lunch hour. Article 7 (B) (4) states, "If the nurse is required to work during the lunch period, such lunch period shall be paid as time worked in addition to payment for the full shift and shall be deemed time worked for the purpose of computing overtime." It does not matter if the nurse agreed to volunteer to skip lunch. The contract requires that a meal period be given.

Exhibit 10-2 Contract Interpretation

This exercise consists of three parts:

1. questions that arise from the contract
2. questions you must ask yourself regarding interpretation
3. questions regarding your reaction to grievance filing

PART I: Read each of the following contract questions:

1. A nurse works through the meal period and puts in for overtime. Is the nurse entitled to such pay?
2. A nurse works from 11 A.M. to 7:30 P.M. and puts in for shift differential. Is the nurse entitled to such pay?
3. A short-hour nurse from ICU requests educational leave for an all-day program on cardiac monitoring. Is the nurse entitled to such paid leave?
4. Two nurses from the same unit, Nurse A with 10 years hospital seniority and 4 years nursing unit seniority and Nurse B with 5 years hospital and nursing unit seniority, request a 1-week vacation at Christmas time. Both are entitled to such vacation. If only one nurse can have such vacation, whom shall you choose?
5. A nurse returns from a 33-day leave of absence without pay. Is the nurse entitled to return to the same shift and classification?

PART II: With each contract question, ask yourself the following questions:

• What CONTRACT provision(s) is/are relevant?
• Is the language CLEAR?
• Is the language AMBIGUOUS?
• What response will you give?

PART III: How would you feel if a grievance were filed against you?
If you are doing this as a small group exercise, choose someone to record and report to the group as a whole.

Question 2: No. The nurse is not entitled to shift differential pay. Article 5(E) (1) states that shift differential pay is paid for nurses who "commence shifts of 4 hours or more at or after 12 noon and prior to 6:00." The nurse began the shift at 11:00 A.M. and is therefore not entitled to shift differential.

Question 3: Probably not. Article 14(D) (1–7) states nothing about short-hour nurses being entitled to educational leave. It reads, "A nurse shall be entitled to 5 days leave with pay each year to attend courses, etc." However, Article 13, Benefits for Nurses Working Less than Full-Time (c) Short-Hour and Casual Nurses, states that "short-hour nurses and casual nurses are ineligible for all fringe benefits such as, but not necessarily limited to, the following . . . ." Educational leave is not included in the list of benefits. Because Article 14 states that nurses are entitled to educational leave and

Article 13 indicates that short-hour nurses are not eligible for this benefit, you may wish to check with the personnel department or your supervisor to verify the correct interpretation.

Question 4: It depends. Article 9(C), Scheduling of Vacation, states, "If staffing and patient care requirements do not permit all nurses requesting a certain vacation preference to take their vacations over the same time period, length of service in the hospital shall be the determining factor within each unit." Article 8(C) (4) states, "A request for vacation shall not unreasonably be denied because of the season of the year." Ability to staff is the determining factor. If the nurse manager could not accommodate both vacation requests, the nurse with greater seniority in the Hospital, Nurse A, would get the vacation. Nurse B has less hospital-wide seniority and therefore would not be granted vacation time.

Question 5: On the face of it, no. The nurse would not be entitled to return to the same shift and classification. The contract provides different return to work guarantees depending upon whether the leave exceeds 30 days. Article 14 (I), Leaves of Absence, states, "If the leave is in excess of 30 days and the nurse returns in compliance with the approved terms of the leave, the Hospital will use its best efforts to, and will not unreasonably deny, return of the nurse to the same classification, position, unit, or shift as occupied at the commencement of the leave".

The following was learned from the contract interpretation exercise in Exhibit 10-2:

- When the language is clear, as in Question 2, the answer is easy.
- When the language is apparently clear, you need to look for answers in more than one place. To answer Question 3, it was necessary to clarify the term "nurse" and to review short-hour nurse benefits. Did the term "nurse" refer to all nurses? Looking further, it was noted that short-hour nurses are not entitled to fringe benefits but that educational leave was not included among them.
- When the language is clear, as in Question 5, a qualifier, such as "will not be unreasonably denied," is left to interpretation.
- A wrong answer could lead to a grievance.
- If you are doubtful of the correct answer, it is appropriate to say, "I'll get back to you," rather than to give an immediate response and be wrong.
- It is not important to memorize the contract but you should be well versed in those areas that affect you on a regular basis and know how to find the appropriate contract provision.

For the most part, nurse managers who were asked the question—How would you feel if a grievance were filed?—felt more comfortable with employees who came individually or as a group to discuss a problem or a complaint than with those who came to file grievances. With grievances they felt "attacked" and "vulnerable" and that "their authority had been challenged." They explained that some of their concerns stemmed from their lack of preparation for the grievance and the approach used by the union steward. Beletz and Meng (1977) suggest that the "sudden feeling in the pit of the stomach and that sudden urge to run when involved in a grievance is normal." However, with education and experience these reactions should lessen in intensity.

Rather than feeling attacked, consider the grievance procedure as a channel of communication that can provide the impetus for instituting change and discovering needs that can lead to policy and/or contract reform. The grievance procedure, if a part of your contract, is an acceptable and agreed-upon mechanism for employees to question the responses of management. Remember, it is not the only mechanism of communication available to you. Finally, and most important, employees who come to you in this fashion are exercising their protected rights under Section 7 of the Act. Your wisest approach is an open one: Listen to what they have to say, do not act defensively, clarify the data presented, and indicate that you will get back to them.

SECTION 7: EMPLOYEE RIGHTS

Section 7 is considered to be the foundation of the Act. It protects the rights of employees to band together by stating that:

Employees shall have the right to self-organization, to form, join, or assist labor organizations, to bargain collectively through representatives of their own choosing, and to engage in other *concerted activities* (italics added) for the purpose of collective bargaining or other mutual aid or protection.

Section 7 also provides that employees shall have the right to refrain from any or all of these same concerted activities except to the extent that a collective bargaining contract may require membership in a labor organization (or payment of dues) as a condition of employment.

Under Section 7, employees have the right to:

- complain about working conditions with, or to, or on behalf of other employees
- discuss, advocate, and actively strive toward unionization

- strike on their own behalf, or honor a picket line established by another group of employees or unions, even if the employees striking or honoring another picket line are nonunion

There is no set definition of protected concerted activity, but it must contain two elements: (1) the activity must be concerted and (2) it must be, in the language of Section 7 "for the purposes of collective bargaining or other mutual aid or protection" (Henry, 1984).

Some examples of concerted activity include (Henry, 1984):

- A union files a complaint concerning the employer's alleged violation of state safety provisions that affected all employees.
- A union attempts to enforce rights contained in the collective bargaining agreement.
- A union files claims for state unemployment benefits.

Because the exact application of the term "concerted activity" is constantly being tested with the NLRB and in the courts, particularly with respect to whether the activity or individual is protected, no retaliatory action should be taken by a supervisor against an individual or group of employees who act in concerted fashion. Consult your personnel director for guidance. It would be far better to do nothing than to risk committing an unfair labor practice and litigation.

Mutual Aid or Protection

Protected concerted activity must not only be concerted—that is, acting together or in concert with others for mutual aid and protection—but it must be for the purposes of self-organization. The term "self-organization" is not precisely defined, but the following activities have been found by the courts to be legitimate examples of self-organization:

- distributing literature concerning legislation affecting working conditions
- criticizing the employer in public during organizational efforts
- protesting changes in operating room assignments and on-call procedures
- seeking improvements in wages, hours, and other terms and conditions of employment

Be aware that nonunion employees, as well as organized employees, are protected by Section 7 of the Act. Henry (1984) cites cases where the same standards and guidelines that apply to unionized employees regarding protected concerted activity apply to nonunionized employees as well.

GRIEVANCES

As a nurse manager, you are in a position to prevent or at least reduce the filing of grievances by your staff.

There are both general and specific sources of grievances (Trotta, 1976) (Exhibit 10-3). Exhibit 10-4 offers suggested guidelines for the recognition and prevention of grievances.

Exhibit 10-3 Causes of Grievances

GENERAL CAUSES

Common Human Characteristics

- self-interest
- authority complex
- communication barrier
- self-justification
- gut reactions

Organizational Climate—The Character of Interpersonal Relationships That Permeates the Organization

- attitude of top management
- personnel policies
- supervisor selection process
- training policies

Union Attitudes

- attitude of state representatives
- attitude of local officials

SPECIFIC CAUSES

The Employee

- qualifications do not match the job
- personal problem
- unreliable, uncooperative, and antagonistic
- linguistic, racial, and cultural problems
- union membership

continues

Exhibit 10-3 continued

> **The Supervisor**
>
> - wrong attitudes (e.g., arrogant, antagonistic toward union)
> - weak supervision
> - favoritism, inconsistency
> - promises to employees
> - failure to eliminate sources of irritation
> - unclear orders and inadequate instructions
> - failure to keep employees informed
> - failure to dispel rumors
> - failure to listen and consider employee's viewpoint
> - failure to consider employee's best interest
> - incomplete understanding of labor contract
>
> **The Union Steward**
>
> - incomplete knowledge of the labor contract
> - making unwarranted promises to members
> - failure to act on union members' complaints
> - showing favoritism
> - failure to set a good example
> - playing union politics
> - allowing rumors to circulate

The provisions of each collective bargaining agreement will determine whether a complaint is a contractual violation as opposed to a general complaint. Although it is important to make a distinction between the two, it is recommended that all complaints be treated as potential grievances in terms of your approach and method of handling. If your agreement is silent over the definition of a grievance, the definition of what may go to arbitration, may itself be referred to an arbitrator. Some contracts, however, specify that a grievance is defined as a misapplication or misinterpretation of the Agreement. Your hospital's labor relations staff can assist you should this differentiation be necessary.

Grievance Investigation

A full, comprehensive, and unbiased investigation is essential to effective grievance management. Key to the effectiveness of this investigation is knowing the difference between a fact, opinion, allegation, and assumption. Trotta (1976) offers the following definitions:

Exhibit 10-4 Recognition and Prevention of Grievances: Guidelines for Nurse Managers

1. Deal with each employee as an individual and as a "whole person."
2. Respect all employees and treat them in a dignified manner.
3. Recognize superior performance and give credit to employees who make good suggestions.
4. Seek and make an effort to understand the employee's point of view as a problem develops.
5. Be alert to sources of employee irritation.
6. Take prompt and effective action to eliminate the causes of irritation.
7. Train employees, especially new ones, to do their job properly.
8. Issue clear orders with reasons why they are necessary and make sure they are understood.
9. Administer discipline objectively, equitably, and consistently.
10. Enforce hospital policies consistently.
11. Avoid favoritism.
12. Cooperate with the union steward in eliminating causes of grievances.
13. Know the provisions of the labor contract.

Source: From *Handling Grievances: A Guide for Management and Labor* by M.S. Trotta, 1976, Washington, D.C.: The Bureau of National Affairs. Copyright 1976 by The Bureau of National Affairs.

- *Fact*—something that is not in dispute, such as an employee's date of hire, age, the date, time of day. It exists as true and cannot be denied.
- *Opinion*—conclusions arrived at by persons who have technical or professional ability to evaluate the situation. It can be a belief or conclusion that may be questioned.
- *Allegation*—a claim or charge made against someone. It is an unsupported assertion and must be distinguished from a fact.
- *Assumption*—something taken for granted as true and a concept one assumes to be true without proof.

There is no method or checklist that can guarantee success in grievance handling. However, just as the nursing process is an orderly way to determine a nursing diagnosis and a plan of intervention that has a high probability of success, guidelines in Appendix 10-A can be invaluable in your investigatory and decision-making process.

SPECIAL CONSIDERATIONS IN DISCIPLINE AND DISCHARGE

What are the grievances that give you the most concern? If you answered, "Discipline and Discharge," you agreed with many of your counterparts.

It *is* possible to terminate someone for poor performance, but nurse managers must be willing first to set performance standards, counsel, evaluate, and assist staff to meet those expected standards. Performance standards must be outlined with a plan of what you and the employee are going to do to achieve those standards. When these methods do not motivate a change in behavior, employees need to be informed of the consequences of lack of change on their part. The Latin root of the word "discipline" is teaching and educating. Therefore, when we discipline we also teach. It is not enough merely to warn. Terminations that occur without due process will be seen by an arbitrator as arbitrary, capricious, and without just cause. These are the types of arbitrations that will be overturned in favor of the employee. However, there are circumstances involving health, safety and other serious matters when it is appropriate for you to suspend and/or remove employees from the work setting without having given an oral or written warning. These exceptions are discussed later in this chapter.

Good and Just Cause

In all other grievances but in discipline cases, the burden of proof is on the employee or the union; that is, the union must prove that the hospital violated the contract. However, the burden of proof in discipline cases rests with management. The hospital must prove that it had sufficient grounds to discipline or terminate the employee.

The guidelines presented below have been used by expert arbitrators as the benchmarks by which they evaluate the substance and process of the termination procedure. In addition to following these guidelines it is imperative that you have a clear understanding of the scope of your authority to act. That is, does your job description give you the authority to carry out discipline, including issuing an oral warning, written reprimand, suspension, and/or termination? Or, can you merely recommend such action? So, before you proceed to discipline, verify your authority to act.

Justin (1969), a prominent labor arbitrator, lists some noteworthy rules of corrective discipline:

- To be meaningful, discipline must be corrective, not punitive.
- When you discipline one, you discipline all.
- Corrective discipline satisfies the rule of equality of treatment by enforcing equally among all employees established rules, safety practices, and responsibility on the job.
- It is the job of the supervisor, not the shop steward, to make the worker toe the line or increase efficiency.
- Just cause or any other comparable standard for justifying disciplinary action under the labor contract consists of three parts: (1) Did the employee breach the rule or commit the offense charged against him or her? (2) Did the employee's act or misconduct warrant corrective

action or punishment? and (3) Is the penalty just and appropriate to the act or offense as corrective punishment?

- The burden of proof rests on the supervisor. He or she must justify each of the three parts that make up the standard of just cause under the labor contract.

Supervisors who act according to the following guidelines will be in a better position to have their case sustained by an arbitrator (Trotta, 1976):

- distinguish between facts and allegations and investigate every allegation thoroughly
- do not make a decision based upon assumptions
- check opinions for accuracy before making a decision
- distinguish between serious and minor offenses
- follow the concepts of progressive discipline
- distinguish between long-service employees and those recently employed
- are sure the penalty fits the offense
- are consistent for similar offenses involving different employees; similar penalties are imposed

Using the contract language in Item 15 of Exhibit 10-5 as the collective bargaining agreement for "Hospital X," the guidelines above, and those outlined in Appendix 10-A, think about how you would handle the following situation.

Case Study—To Discipline or Not to Discipline?

You are the nurse manager of the obstetric units. Your scope of authority covers all three shifts in Labor and Delivery, Postpartum, and Newborn Nursery. One morning a physician comes to you and says, "I want Nurse Y who worked last night on the P.M. shift fired. Did you know that she gave Syntocin IV and the baby delivered in the patient's bed? I will take this to the Medical Executive Committee if she's not fired." Shortly after the physician leaves your office, Nurse Y asks to meet with you. In your office she informs you that she is meeting with you as Step One of the Grievance Procedure. She indicates that she believes Appendix A of the Agreement has been violated. She was assigned to float to OB and does not have appropriate training or experience in this area. She states she went because she did not want to be fired. What would you do?

First, tell the physician that you will conduct a thorough investigation, and if discipline is necessary, you will decide at what level to impose it. Second, when the nurse comes to you to file the grievance, before you start your investigatory interview with her, be aware that although she is there as a grievant she is also an employee whom you may discipline. You will need to inform her that this is an investigatory interview and may inform her of her Weingarten Rights (*NLRB v. Weingarten* 88 LRRM 2689), which are covered in detail later in this chapter. Exhibit 10-5 is a fact sheet that neither the grievant nor the employer dispute.

What do you think should be done? Using the guidelines suggested in Appendix 10-A, you may conclude the following:

- The nurse should not be fired. There are too many factors indicating shared responsibility for the medication error. Neither the baby nor the mother was harmed. The nurse has a good employment record. At best, a counseling session should be held for the supervisor who made the assignment and the nurse for not remembering information covered in her basic nursing program.
- Until the definition of emergency can be determined, it is premature to determine if there had been a violation of the Agreement. Did emergency refer to a sudden influx of patients, a staffing shortage, or a natural disaster, such as a flood, fire, or earthquake?
- Regardless, before floating any nurse, supervisors should determine her level of knowledge, the skills necessary, and functions required in the new assignment, and provide adequate orientation.
- To avoid further confusion, a sign should be posted in the OB medication area regarding the appropriate method of Syntocin administration.
- The nurse manager should verify her response to Nurse Y with the Labor Relations staff.
- Although this particular Agreement requires a response within 7 days of the meeting, in disciplinary situations the response should take less time. This matter would take top priority.

Progressive Discipline

In contemporary employee-employer relations, particularly those in an organized setting, discipline is seen as corrective. That is, the employer identifies the behavior that is unacceptable and the corrections that need to be made and assists the employee to meet acceptable standards of behavior. The counseling component of performance appraisal, this corrective action is seen by arbitrators as the first element of progressive discipline. The steps in progressive discipline are:

Exhibit 10-5 Grievance Summary—Nurse Y

1. Nurse Y has been an ICU nurse for 5 years and has worked in ICU at Hospital X for 1 year. She has a good performance record and has no record of medication errors. In the ICU, Pitocin is given both diluted in an IV and directly IV. Standing orders in the ICU outline the procedures. Nurse Y's exposure to OB occurred 8 years ago in her basic educational training.
2. Supervisor did call Nurse Y shortly after the shift started at 3:00 P.M. and did indeed tell her to go to the Labor and Delivery department to relieve the day nurse who had stayed over. The Supervisor apologized for having to float Nurse Y, but it was an emergency and Nurse Y was the only person available to float.
3. Supervisor told Nurse Y that she would keep herself available for support.
4. Supervisor told Nurse Y that she would have an OB Technician in the unit.
5. Nurse Y did not say that she would refuse to go, neither did she say that she was not qualified to go.
6. The MD order read, "IV Syntocin, Amp I, stat." There was no notation that it was to be mixed in an IV solution.
7. The doctor was leaving the unit as Nurse Y was coming on duty and told the nurse about the order, but did not say that he was coming back to start the IV.
8. After Nurse Y received report from the day nurse, she proceeded to administer the Syntocin IV.
9. When the physician returned to start the IV Nurse "Y" told him that she had already given the drug as ordered.
10. Neither the baby nor the mother was harmed by the medication.
11. There are no posted guidelines in the OB medication area regarding the appropriate administration of this medication.
12. Faculty of both an associate and baccalaureate program who use the hospital for clinical teaching indicated that students are taught to prepare Syntocin in an IV solution, usually one of 5% D/W when used in OB.
13. A review of ICU guidelines indicates that there are protocols and standing orders for administering Syntocin directly into the vein.
14. A review of other charts indicates that the physician in question writes sloppy and incomplete orders.
15. Appendix A of the Agreement states:

    The Hospitals and the CNA recognize that nurses may or may not have training and/or experience in Intensive Care Unit (ICU), Burn ICU, Respiratory ICU, Intensive Care Nursery (ICN), Coronary Care Unit (CCU), Post Anesthesia Recovery Room (PAR), Renal Dialysis, or in other areas when special training and/or experience may be needed. Except in case of emergency, nurses without appropriate training and/or experience shall not be assigned to such areas.

    Appendix B of the agreement further states that Obstetrics and Nursery are to be considered Special Units at one of the hospitals.

- oral reprimand—corrective in nature
- written warning—explaining the expected behavior change and by what date (change expected may be immediate)
- suspension—time off without pay
- termination

Earlier in this chapter substance and procedure were described as two essential components of sustaining any action to terminate an employee. According to Henry (1984), procedure means that you must consider whether all of the notice or due process preconditions to supervisory action have been met. Substance involves whether or not you and your employer can prove that the employee did or did not do whatever you claim to be the case. You must pay equal attention to each of these components of discipline.

Group Notice

Employees can be notified about appropriate performance standards in a variety of ways:

- group meetings
- posted notices
- communication journals or logs
- policies and procedures manuals
- employee handbooks
- orientation sessions
- consistent enforcement of rules
- union contracts

As you review this list of how one gives notice to employees of policies that govern behavior or of appropriate rules and regulations, keep these points in mind:

- Keep a record of when the policies, procedures, and practices were given to the individual or the group.
- Have employees sign in for the informational meetings that they attend and prepare a brief summary of the meetings held.
- Have staff sign for the receipt of meeting minutes and keep the receipts for your records.
- Include a policy in the employee handbook that requires employees to be responsible for reading posted information, journals, and logs, because some employees may not read them.

- Review procedure manuals and employee handbooks on a regular basis, keep a record of the date when the policies are changed, and keep informed of all the changes you have made.
- Include in orientation sessions a checklist of material to be covered and logs or registers for employees to sign. Retain all orientation documents.
- Enforce hospital rules consistently and continually.
- Apply the contract consistently and continually.
- Use good communication skills when counseling employees.
- Get their feedback about their impressions of the session.

Individual Notice

Employees may be told about employee performance standards on an individual basis. You will inform an employee about a needed change in behavior in a number of ways, including:

- Counseling sessions
- Performance appraisals
- Oral reprimands
- Written warnings

Exceptions to Progressive Discipline

You may be faced with a situation in which having an employee remain on the job presents a potential danger to patients and other employees, such as in cases of suspected substance abuse or physical abuse. As a supervisor, to fulfill your responsibility of maintaining a safe environment for patients and staff, you may have to remove the person from the workplace without the opportunity to carry out the sequence of progressive discipline. You should consult the personnel or labor relations director in your facility about the policies in your hospital governing your behavior in cases of patient and staff safety.

EMPLOYEE INSUBORDINATION

To sustain a charge of insubordination you are required to answer these three questions in the affirmative:

1. Was the employee actually given and did she hear a DIRECT order, or was the employee given a suggestion, advice, or a request?
2. If a direct order was given, was it CLEAR?
3. Did the employee REFUSE?

These next two questions, although not required, should also be answered in the affirmative:

1. Was the employee given adequate FOREWARNING of the possible consequences of the alleged refusal to carry out the order?
2. Was the order reasonable and necessary to the SAFE, ORDERLY, and EFFICIENT operation of the organization?

There is a generally accepted rule among arbitrators called "obey now and grieve later." Do not react too quickly when an employee refuses to perform a task. Take time to find out the nature of the refusal, and learn to distinguish between refusal as insubordination and refusal because the person is afraid or unprepared for the task. It is legitimate for an employee to refuse to obey an order that she genuinely believes is an imminent danger to health and safety. One, however, cannot use a defense of fear when one has routinely been doing the task in question.

In addition to not being able to require an employee to do something that places her health or safety in jeopardy, one cannot ask an employee to violate a statute or established standards of practice. However, Henry (1984) states that, where the issue is one of judgment, "then even a professional or licensed employee is not entitled to refuse and if the person does, disciplinary action may be appropriate . . . it is appropriate to establish a procedure to handle preimplementation inquiries as to the accuracy of the judgment through increasingly higher supervisory levels." Therefore, staff nurses on your unit should be encouraged to consult with you or in your absence with the supervisor to validate the judgment being made. Hospital policies should be in place to provide guidance in cases where the judgments of professionals differ.

WEINGARTEN RIGHTS*

In 1975, the Supreme Court of the United States upheld the National Labor Relations Board (NLRB) in the decision *NLRB v. Weingarten* (88 LRRM 2689), thus establishing the Weingarten doctrine. This case is impor-

* Appreciation to William J. Neff, Director, Labor Relations, University of California, San Francisco, for his assistance in the preparation of this section on Weingarten Rights.

tant to you as a nurse manager because you may be faced with a situation where an employee in an organized or unorganized facility requests the presence of her union steward or a representative. The NLRB holds that, under Section 7 of the Act, the employee has a right "to union representation, or to another employee to represent her or him, at an investigatory interview which the employee reasonably believes might result in disciplinary action."

This Supreme Court decision holds that an employee is entitled to union representation under the following circumstances: (1) upon request, (2) at an investigatory interview, and (3) when the employee reasonably believes that the investigatory interview will result in disciplinary action (Henry, 1984). The above provisions apply then in any situation when the employer—any supervisor or other member of management, including security personnel—wishes to conduct an investigatory interview with an employee and the circumstances are such that the employee reasonably believes that disciplinary action could be taken against her and IF and ONLY IF the employee requests a representative (there is no obligation to offer a representative).

The supervisor then has two options. One, tell the employee that there will be no interview if a representative is present. Then the employee has two options at her discretion: (1) have the interview without a representative, or (2) have no interview and forego any benefits that might result from the interview. It is important that this not appear to be a reprisal or retaliatory in nature.

The supervisor also has the option to allow a representative to be present during the interview. It is important to note that the representative may assist the employee in presenting the facts, but may not bargain or negotiate with the supervisor or manager. In no event is the representative permitted to disrupt or interfere with the interview. Too, the supervisor can and should terminate this interview if it is not serving a useful purpose.

Since the Weingarten decision in 1975, the doctrine has been modified somewhat by the NLRB and the courts. The following principles have since been established:

- The Weingarten right to representation includes the right to consult a representative BEFORE the interview. Either the representative or the employee has the right to invoke the right of prior consultation.
- The Weingarten right does NOT require that a supervisor postpone the interview with the employee because a PARTICULAR representative is unavailable when another representative is available.
- The Weingarten right applies whether or not the employee is represented by a union.

- The Weingarten right does not apply to interviews "conducted for the purpose of notifying an employee of a previously determined disciplinary action."

- Counseling sessions are generally not subject to the Weingarten right UNLESS the session(s) are found to be a "preliminary step to the imposition of discipline" in which case, the Weingarten right should apply (Alfred M. Lewis, 95 LRRM 1216).

- The Weingarten right does not apply to counseling and interview sessions when a supervisor gives assurances that the sessions are not disciplinary and WILL NOT be recorded or used for disciplinary purposes.

- The Weingarten right does not arise until the employee requests representation at the beginning of the interview.

- A union cannot invoke the right of employees to Weingarten representation (*Appalachian Power Company v. NLRB*, 106 LRRM 1041, 1980).

- The Weingarten right does not mature until the interview begins (Roadway Express, NLRB, 103 LRRM 1050, 1980).

The decision whether to hold an interview, once a request for representation is made, must be made on a case-by-case basis. Sometimes, the facts on hand may be conclusive enough to make a decision without an interview. On the other hand, the interview may be pertinent to the decision-making process. In either case, you should still schedule the interview with the employee. If the employee then REQUESTS representation for the interview, evaluate the matter fully before deciding whether to hold the interview.

NEGOTIATION PHASE OF THE COLLECTIVE BARGAINING PROCESS

The final section of this chapter presents the legal framework that governs the behavior of all parties in the negotiations, appropriate topics for bargaining, third party intervention as mandated by law, and voluntary third party intervention as a strategy to settle an impasse or a work stoppage. Finally, it addresses the legal right to strike, the dilemmas faced by the parties, and the implications for your behavior as a nurse leader and as the manager or supervisor of your unit.

Views of Bargaining

What impressions do you have of collective bargaining? Do you see it as a poker game, a political struggle full of power tactics? Or, do you see it as a problem-solving process? Nurse leaders have described it in all these ways.

Walton and McKersie (1965) describe the bargaining process according to two models: (1) distributive bargaining and (2) integrative bargaining. The premise underlying distributive bargaining is that there is a limited amount of resources that must be divided between labor and management; when one gains, another loses, and both parties are out to maximize their own share of the limited resources. The objectives in this model are economic; they emphasize rights and obligations. The parties choose how the pie is to be divided. The integrative model, in contrast, is built on the premise of problem solving. The objective is for both parties to win or to select solutions that offer both parties a gain over their current status or no improvement to either. One of the solutions examined is examining the size of the pie. It is critical in this model that there be an open exchange of information, a search for solutions, and determination of their consequences and that both parties are equally motivated to work at the process.

Both the distributive model and integrative model are used when discussing economic items, whereas the integrative method may be more appropriate in resolving noneconomic issues. What is important to remember is that the attitudes of the parties during negotiations cannot be separated from the relationship that exists between the parties in the time between bargaining.

Implications for Nursing Leadership

Your behavior both as a manager and leader is critical to the employee-employer relationship. While reasons for strikes vary, early strikes were generally over economic issues (Miller, 1975; Miller & Dodson, 1975). A shift took place in the early seventies when nurses used collective bargaining to make major changes in fundamental professional issues such as quality of patient care, safety, and input. Major issues today are fundamentally non-economic (although dollar value can be attached to most issues); rather, strikes may occur because of nurses' inability to communicate with management and their perceptions of authoritarian behavior on the part of management. Your day-to-day handling of the concerns of those under your supervision can play a critical role in how management is perceived by employees. Using the integrative approach in your routine interactions with employees is of benefit.

Legal Framework

The legal obligation to bargain in good faith is imposed by Section 8(d) of the NLRA:

> To bargain collectively is the performance of mutual obligation of the employer and the representatives of the employees to meet at reasonable times and confer in good faith with respect to wages, hours, and other terms and conditions of employment, or the negotiation of an agreement or any question arising thereunder, and the execution of a written contract incorporating any agreement reached if requested by either party, but such obligation does not compel either party to require the making of a concession.

Section 8(d) is enforced by sections 8(a) (5) and 8(b) (3) of the Act, which make it an unfair labor practice for either the union or the employer to refuse to bargain in good faith. Section 8(d) has two separate elements:

The employer has the obligation to bargain with the union once it has been designated as the exclusive bargaining representative for a group of employees and once the employer receives a request from the union to begin collective bargaining negotiations. The parties bargain in good faith when they enter into negotiations with an open mind and make a sincere effort to reach an agreement on mutually acceptable terms. These obligations are binding on employees in all organized work settings.

Issues subject to bargaining can be divided into three categories:

1. *Mandatory*—items falling within the category of wages, hours, and other terms and conditions of employment; those items reviewed earlier under the democracy, content, and conditions of work; can be bargained to impasse and any subsequent settlement reached on these items will be included in any subsequent contract.
2. *Permissive*—any topic that falls outside wages, hours, and other terms and conditions of employment, e.g., procedures for contract ratification and demands of each other as to who is on the bargaining team; cannot go to impasse over such a topic; it can be included in the final settlement or under certain circumstances be included in the final settlement by mutual agreement.
3. *Illegal*—an inclusion of any topic for bargaining that is a violation of law; for example, a closed shop.

Conduct During Negotiations

Your behavior as a manager and therefore as an agent of the employer during negotiations is governed by Section 8(a) (1) of the Act, which prohibits unfair labor practices of both employers and unions. Employers may not (Rutkowski & Rutkowski, 1984):

- dominate or interfere with the formation or administration of a union nor contribute financial or other support to it
- discriminate against employees in hiring, retention, or conditions of employment as a means of encouraging or discouraging labor organization membership or activities
- discriminate against an employee for filing charges with the NLRB and for providing testimony under the Act
- refuse to bargain in good faith

Section 8(b) describes similar unfair labor practices by unions. Rutkowski and Rutkowski (1984) use the acronym SPIT to alert supervisors to inappropriate behavior during organizing campaigns. This same acronym applies to conduct during negotiations. As a manager, you cannot:

- *S*py: You cannot attend union meetings or inquire about the nature of the meeting and its outcome.
- *P*romise: You cannot promise an employee any reward for staying out of a union or for not going on strike.
- *I*nterrogate: You cannot interrogate employees about their preferences for a union or their intent to strike or not to strike.
- *T*hreaten: You cannot threaten them with reprisals of any kind (we suggest that you not threaten them at other times either).

Therefore, during negotiations and organizing campaigns you must refrain from any activity that interferes with the employees' rights under Section 7. According to Henry (1984), however, you may question employees regarding their intention to work if a strike does occur. Yet, it is imperative that these questions be neutral and not be accompanied by any threats or promises. A more detailed list of "do's and don'ts" for supervisors during an organizing campaign or during negotiations and a strike can be found in Appendix 10-B.

Although strikes are not the most effective method for resolving labor disputes, they do occur because the parties (1) are unable to agree, (2) miscalculate the other's interests, or (3) run out of time (Sloan & Witney, 1977). Remember, the Act does not compel parties to agree.

Voluntary and Mandatory Resolution of Impasse

It is important to become familiar with the variety of mechanisms available to assist the parties to move toward a collective bargaining agreement that will achieve a peaceful settlement. Traditionally, nurses' labor organizations have exhausted all of these remedies before a strike (Foley, 1985; Miller, 1975). Some mechanisms are voluntary and some are compulsory under the health care amendments to the Act.

One voluntary mechanism is *arbitration*. The parties may wish to submit all outstanding issues to a neutral third party who has the authority to settle the dispute. Any settlement reached by this mechanism is binding and enforceable on and by both parties.

Rights arbitration refers to those disputes over the meaning or proper applications of a particular contract provision or to a specific situation. The claim is to rights already accrued, not merely to create new ones for the future. Rights arbitration was the mechanism described earlier in the discussion of grievances that may be settled under binding arbitration.

Interest arbitration refers to disputes over the formation of collective agreements or efforts to secure them. Their objective is the acquisition of rights for the future, not the assertion of rights claimed to have been vested in the past.

Another voluntary mechanism—*mediation*—occurs when an individual assists the parties by using persuasion and logic to effect a compromise. Mediators are third party neutrals who assist the parties to resolve their differences. Health-related parts of Section 213(a) of the act now require the parties to accept the services of the Federal Mediation Service to assist in the resolution of negotiations that are at impasse. Their recommendations have no binding effect on the parties.

Sam Kagel (1973), an outstanding arbitrator and a charter member of the Royal Academy of Arbitrators, advocates an approach that he termed "med-arb." Under this approach the parties select a neutral party who first mediates and attempts to get the parties to resolve as many issues as possible. When it is felt that further mediation will prove fruitless, the mediator "dons the arbitrator cap" and disposes of the remaining, unresolved issues (Corbett, 1973). A fuller discussion of third party intervention, is found in Corbett (1973), Dunlap (1973), Kagel (1973), and Polland (1973).

There is no substitute for good faith bargaining. In arbitration settlements of impasse situations unions have more to gain than do the employers (Henry, 1984). When the parties agree to arbitration, employers lose the ability to control such issues as cost, new employee work rules, and new worker classifications.

Management Preparation for a Strike

In the event that the parties are not able to reach an agreement, under the health care amendments to the Act (Section 8(d) (g)), the labor organization is obligated to give the employer a written 10-day notice of its intent to strike. Failure to do so precludes the labor organization from going on strike. If a union goes on strike without the required 10-day notice it has committed an unfair labor practice (ULP) and is subject to court injunction, and the strike, if it occurs, becomes unprotected activity. Although hospital administrators should not wait until the strike is called to prepare their strike plan, they can use the 10-day notice period to:

- determine the level of patient census that can be properly cared for by management and nonstriking staff and reducing the census to the number necessary
- have the community relations department prepare the public for any inconvenience
- gain public support for a fair and equitable settlement

As a member of the management team, you will be called upon to assist the organization in the development of a strike plan. Bloom (1975), Coulton (1976) and Rutkowski & Rutkowski (1984) are excellent resources to consult. Nurse managers are in an excellent position to serve as a communication channel between employees and the employer.

Strikes—A Professional Dilemma

What have been your thoughts while reading this section on strikes? What kinds of feelings does the word "strike" evoke in you? Consider these thoughts and feelings expressed by nurses, some of whom have been staff nurses on strike, in a recent leadership seminar:

- "I am dedicated to serving the patient. I think it's wrong to abandon the patient."
- "I feel we had no choice but to strike. I can't let them make me feel guilty for wanting decent working conditions, better patient care, and a salary my children and I can live on."

The very nature of any dilemma requires that one make a choice between equally undesirable alternatives (Curtin & Flaherty, 1982). Curtin and Flaherty tell us that "a dilemma may not be solvable, but it is resolvable.

Nurses who are faced with a dilemma to strike or not to strike are experiencing a values conflict: a struggle between the needs of the patient, the employer, professional autonomy, professional friendships, and their needs and those of their families. Which should take precedence?

Nursing is a service-oriented profession, and there are two behaviors available to dissatisfied workers—"voice" and "exit" (Miller & Dodson, 1976). Behaviors associated with "voice" are strike, demonstration, and picketing. In addition, "voice" can also be demonstrated by dealing directly and forthrightly with issues as they arise and working together with nurse managers throughout the term of the contract in order to make a true impact on the standards of care.

Your conduct during a prestrike and strike period is guided by the same factors discussed in the section on negotiations. A nursing administrator who went through a strike said:

> By communicating openly and respecting each other's rights to our moral and professional values, we were able to talk through the problems and reach solutions . . . . Open communication was the key factor in minimizing what could have become an irreparable division in this community of professional nurses (Bloom, 1975).

Values concerning collective bargaining and all that it entails are deeply held. According to Katz and Lawyer (1985), these values cannot be changed through argument, logic, or persuasion. Rather, the goal should be to "hear, understand, and consider the other's view, respect the person, and accept the reality that another may see, hear and feel things differently than you." The challenge then, is how people who differ can find a basis for agreement. Could it be that care of the patient is the unifying theme?

REFERENCES

Beletz, E.E., & Meng, M.T. (1977). The grievance process. *American Journal of Nursing, 2,* 256–260.

Bloom, I. (1975). Strike with honor. *Journal of Nursing Administration, 3,* 19–20.

Cleland, V.A. (1975). Taft-Hartley amended: Implications for nursing and the professional model. *American Journal of Nursing, 2,* 288–296.

Corbett, L. (1973). Mediation/arbitration from the employer's standpoint. *Monthly Labor Review, 96,* 65.

Coulton, M.R. (1976). Labor disputes: A challenge to nurse staffing. *Journal of Nursing Administration, 5,* 15–20.

Curtin, L., & Flaherty, M.J. (1982). *Nursing ethics: Theories and pragmatics.* Bowie, MD: Robert J. Brady Co.

Dunlap, K. (1973). Med-Arb: Reactions from the rank and file. *Monthly Labor Review, 96,* 66.

Foley, M.E. (1985) In D.J. Mason & S.W. Talbott (Eds.), *Political action: Handbook for nurses* (pp. 265–282). Menlo Park, CA: Addison-Wesley.

Fralic, M. (1977). The nursing director prepares for labor negotiations. *Journal of Nursing Administration, 7/8,* 4–8.

Henry, K.H. (1984). *The health care supervisor's legal guide.* Rockville, MD: Aspen Publishers, Inc.

Hunter, J., Bamberg, D., Castiglia, P., & McCausland, L. (1986). Job satisfaction: Is collective bargaining the answer? *Nursing Management 17.3,* 56–60.

Jacox, A. (1980). Collective action: The basis for professionalism. *Supervisor Nurse, 8,* 22–24.

Justin, J. (1969). *How to manage with a union, book one.* New York: Industrial Relations Workshop Seminars, Inc. 294–295, 301–302.

Kagel, S. (1973). Combining mediation and arbitration. *Monthly Labor Review, 96,* 62.

Katz, N.H., & Lawyer, J.W. (1985). *Communication and conflict management skills* (p. 116). Dubuque, IA: Kendall/Hunt Publishing.

Longest, B.B. (1974). Job satisfaction for registered nurses in the hospital setting. *Journal of Nursing Administration, 4/5,* 46.

Miller, M.H. (1975). Nurses' right to strike. *Journal of Nursing Administration, 2,* 35–39.

Miller, M.H., & Dodson, L. (1976). Work stoppage among nurses. *Journal of Nursing Administration, 12,* 41–45.

Polland, H. (1973). Mediation-arbitration: A trade union view. *Monthly Labor Review, 96,* 65.

Rakich, J.S., Longest, B.B., & O'Donovan, T.R. (1977). *Managing health care organizations.* Philadelphia: W.B. Saunders.

Rotkovitch, R. (1980). Do labor unions' activities decrease professionalism? *Supervisor Nurse, 8,* 16–18.

Rutkowski, A.D., & Rutkowski, B.L. (1984). *Labor relations in hospitals.* Rockville, MD: Aspen Publishers, Inc.

Sloan, A.A., & Witney, F. (1977). *Labor relations* (3rd ed.). Englewood Cliffs, NJ: Prentice-Hall.

Trotta, M.S. (1976). *Handling grievances: A guide for management and labor.* Washington, DC: The Bureau of National Affairs.

Walton, R. & McKersie, R. (1965). *A behavioral theory of labor negotiations.* New York: McGraw-Hill.

SUGGESTED READINGS

Beletz, E. (1980). Organized nurses view their collective bargaining agent. *Supervisor Nurse, 11,* 39–46.

Bryant, Y. (1978). Labor relations in health care institutions: An analysis of Public Law 93-360. *Journal of Nursing Administration, 3,* 28–39.

Cannon, P. (1980). Administering a contract, *Journal of Nursing Administration, 10,* 13–19.

Cleland, V.A. (1974). The supervisor and collective bargaining. *Journal of Nursing Administration, 9/10,* 33–35.

Cleland, V.A. (1978). Shared governance in a professional model of collective bargaining. *Journal of Nursing Administration, 9,* 10–15.

Coletta, S.S. (1978). Values clarification in nursing: Why. *American Journal of Nursing, 12,* 2057.

Conta, L.A. (1972). Bargaining by professionals. *American Journal of Nursing, 2,* 309–312.

Creighton, H. (1976). Law for the nurse supervisor. *Supervisor Nurse, 7,* 48–53.

Elkouri, F., & Elkouri, E.A. (1973). *How arbitration works.* (3rd ed.). Washington, DC: Bureau of National Affairs.

Gaynor, D. RN's strike. *Health PAC Bulletin, 60,* 1–8, 10–14.

Godfrey, M. (1976). Someone should represent nurses. *Nursing '76, 6,* 73–84.

Grand, N.K. (1973). Nurse ideologies and collective bargaining. *Journal of Nursing Administration, 3/4,* 29–33.

Jacox, A. (1969). Who defines and controls nursing practice. *American Journal of Nursing, 5,* 977–982.

Kossoris, M.D. (1967). The San Francisco Bay Area nurses' negotiations. *Monthly Labor Review, 6,* 8–12.

Kralewski, J.E. (1974). Collective bargaining among professional employees. *Hospital Administration, Summer,* 30–41.

Parlette, G.N., O'Reilly, C.A., & Bloom, J.R. (1980). The nurse and the union. *Hospital Forum, 23,* 14–15.

Stickler, V.B., & Velghe, J.C. (1980). Why nurses join unions. *Hospital Forum, 23,* 14–15.

Zimmerman, A. (1975). Taft-Hartley amended: Implications for Nursing—the industrial model. *American Journal of Nursing, 2,* 284–288.

Appendix 10-A

Checklist of Issues for Supervisory Decision Making

A. Procedural Issues To Consider

1. Did employee have notice of:
   _____ The applicable policy, procedure, or other requirement of your employer?
   _____ The work-related expectations you may have concerning the person's job performance, conduct, or attendance?
   _____ The dissatisfaction you have with an employee's conduct, performance, or attendance, and of the corrective action the individual must take?
   _____ The consequences, including the possibility of disciplinary action, if the unsatisfactory conduct, performance, or attendance continues?
   _____ The relevant changes in your employer's policies, procedures, or other requirements?

2. Did you investigate the facts before taking disciplinary action?
   _____ Did you interview witnesses, obtain their statements or your own investigatory notes of what they knew, saw, or heard, and did you verify or discount any conflicting "facts" that arose?
   _____ Did you review all the documentation for discrepancies, missing facts, omitted dates or signatures, etc.?
   _____ Did you review the employee's prior record?
   _____ Did you speak to the employee to determine that person's version of the events or problem?

Source: From *The Health Care Supervisor's Legal Guide* (pp. 281–284) by K.H. Henry, 1984, Rockville, MD: Aspen Publishers, Inc. Copyright 1984 by Aspen Publishers, Inc.

_____ Did you review your documents or double-check with your witnesses or other individuals with firsthand knowledge of any inconsistency emerged between the employee's version and that of other witnesses (or your own understanding of the facts) to determine whether the differences could be resolved?

_____ Did you evaluate the facts (outlining your facts can be extremely helpful in this regard) so as to discard irrelevant ones and those that could not be proved or did not appear credible?

3. Have your employer's policies, procedures, or requirements been enforced consistently and evenly?

_____ What type of disciplinary action has been taken for past infractions?

_____ Have you considered the possibility of deferring disciplinary action in this case, if enforcement has not been consistent, in favor of informing all employees that the policy, etc., will be enforced in the future (group notice), and proceeding with disciplinary action only for future infractions?

_____ Are there any aggravating factors that support disciplinary action if there has not been consistent enforcement and, if so, can you still comply with other applicable notice requirements?

4. Have you obtained advice, direction, or approval as required by your employer's own procedures or requirements, e.g., from personnel, your superior, legal counsel, etc.?

5. Was the employee notified of the right to union representation for the investigatory interview, if applicable, and was the union given notice of the disciplinary action, if applicable?

6. Have you prepared an appropriate written notice of your final disciplinary action, discussed it with the employee, asked the person to sign the notice to acknowledge receipt of a copy, and provided a copy for the worker's personnel file? Remember, if your disciplinary action is to terminate an employee, then double-check your own internal procedures since they may not require a meeting or that a copy be provided to the employee.

7. Have you followed progressive discipline, if it is appropriate (for example, is the infraction not so serious that termination for a first-time offense is warranted) and is your intended disciplinary action the next appropriate step to take?

B. Substantive Issues to Consider

1. What is the general nature of the problem you are facing: unsatisfactory performance, misconduct, or absenteeism/attendance?

2. Can you determine, if the issue is unsatisfactory performance:

    _____ How the employee's performance is unsatisfactory?

    _____ What the employee must do to correct the performance?

    _____ Whether the employee appears to be unable or unwilling to perform (since your plan of action may be influenced by this distinction)?

    _____ Whether the employee's performance fluctuates between satisfactory (or even excellent) to poor, indicating the ability to do the work but a lack of concern or consistency (again, this distinction may influence your decision)?

    _____ Whether your expectations are consistent with how other employees perform the job (if not, you may need to establish revised standards or give notice to all employees that existing ones will be enforced before you proceed to any disciplinary action)?

    _____ Whether the employee has received any assistance from you or others and whether any such aid (or external sources of help), such as written materials, continuing education programs, seminars, etc., would be helpful?

3. Can you identify, if the issue is misconduct:

    _____ What type of misconduct is involved, such as theft, sleeping on duty, under the influence of alcohol or drugs, insubordination, unauthorized absences, destruction of property, fighting, etc. (remember, there may be more than one type of misconduct)?

    _____ What requirements you must meet to prove that type of misconduct and whether your facts establish each such activity (for example, sleeping on duty requires sleeping, not merely closing one's eyes, and on duty time, excluding rest breaks, meal periods, etc.)?

4. Have you considered, if dependability (absenteeism or tardiness) is the problem:

    _____ Whether the primary problem is extensive absences (long absences because of health problems), one- or two-day absences (may be health but the employee may have personal problems or is deliberately using up sick leave as it accumulates), or tardiness (the easiest to deal with from a disciplinary standpoint)?

_____ Whether you are contesting, or conceding, that the absences are health-related?

_____ Whether there is any factual basis for contesting the legitimacy of any claims that the absences are health-related?

_____ Whether your facts support a conclusion that the employee is engaging in a deliberate pattern of absenteeism/attendance akin to misconduct (such as not calling in sufficiently in advance of an absence, not returning to work at the end of an approved leave, being absent on days adjacent to days off, holidays, etc.)?

_____ Whether any medical verification or information is necessary, whether it has been obtained, and whether your policies allow mandatory referral to employee health or to an employer-selected physician?

_____ Whether any of the absences were the result of workers' compensation illness or injuries?

5. Have you identified whether any legal do's and don'ts apply to your problem and, if so, will your intended action comply with those legal standards?

6. Do any of your employer's policies or procedures speak to the problem you are facing; if so, is your intended action consistent with those policies?

7. What has been your employer's response to past occurrences of the same type of problem at issue here and is your intended action consistent with those responses?

8. Have you checked and double-checked:
   • any relevant employer policies, rules, or procedures, as enforced and as communicated to employees
   • any applicable outside standards (such as those of the Joint Commission on Accreditation of Hospitals, etc.)
   • any pertinent union contract provisions
   • your employer's own past practices, etc.?

9. Has supervisory action been taken for this incident (whether disciplinary, a performance review detailing deficient areas of performance, or counseling, etc.); if so, is a follow-up appropriate and, again, if so, have you flagged a follow-up date to ensure that it will occur?

Appendix 10-B

Appropriate Supervisor Behavior During Negotiations and Organizing

An Employer or Supervisor Can Legitimately Do All of the Following:

1. Tell employees how their wages, benefits, and working conditions compare with other employers (whether unionized or not) and how those factors in your facility are superior to those in union contracts negotiated with other employers.
2. Tell employees of the disadvantages that may result in belonging to a union, such as loss of income because of strikes, requirements to serve in picket line, expensive dues, fines, and assessments.
3. Tell employees that the law permits the employer to hire a permanent replacement for anyone who engages in an economic strike.
4. Tell employees that no union can make the employer pay more than it is willing or able to pay.
5. Tell employees about the benefits they enjoy now as nonunion employees but be sure to avoid any veiled threats or promises as to how your employer will react if a union wins the election.
6. Tell employees that merely signing the union authorization card or application for membership does not mean that they must vote for the union in an NLRB election but that they are free to cast a vote that is in their own best interests. Furthermore, tell employees that NLRB elections are determined by the majority vote of the employees *actually voting*—not the total number of employees who are eligible. Therefore, it is essential that all employees vote.

Note: Guidelines for supervisory conduct during union organizing drives or NLRB election campaigns should be reviewed with your employer's legal counsel.

Source: From *The Health Care Supervisor's Legal Guide* (pp. 72–74) by K.H. Henry, 1984, Rockville, MD: Aspen Publishers, Inc. Copyright 1984 by Aspen Publishers, Inc.

7. Tell employees about the NLRB election procedures, the importance of voting, and the secrecy of the ballots.
8. Tell employees that the employer opposes the principle of compulsory union membership but that the union would have the right to request that a collective bargaining contract require employees to pay dues or be terminated from employment.
9. Hold group meetings of employees to explain the employer's position. These meetings can be held on worktime without having to give equal time for union-scheduled meetings. However, these meetings cannot be held during the 24-hour period immediately preceding the election and they should never be held unless they have been planned and scheduled by management.

An Employer or Supervisor Cannot Do Any of the Following:

1. Promise employees a pay increase, promotion, benefit, or special favor if they stay out of a union or vote against it.
2. Threaten loss of jobs, reduction of income, discontinuance of any privileges or benefits, or use any intimidating language that may be designed to influence employees in the exercise of their right to belong, or refrain from belonging, to a union.
3. Threaten, through a third party, any of the above acts of interference.
4. Spy on union meetings or conduct yourself in a way that would indicate to the employees that you are watching them to determine whether or not they are participating in union activities. Surveillance of an employee's union activities is considered to be inherently coercive or threatening.
5. Engage in any partiality favoring nonunion employees over employees active on behalf of a union.
6. Discipline or penalize employees actively supporting a union for an infraction that nonunion employees are permitted to commit without being similarly disciplined. REMEMBER: You can discipline employees for violating a valid employer policy in accordance with your normal procedures *if* the violation is the real reason for the employer's action. The violation cannot be a pretext for a real reason of antiunion motivation because of the employee's union activities. It is suggested that legal counsel be consulted before any disciplinary action is taken against any employee during preelection time.
7. Select employees for layoff or reclassification with the intention of curbing the union's strength or of discouraging affiliation with it.
8. Ask employees for an expression of their thoughts about a union or its officers.

9. Ask employees at the time of hiring or thereafter whether they belong to a union or have signed a union application or authorization card.

10. Ask employees about the internal affairs of unions, such as meetings, etc. Remember that it is not an unfair labor practice to listen if employees tell you of such matters of their own accord but you must not ask questions to obtain additional information.

11. Make a statement that you will not deal with a union or that the employer will shut down if the union wins.

12. Enforce an invalid solicitation-distribution policy—for example, by preventing employees from soliciting union membership or discussing the election or union activities during their nonworking time, including breaks and lunch periods.

Chapter 11

Problem Solving and Decision Making

written with JoAnn G. Ford and Bobbie C. Nelms

Nurses need to use a systematic decision-making process. The newer state nurse practice acts and the expanded roles of the nurse demand increased responsibility and accountability. Many of the nurse's responsibilities require nursing judgment and decision making. Your effectiveness as a nurse leader is determined in part by the quality of your decisions.

The end result of problem solving and decision making should be a good decision, which must be distinguished from a good outcome. A good decision is a decision that is made systematically using good decision-making skills (Gelatt et al., 1973). A good outcome is getting what you want. What you want, of course, is based on your values and preferences.

Over time, good decision making should lead to improved outcomes. However, any one good decision may lead either to a desired or undesired outcome. In the same way, a poor decision-making process can lead to either a desired or undesired outcome. For example, a systematically made decision to hire a staff nurse based on interviews and references could result in an outcome of staff conflict leading to resignations—a good decision leading to an undesired outcome. On the other hand, a spontaneous decision made after a social meeting to hire a staff nurse could result in a respected, effective addition to the staff—a desired outcome. However, making decisions systematically increases the probability of a good outcome.

This section presents one model of decision making (Ford, Trygstad-Durland, & Nelms, 1979). Its components are:

- *values,* which underlie all decision making
- *behavioral objectives,* which are a statement of what is desired

This chapter is adapted from *Applied Decision Making for Nurses,* by J.A. Ford, L.N. Trygstad-Durland, and B.C. Nelms, 1979, St. Louis, MO: The C.V. Mosby Company. Reprinted by permission of the authors.

- identification of the *problem*
- *gathering* of *information* about the problem
- identification of *options*
- identification of *alternatives*
- *analysis* of *alternatives* according to probability, desirability, and risk
- *the decision* itself
- *evaluation* of the decision

Each component is described and exercises are included to assist you in understanding and using each component of the decision-making process.

CLARIFYING VALUES

The first step in the decision-making process is identifying the values involved in this particular decision. Values influence our perceptions and our actions. As children, we learn values from our family of origin. As we grow and develop, our values may change. With education and experience, we may develop new values.

Three exercises are included here to assist you in identifying and clarifying your own values. The first exercise helps you recognize your values as you make choices based on those values. Read each of the questions in Exhibit 11-1 and then rank order your responses, with 1 being your most preferable and 3 being your least preferable.

Exhibit 11-2 enables you to rank order life values according to their importance for you. This exercise gives you another opportunity to make choices from competing possibilities. Read over the list and then rank your values, with 1 being the most important, 2 being the second most important, and so on, until you have numbered all the possibilities (Simon, Howe, and Kirschenbaum, 1972).

Exhibit 11-3 provides you with an opportunity to write your own obituary. After completing this exercise, you may want to consider whether your current behavior is compatible with achieving the outcomes you describe in your own obituary. For instance, leaving behind a circle of close friends and family suggests a life pattern of time and energy devoted to developing and maintaining relationships.

These three exercises use non-nursing examples to help you with the process of clarifying life values. Now, you may want to list your values as they relate more specifically to your work setting and nursing career. Remember that values are not merely hopes or dreams. A value must be chosen freely from alternatives and be enacted in behavior. Check your values against the

Exhibit 11-1 Identifying Values

1. Whom would you prefer to marry? A person with:
   _____ Intelligence
   _____ Personality
   _____ Sex appeal
2. Which would you most like to improve:
   _____ Your looks
   _____ The way you use your time
   _____ Your social life
3. You've spent a great deal of time picking a gift for a friend. You give it to him personally. If your friend does not like the gift, what would you rather he do?
   _____ Keep the gift and thank you politely
   _____ Tell you he does not like it
   _____ Return the gift to the store without telling you
4. What is the worst thing you could find out about your teenager? (Does the sex of the teenager make any difference?)
   _____ That he has been shoplifting
   _____ That he has experimented with several kinds of drugs
   _____ That he has been or is promiscuous
5. Which would you least like to be?
   _____ Very sickly
   _____ Very poor
   _____ Disfigured
6. When you worry about a grade on an exam, what do you think about?
   _____ Yourself
   _____ Peers
   _____ Family
   _____ The teacher
   _____ Graduate school
7. Which of these would be most difficult for you to accept?
   _____ Death of a parent
   _____ Death of your spouse
   _____ Your own death
8. Which are you more concerned about as you grow older?
   _____ Cancer
   _____ Immobility
   _____ Loneliness
9. Where would you rather be on Saturday?
   _____ At the beach
   _____ In the woods
   _____ In a department store
10. Which would you be most likely to take a course in?
    _____ Sex education
    _____ Race relations
    _____ Ecology

Source: Reprinted by permission of Dodd, Mead & Co., Inc. from *Values Clarification* by Simon, Howe, and Kirschenbaum. Copyright 1972 by Dodd, Mead & Company, Inc.

Exhibit 11-2 Present Life Values

_____ Make a new discovery
_____ Complete my education
_____ Achieve the goals of my religion (salvation, nirvana)
_____ Be at peace with myself
_____ Learn to resolve conflicts I have with others
_____ Have a close love relationship with another adult
_____ Have and rear children
_____ Be accepted by my parents for the person I am
_____ Accept my parents for the people they are
_____ Be in excellent health
_____ Change my appearance to be the beautiful person I want to be
_____ Live in a world at peace
_____ Understand human behavior
_____ Know myself
_____ Be aware of my own feelings
_____ Express my own feelings
_____ Live in a clean environment
_____ Develop close friendships
_____ Live a peaceful life
_____ Live an exciting, stimulating life
_____ Work/study part-time so I have time for other important activities
_____ Have a challenging job even if it takes more than 40 hours a week
_____ Gain recognition, be an expert and authority in my chosen field
_____ Develop an active fantasy life
_____ Feel I have contributed to the well-being of mankind
_____ Travel at will, be free of commitments and responsibilities

Source: Reprinted by permission of Dodd, Mead & Co., Inc. from _Values Clarification_ by Simon, Howe, and Kirschenbaum. Copyright 1972 by Dodd, Mead & Company, Inc.

following criteria (Raths, Harmin, & Simon, 1979):
Choosing
  1. Freely
  2. From possibilities
  3. After consideration of consequences of these possibilities
Prizing
  4. Being happy with the choice
  5. Being willing to affirm the choice to others
Acting
  6. Behaving on the basis of the choice
  7. Behaving repeatedly on the basis of the choice

After listing your values, rank them as you ranked your present life values in Exhibit 11-2.

Exhibit 11-3 Writing Your Own Obituary

_____ age _____ died today of _____.
He (she) is survived by _____. Until death, his (her) principal endeavor
was _____
_____.

He (she) will be remembered by _____
because _____.
 Notable contributions were made in the area of _____
_____.

He (she) always hoped that _____. He (she) was a member of
_____.

 Flowers may be sent to _____.
In lieu of flowers please _____,

 Source: Reprinted by permission of Dodd, Mead & Co., Inc. from *Values Clarification* by Simon, Howe, and Kirschenbaum. Copyright 1972 by Dodd, Mead & Company, Inc.

You wrote your obituary to help clarify what you hope to achieve in this lifetime. To help you identify what you hope to achieve professionally, try writing the words to be inscribed on your retirement plaque.

Values clarification is the first step in decision making. The decision will direct you in enacting the values underlying it.

WRITING BEHAVIORAL OBJECTIVES

The second step in the decision-making process is writing behavioral objectives. The behavioral objective is a guideline for enacting a value, for translating it into behavior. It contains a subject, an object reference, and an action verb and answers the question: "Who will do what, where, when, and how well?" Another way of describing a behavioral objective is that it (1) states the terminal behavior, what the person will be able to do; 2) specifies the conditions under which the behavior will be performed; and (3) defines the degree or level of proficiency that will be exhibited by the appropriate behavior (Mager, 1975). The following are examples of behavioral objectives:

- Given a dictionary, the student will correctly define the word "analyze."
- By the end of the 3-hour class time, the student will discuss four essentials of stress management.
- After reading and doing the exercises in this chapter, the nurse leader will make a work-related decision according to this process.

If you are unfamiliar with writing behavioral objectives, you may want to stop at this point to practice writing them according to these guidelines. See the discussion of management by objectives in Chapter 2 for additional examples of objectives.

IDENTIFYING PROBLEMS

A problem is a threatened value, an unmet behavioral objective, an unmet expectation, or a discrepancy between what is real and what is ideal or desired. We usually identify the need to make a decision because we experience a problem. Problems are often the entry point for the decision-making process. However, because the decision-making process depends on understanding our values and can be enhanced by writing a behavioral objective based on these values, this discussion of the process began with values.

The problem statement is a pivotal point in the decision-making process. The way we identify a problem limits the possibilities for solution. Exhibit 11-4 is an exercise in identifying a problem and possible solutions depending on the way the problem is identified.

Identify the problem in Exhibit 11-4 in as many ways as you can. Make a list of all the possible ways you could state the problem of tying together the two strings suspended from the ceiling.

When this exercise is done by a group, the list of problem statements generated inevitably includes at least the following six problem statements:

1. The string is too short.
2. The arms are too short.
3. The legs are too short.
4. The room is too big.
5. Being alone, there is no one there to help.
6. There is no furniture in the room—nothing to stand on to gain better access to the string.

If we identify the problem as not having furniture in the room or needing a chair to stand on to reach the strings, nothing can be done and the problem is insoluble. Similarly if the problem is defined as being alone in the room with no one else available to help, the problem cannot be solved. The same is true of stating that the room is too big, or the arms or legs are too short because we do not have the power to make the room smaller or our arms or legs longer.

However, when the problem is identified as the string being too short, possibilities for a solution emerge. The question needs reframing. One way of reframing the problem is to ask how the string can be lengthened, by using

Exhibit 11-4 Problem Identification

Look at the sketch below and imagine that you are the person shown standing in this room. You have been given the task of tying together the ends of the two strings suspended from the ceiling. The strings are located so that you cannot reach one string with your outstretched hand while holding the second in your hand. The room is totally bare, and you have only the resources you would normally have in your pocket or handbag. How do you solve this problem?

Source: From *Creative Growth Games* (p. 22) by E. Raudsepp, 1977, New York: Harcourt Brace Jovanovich, Inc. Copyright 1977 by Harcourt Brace Jovanovich, Inc. Reprinted by permission.

what is available on your person or in your pocket or handbag? One solution to the problem is to remove your shoelaces, your shirt, or another available object and tie it onto the string to lengthen it, thereby making it possible to hold and tie together the two ends of the string suspended from the ceiling.

The way the problem is stated both suggests solutions and limits the possibility of solution. An obvious conclusion that can be drawn from this exercise is that we should first consider various ways to describe the problem before we look for options and alternatives to solve the problem.

GATHERING PERTINENT INFORMATION ABOUT THE PROBLEM

To assist you with this step of the decision-making process, think of a time when you made a decision with which you were not happy. The decision may have been personal or professional. It may have been made 30 years ago, or it may have been made yesterday. As you remember this decision with which you were not pleased, consider the following five common mistakes that are made in information gathering (Gelatt et al, 1973). Doing so may enable you to discover mistakes that you may have made in that particular decision-making process. The five most commonly made mistakes in gathering information are:

1. collecting useless or irrelevant information
2. misinterpreting the importance of data
3. generalizing from the past, particularly from emotional experiences of the past
4. not knowing alternatives
5. not knowing possible outcomes

We never intentionally gather useless or irrelevant information. Rather, we gather such information because we mistakenly think that it would be useful or relevant. In the problem situation in Exhibit 11-4, it is useless or irrelevant to measure the height or the width of the walls. However, if the problem-solving focus is placed on the room being too big, that information might appear to be relevant at the time.

We may misinterpret the importance of particular data because of our knowledge or skill level or our past experience. For example, consider the patient in the emergency department who is receiving fluids intravenously. When the fluid has run in and the IV bottle is empty, the patient may think, "Oh, good, the bottle is empty. Now I can get rid of this uncomfortable IV feeding." A student nurse in her first month of nursing practice may walk in and see that the IV bottle is empty. She may say to herself, "That is something I should tell somebody. It probably needs to be removed." The experienced staff nurse may walk in and say, "Oh good grief, we had a very difficult cut-down to do on this man, the IV has now run out, and we will probably have to do another cut-down. This is a terrible situation." The nurse leader may say to herself, "Where is the problem in our organization and follow-up that we allowed this to happen?" The information—that the IV bottle is now empty—is interpreted differently by the patient, the new student nurse, the experienced staff nurse, and the nurse leader. The relevance of the situation to the patient and the need for action are misinterpreted by the patient and student.

When we generalize from the past, we make the assumption that what was learned in one experience can and should be applied in the current situation. This may or may not be true. It is least likely to be true when the past experience was traumatic.

GENERATING OPTIONS

Options are all the possible responses we could make to a particular problem. Not all will be practical, not all will work, and not all will lead to a desired outcome. In this step of the decision-making process, our goal is to generate as many options as possible so they can then be screened or altered to identify as many alternative solutions as possible.

Creative or lateral thinking is an important process in the generation of options. Of the many which can be used, five creative thinking techniques are described here to assist you in generating options. The exercises will enhance your understanding of these techniques.

The first technique is the shift of attention.

> In a tennis tournament there are 111 entrants. It is a singles knockout tournament, and you as secretary have to arrange the matches. What is the minimum number of matches that would have to be arranged with this number of entrants (de Bono, 1970).

When faced with this problem most people draw little diagrams showing the actual pairings in each match and the number of byes. Others try to work it out by reference to 2n, i.e., 4,8,16,32, etc. In fact, the answer—110 matches—can be determined at once without any complicated mathematics. To work it our one must shift attention from the winners of each match to the losers (in whom no one is usually very interested). Because there can only be 1 winner there must be 110 losers. Each loser can only lose once so there must be 110 matches.

The above problem is an example of the usefulness of shifting the entry point. Very often it is not just a matter of the order in which the parts are attended to, but the choice of parts that are going to be considered at all. If some part of the problem is left out of consideration, then it is very unlikely that it will ever come into play in finding a solution.

For these reasons, the choice of attention focus can make a huge difference to the way we view the situation. To restructure the situation, one may need no more than a slight shift in attention. Without a shift in attention, it may be very difficult to look at the situation in a different way (de Bono, 1970).

The second creative thinking technique is brainstorming. The purpose of brainstorming is to generate a large quantity of possibilities, with no attention paid to the quality of those options. Each suggested possibility is written down. No judgment of its value is made. Sometimes the wilder the possibility the more useful it can become at a later point. In brainstorming, a time limit is usually set. You probably used the brainstorming process in Exhibit

11-4 when looking for different ways to define the problem of tying the ends of the two strings together.

The third creative thinking technique is reversal. The purpose of reversal is to change the initial way you look at a situation and allow yourself to look at the situation from other points of view. Below are two problems that require reversal in thinking for their solution. Try them.

> *Problem:* It was the sixteenth hole in the annual Bob Hope tournament play. The tall, handsome newcomer, who looked very much like Bing Crosby, had an excellent chance of winning. His iron shot had fallen short of the green, and he had a good chance of making a birdie. Smiling broadly and singing, "Thanks for the Memories," he bounded down the fairway but then stopped short in utter dismay. His ball had rolled into a small paper bag carelessly tossed there by someone in the gallery—although it was whispered that Bob Hope had placed it there. If he removed the ball from the bag, it would cost him a penalty stroke. If he tried to hit the ball and the bag, he would lose control over the shot. For a moment, he stood there pondering the problem. Then, to Bob's chagrin, he solved it. How did he solve it?
>
> *Solution:* He reached into his pocket, extracted a book of matches, lit one, and set fire to the bag. When the bag had burned to ashes, he selected an iron, swung, and watched the ball roll to the rim of the hole. Unable to get the ball away from the paper bag without a penalty, this golfer was imaginative enough to recognize that the problem could be solved by getting the paper bag away from the ball.*
>
> *Problem* (de Bono, 1970, p. 144): A flock of sheep were moving slowly down a country lane that was bounded by high banks. A motorist in a hurry came up behind the flock and urged the shepherd to move his sheep to the side so that the car could drive through. The shepherd refused because he could not be sure of keeping all the sheep out of the way of the car in such a narrow lane.
>
> *Solution:* The shepherd reversed the situation. He told the car to stop, and then he quietly turned the flock around and drove it back past the stationary car.

The fourth creative thinking technique is dialectical thinking, which is a way of bringing together two previously competing ideas. Dialectical think-

---

* The preceding problem and solution are from *Creative Growth Games* (pp. 49 and 137) by E. Raudsepp, 1977, New York: Harcourt Brace Jovanovich. Copyright 1977 by Harcourt Brace Jovanovich. Reprinted by permission.

ing takes us from "either/or" to "both/and." An example comes from a research project. While gathering data about what is stressful to staff nurses, the researcher heard, in the first five interviews, that the greatest source of stress to the staff nurses was the head nurse's behavior. These staff nurses described their head nurses as barriers to solving the stressful situation. Whatever the staff nurses tried to do, they experienced interference from the head nurse. In the next three interviews with different staff nurses, the researcher heard descriptions of how helpful the head nurse had been in stressful situations. Whatever the stressor experienced by the staff nurse, the head nurse's response facilitated the solution to the stressful situation. At the end of eight interviews, the researcher asked herself, "Were head nurses barriers, or were head nurses helpful?" The dialectical understanding is that head nurses were very important in stressful situations faced by the staff nurse. Their response to the staff nurse could either help or hinder her, but what was true of all of these situations was that the head nurse's response was very important.

The fifth creative thinking technique is analogy, in which one situation is compared to another situation. The situations need not seem similar, at least not on the surface, because, in trying to compare even dissimilar situations, we often generate ideas that we would not otherwise have considered. For example, if you are having difficulty teaching a young diabetic how to give himself insulin injections, you might consider how giving an injection is similar to trying to start a car on a cold winter morning or trying to untangle a ball of string or learning to swim. From looking at possible similarities or comparisons, you may generate new ideas on how to approach the diabetic teaching.

Exhibit 11-5 provides you an opportunity to use creative thinking for problem solving.

There are two general approaches to problem solving. The one most often used in business is vertical thinking—a logical analysis in which one step or premise follows another and builds to a conclusion or solution. It may also be described as "straight-line" thinking. The second approach is *lateral thinking,* in which all the factors that relate to the problem are considered. Lateral thinking is typified by the process of brainstorming in which all solutions are considered, no matter how far-fetched they may seem at first. It may be also described as "sideways" thinking. In such cases as the "Pebble Story," vertical thinking may fail to produce a solution, and lateral thinking may be the best approach.

After analyzing the "Pebble Story," vertical thinkers would arrive at three possible solutions:

1. The girl should refuse to take a pebble.

Exhibit 11-5 The Pebble Story

Many years ago, when a debtor could be thrown into jail, a merchant in London had the misfortune to owe a huge sum to a moneylender. The moneylender, who was old and ugly, fancied the merchant's beautiful teenaged daughter. He proposed a bargain. He said that he would cancel the merchant's debt if he could have the girl.

Both the merchant and his daughter were horrified at the proposal. So the cunning moneylender proposed that they let providence decide the matter. He told them that he would put a black pebble and a white pebble into an empty money bag and then the girl would pick out one of the pebbles. If she chose the black pebble, she would become his wife and her father's debt would be canceled. If she chose the white pebble, she would stay with her father and the debt still would be canceled. But if she refused to pick out the pebble, her father would be thrown into jail and she would starve.

Reluctantly, the merchant agreed. They were standing on a pebble-strewn path in the merchant's garden as they talked, and the moneylender stooped down to pick up the two pebbles. As he picked up the pebbles, the girl, sharp-eyed with fright, noticed that he picked up two black pebbles and put them into the money bag. He then told the girl to pick out the pebble that was to decide her fate and that of her father.

Instructions: Picture your self as the girl in the story.

1. How would you have handled the situation?
2. If you had advise her, what would you advise her to do?
3. How did you reach your solution (briefly explain your thinking)?

Source: From *New Think: The Use of Lateral Thinking in the Generation of New Ideas* by E. de Bono, 1968, New York: Basic Books, Inc. Copyright 1968 by Basic Books, Inc. Reprinted by permission.

2. The girl should show that there are two black pebbles in the bag and expose the moneylender as a cheat.
3. The girl should take a black pebble and sacrifice herself in order to save her father from prison.

However, none of these suggestions is very helpful. If the girl does not take a pebble, here father will go to prison; if she does take a pebble, she will be forced to marry the moneylender.

In contrast to vertical thinkers who are concerned with the fact that the girl has to take a pebble, lateral thinkers focus on the pebble that is left behind. Vertical thinkers take the most reasonable view of a situation and then proceed logically and carefully to to work it out. Lateral thinkers tend to explore all the different ways of looking at something, rather than accepting the most promising view and proceeding from that. Therefore, lateral thinkers would be more likely to find this solution to the problem:

The girl in the "Pebble Story" put her hand into the money bag and drew out a pebble. Without looking at it, she fumbled and let it fall to the path, where it immediately was lost among all the other pebbles. "Oh, how clumsy of me," she said, "But never mind, if you look into the bag, you will be able to tell which pebble I took by the color of the one that is left."

Because the remaining pebble was, of course, black, it must be assumed that she had taken out the white pebble—the moneylender dared not admit his dishonesty. By using lateral thinking, the girl changed what seemed to be an impossible situation into an extremely advantageous one. The girl actually was better off now than if the moneylender had been honest and had put one black and one white pebble into the bag, for then she would have had only a 50 percent chance of being saved. As it happened, she was sure of remaining with her father and, at the same time, of having his debt canceled.

ANALYZING ALTERNATIVES AND SETTING PRIORITIES

This step in the decision-making process identifies altenatives and predicts consequences and outcomes according to the evaluation of alternatives. From our list of options, we have a list of possible responses to the problem. However, not all of our options will solve the problem in a way that we desire. Those behaviors that would lead to the desired outcome, that would maintain our values, or that would meet our stated objectives become our alternatives. Each identified alternative must have the potential of solving the problem under consideration and be capable of meeting the behavioral objective. To select the best alternative, each one is then evaluated according to the three criteria of probability, desirability, and personal risk.

Probability

Probability is the likelihood that an alternative will be successful in meeting the objective. Probability is often expressed in terms of percent, with 100 percent representing the certainty that it is going to happen. On the other end, a 1 percent probability means that it is very unlikely that it will happen. For the purposes of this decision-making process, consider probability in terms of low, medium, and high. Table 11-1 gives you an opportunity to assess probability.

Table 11-1 Assessing Probability

What is the Probability That:	Probability
1. A 3-year-old boy will fall out of bed if his siderails are left down?	High Medium Low
2. A patient will have an allergic reaction to the penicillin you gave him if you forgot to take an allergy history?	High Medium Low
3. You will be ill during the next 6 months?	High Medium Low
4. A woman with two children will become pregnant if she does not use contraceptives?	High Medium Low
5. The new staff nurse hired last week will perform adequately if placed in charge of the day shift?	High Medium Low
6. You will go to graduate school in nursing?	High Medium Low
7. A man who says he has a gun at home and wants to commit suicide will actually do so?	High Medium Low
8. Telling a coworker you do not like her attitude will result in a change of attitude?	High Medium Low
9. Listening actively to the complaints of a colleague will improve your working relationship?	High Medium Low

Desirability

Desirability is a subjective measure of your preference for a particular alternative and is determined by your values. The criterion is usually situation dependent.

Risk

Risk can be defined as a hazard or as exposure to possible injury, damage, or loss. It must be assessed from the point of view of everyone involved in the situation: the nurse, the client, the organization, and anyone else who is involved. Risk may involve physical, emotional, social, or economic risk. Exhibit 11-6 is an exercise in assessing risk from your point of view.

MAKING THE DECISION

Now that you have evaluated alternatives, you are ready to make a decision based on your assessment of probability, desirability, and risk taking. Look at your assessment of alternatives and decide what combination of probability, desirability, and risk taking you value in this particular situation. That is, determine which factor is most important, which is second, and which is third in importance for this decision. Probability, desirability, and risk will vary in importance in different problems and different decisions.

Exhibit 11-6 Assessing Risk

Instructions: Below are concentric squares with the words *self, intimates, friends, acquaintances,* and *stranger* written in the successively larger squares. Answer the first question: 1. To whom would you tell your doubts about religion?

If you would only tell yourself, write "1" in the square that says self. If you would tell not only yourself but intimates, friends, and maybe even acquaintances, but not strangers, then put a "1" in the square where acquaintances is written.

For each of the following questions, write the corresponding number in the outermost square where you would be willing to share this information.

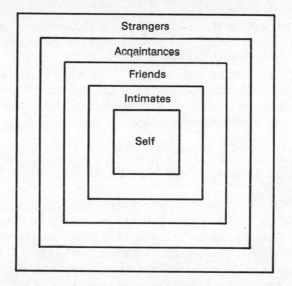

To whom would you tell:

1. Your doubts about religion?
2. You smoke marijuana?
3. What you cried about the last time you wept?
4. Your discontent with some part of your body?
5. Your diminishing respect for your supervisor?
6. You have considered suicide?
7. The major problems in your marriage?
8. When you experienced very profound jealousy?
9. Your desire for your supervisor's job?
10. Your salary?
11. Your lack of confidence in yourself.
12. Your sense of pride in your facilitation of conflict resolution between two colleagues?

Source: Reprinted by permission of Dodd, Mead & Co., Inc. from *Values Clarification* by Simon, Howe, and Kirschenbaum. Copyright 1972 by Dodd, Mead & Company, Inc.

Rank probability, desirability, and risk for each alternative. Then identify the alternative with the best combination of high probability and desirability and low risk for the specific situation.

EVALUATING THE DECISION

A good decision is one that involves each step of the decision-making process and solves the problem in a way that upholds your values and meets the behavioral objective.

Two examples of decisions made according to this model are given below. Read through them to further your understanding of this model of decision making. Then complete the decision outline in Exhibit 11-7 to make a decision by yourself or in a small group. As with any skill, the more you practice, the easier it becomes. At first you will find this process somewhat time consuming, but with practice, you will incorporate it easily into your everyday thinking and decision making.

Example 1 (Table 11-2): Mary and Mark (Ford, Trygstad-Durland, & Nelms, 1979)

Mary is a junior student nurse. It is her second day in the psychiatric-mental health nursing rotation. Yesterday, Mary introduced herself to Mark and began to establish a therapeutic relationship. Mary told Mark who she was and why she was there and said she would like to spend time with him learning to understand him from his point of view. She told him the days and times when she would be available. They discussed confidentiality, and Mark asked several questions as if to reassure himself that confidentiality really would exist.

Today Mary found Mark in the lounge and asked if she could sit next to him. He nodded and said "Yes." As Mary sat down, Mark yawned. "Sleepy?" Mary said. "Mmmmmm," Mark responded. As Mary looked more closely at Mark, he leaned toward her and said, "Don't tell anyone, OK?" "OK," said Mary. Mark began, "My roommate had some really good grass last night so we went outside and got loaded. Just as we were about to come in, our other roommate came up with a bottle of vodka. We had another joint, then brought the bottle into our room. We drank most of the night. I'm still really ripped."

As Mark finished talking, the team nurse came by with the medicine cart. She handed Mark his medicine, which he swallowed.

It took a moment before Mary realized the significance of what she had heard and seen. Then she realized that drugs, alcohol, and medications should not be combined. She recalled reading about the harmful affects of combining phenothiazines and alcohol. She simultaneously experienced the desire to say something about what she had seen and heard and the desire to remain quiet.

Mary felt her heart begin to pound, and perspiration crept across her body. She opened her mouth to speak, but nothing came out. The patient had swallowed the medication, and the nurse had moved on. In Mary's imagination she saw Mark sprawled on the floor convulsing or dying. Her next thought was of his glaring at her and saying angrily, "Get away from me, you betrayed my trust."

"Where is my instructor? " Mary thought. Then she got up to look for her.

In this example, Mary experiences discomfort as soon as she realizes her conflict between wanting to say something and wanting to keep quiet. She has a conflict between ensuring patient safety and physical integrity and building and maintaining a trusting relationship. All of her nursing education, as well as the hospital, has emphasized the former. Yet, Mary has read that building and maintaining a trusting relationship will be the basis of her learning experience in psychiatric-mental health nursing. Her instructor has said that physical needs are not the primary focus of this rotation and that her own learning is most important. Mary is not sure if this is a conflict among service, institution, and educational values. She is sure that there is a conflict in her own values.

Mary's feelings include ambivalence and anxiety. There is also fear as she fantasizes possible outcomes. Her bodily responses include tachycardia and perspiration. Her thought process is first clouded and then preoccupied with the problem. Her initial behavior is immobilization, followed by the typical student coping behavior of seeking help from her instructor. The discomfort is intensified by the conflict in values and the possibility of a severe consequence of physical danger, perhaps even death.

In a brief discussion with her instructor, Mary is quickly able to identify that her values underlying the desire to speak to the staff nurse are providing for physical safety and maintaining life. Her values underlying her desire to say nothing are keeping to herself something said in confidence and maintaining a trusting relationship. She rank orders these four values for herself as:

1. maintaining life
2. providing for physical safety
3. maintaining a confidence
4. building a trusting relationship

Table 11-2 Summary of Decision-Making Process in the Example of Mary and Mark

1. Values in Rank Order	2. Behavioral Objective	3. Problem Statement	4. Options
1. Maintaining life 2. Providing for physical safety 3. Maintaining a confidence 4. Building a trusting relationship	When giving patient care I will consistently perform nursing functions that promote the maintenance of life.	How do I manage a potential threat to Mark's life?	1. Contact the clinical pharmacist to determine if the dosage of phenothiazines and the amount of alcohol and marijuana are harmful. 2. Say nothing and assume that the drug interaction is not harmful. 3. Give Mark Ipecac to induce vomiting. 4. Wait for signs of physical distress. 5. Call the cardiac arrest team. 6. Educate Mark about the dangers of combining marijuana, alcohol, and medication. 7. Teach the nurse to be more observant when giving medications. 8. Ask the instructor for advice. 9. Tell the staff nurse about a hypothetical situation involving a patient taking marijuana, alcohol, and medication. 10. Tell the staff nurse about this situation. 11. Tell Mark about the possible interaction of drugs and find out what he would want to do.

Table 11-2 continued

5. Alternatives	6. Analysis of Alternatives			7. Decision	8. Evaluation	If Yes, Go to Next Question
	Probability of Success (Percent)	Risk (Highest, 1; Lowest, 7)	Desirability (Highest, 1; Lowest, 7)			
1. Contact the clinical pharmacist to determine if the dosage of phenothiazine and the amount of alcohol and marijuana are harmful.	High 75	Moderate 4	Very high 1	Alternative 1: Contact the clinical pharmacist to determine if the dosage of phenothiazine and the amount of alcohol and marijuana are harmful.	1. Does the decision, analyzed in terms of desirability, probability, and personal risk, correlate with the priority areas assessed in the problem?	Yes
3. Give Mark Ipecac to induce vomiting.	Low 25	High 2	Moderate 4			
5. Call the cardiac arrest team.					2. Does the decision reflect your stated behavior objective?	Yes
6. Educate Mark about the dangers of combining marijuana, alcohol, and medication.	Low 10 Very low 5	Very high 1 Very low 7	Low 7 High 3			
8. Ask the instructor for advice.	Moderate 50 Low 15	Moderate 3 Low 6	High 4 Low 6		3. Does your behavioral objective reflect your priority value for this situation?	Yes
9. Tell the staff nurse about a hypothetical situation involving a patient taking marijuana, alcohol, and medication.						
10. Tell the staff nurse about this situation.	Low 20	Low-moderate 5	Moderate 5			

Source: Reproduced by permission from *Applied Decision Making for Nurses* by J.A. Ford, L.N. Trygstad-Durland and B.C. Nelms, 1979, St. Louis, MO: The C.V. Mosby Company. Copyright 1979 by the C.V. Mosby Company.

The objective for Mary's highest-ranked value is: When giving patient care I will consistently perform nursing functions that promote the maintenance of life. The problem statement then becomes: How do I manage a potential threat to Mark's life?

In consultation with her instructor, Mary evaluates several alternatives.

On re-examination of the problem situation, it is determined that probability is the most important criterion. In this instance, Mary wants an alternative that has the highest probability of success. She is least concerned with the desirability of the alternative and moderately concerned with the risk involved.

Mary's decision is to contact the clinical pharmacist to determine if the dosage of phenothiazine and the amount of alcohol and marijuana are harmful—alternative 1. This alternative best correlates with Mary's ranking of the criteria for the problem situation. When evaluating the decision, Mary considers the following questions:

- Does the decision, analyzed in terms of desirability, probability, and personal risk, correlate with the priority areas assessed in the problem? Yes.
- Does the decision reflect her stated behavioral objective? Yes.
- Does her behavioral objective reflect her priority value for this situation? Yes.

Mary's decision is derived from all elements of the process and is by definition a good decision!

Example 2: Sibling Visitation

Now try the decision-making process with this problem involving Timmy, a pediatric patient; Ms. Browning, his primary nurse; and yourself, the Assistant Head Nurse in charge this evening. After reading the problem description below, complete the decision outline in Exhibit 11-7.

Six-year-old Timmy had surgery 5 days ago. He has had several complications, and his life now seems to hang by a thin thread. Ms. Browning has cared for Timmy since before his surgery and knows it is important to his recovery to encourage him and his will to live. This evening Timmy says to Ms. Browning, "Mom says John (9-year-old idolized older brother) came with her tonight. He's downstairs in the lobby. I want to see him so much. I know he's not allowed to visit, but please sneak him up here for just a few minutes." Ms. Browning came to you for help in making this decision.

Exhibit 11-7 Decision Outline

1. Rank-order your values for this situation.
2. Write a behavioral objective from your most important values.
3. Write a problem statement for this situation.
4. Make a list of all possible options.
5. Select viable alternatives from the list of options.
6. Rank each alternative in terms of desirability, probability, and personal risk.
7. State your decision.
8. Evaluate your decision according to these questions:

- Does the decision, analyzed in terms of desirability, probability, and personal risk, correlate with the priority areas assessed in the problem? If it does not, return to the list of analyzed alternatives and select one that does coincide. Then continue with the evaluation by considering the next question.

- Does the decision reflect your stated behavioral objective? If it does not, return to the alternative analysis phase and consider the remaining alternatives. If it does, continue with the evaluation by considering the final question.

- Does your behavioral objective reflect your priority value for this situation? If it does not, restate the behavioral objective to reflect the value. If it does, the decision is derived from all of the decision-making elements and is by definition a good decision.

DECISION MAKING IN GROUPS

Thus far, this chapter has addressed only individual decision making. However, nurses work primarily in groups, whether they are staff nurses in hospitals and clinics or nurses in management positions. Even nurses working alone in schools, industry, and private practice work in collaboration with others. Too, when nurses do make decisions alone, others are likely to be involved in implementing the decisions.

Nurses also work with patient groups and families. Hospital and community nursing can be family-centered. Rehabilitation and therapy groups are common in psychiatric nursing.

Working with groups inevitably means decision making with groups. Therefore, this chapter includes a summary of group dynamics as they are related to decision making and a discussion of the advantages and disadvantages of group decision making. The decision-making process described earlier for individual decisions is applicable to group decisions as well. The differences in the process are those brought about by the dynamics of the group.

Nurses work in two different types of groups: ongoing and ad hoc. Ongoing groups are established groups that meet together over time, such as a head nurses group, a cardiopulmonary resuscitation team, or the maternal-child health interest group of the state nurses' association. Ad hoc groups meet together for a particular purpose and then disband; a discharge planning meeting with a family is an example of such a group.

The dynamics of the two types of groups are different because of the differences in (1) the amount of time that members devote to them, (2) the importance of the group to its members, and (3) their commitment to the group. However, knowledge of group dynamics is helpful in understanding group behavior and your role in any type of group. When you understand group forces and your position, you are better able to make constructive contributions to the group and choose to accept alternatives without feeling that you have compromised yourself or been manipulated by subtle social pressures.

A clear, agreed-upon goal is a chief determinant of group effectiveness. Agreement on means to reach this goal and the investment of individual energies by each member into this group goal are then needed. The organization of the group, coordination of tasks, and availability of resources also influence its effectiveness. The effectiveness of any group can be enhanced by examining and discussing the current group process and by trying new ways of working together (Knowles & Knowles, 1972). See Chapter 8, Developing Healthy Work Groups, for a more extensive discussion of group dynamics.

Conflict in groups is caused by different response tendencies elicited in various members by a single situation. Conflict enhances the effectiveness of decisions in an ongoing group. Because the different responses take place in a group which has a shared commitment, the differences are unlikely to be perceived as a threat to the group or as hostility. Rather, because of the differences, more alternatives are explored and the result is likely to be a creative, workable solution.

In contrast, strong differences may be disruptive to an ad hoc group where shared process and commitment have not been achieved. Strong leadership may be needed to foster tolerance and valuing of differences until disparate viewpoints are seen as contributing to a greater whole. Otherwise, the ad hoc group's resolution of conflict is likely to be a compromise that is less workable than already proposed alternatives (Hall, 1971).

Group decision making can offer the benefit of better decisions and more effective implementation. Several individuals working together necessarily have broader experience and a wider range of knowledge than any single individual. A greater number of options and consequences can be identified by a group and analyzed from several critical viewpoints. Research findings support the superiority of a group's final decision over the average individual's alternative solution (Hall, 1971).

Participation in and shared responsibility for a decision have the advantage of leading to the members' greater understanding of and commitment to the final choice. This is especially helpful when the group responsible for the decision is also responsible for its implementation.

Disadvantages of group decision making include time and social pressures. It takes more time for a group to discuss alternatives and arrive at a consensus than for an individual to make a decision. This process may be frustrating to task-oriented members. The dynamics of the group may include social pressure toward conformity. If an individual sees her position as subordinate in a group and/or if the group has great value to her, she will be more vulnerable to group pressures toward conformity. "Groupthink" is the name given by Janis (1971) to the process by which individual group members suppress their own critical thinking and questioning of an alternative. This process comes into play when the individual has internalized a group norm for agreement and values agreement more highly than thorough consideration of alternatives (Janis, 1971).

The diffusion of responsibility that occurs with group versus individual decisions may be an advantage or a disadvantage. Individuals within a group may be more open to a variety of possible solutions because the possibility of personal criticism is lessened. However, diffusion of responsibility may decrease commitment to the final decision.

Shifts in choice, especially to risky choices, are another possible disadvantage of group decision making. The process of group decision making may encourage individual members to take a more extreme position and course of action than they would take individually (Main & Walker, 1973). Thus, there is the possibility of unnecessary risk or unhelpful conservatism from a group decision.

Roles played by the leader and group members may prove to be a disadvantage in decision making. Some patterns of leadership, especially disorganized leadership that lacks direction, may contribute to difficulty in the group decision process. Group member roles that focus attention on the individual, rather than on the group and its task, are a hindrance to decision making. Individual group members who do not understand the decision-making process can also hamper group decision making.

Some types of decisions are more advantageously made in groups, whereas others are more effectively made by individuals (Harrison, 1975). Decisions most effectively and efficiently made by individuals are routine, recurrent ones that have a degree of certainty. Decisions that are neither routine nor recurrent or predictable are best made in a group. Group decision making offers an advantage in setting objectives because of the broader knowledge base of its members. Evaluating alternatives within a group is also facilitated by the broader range of critical analysis available (Harrison, 1975).

To make group decisions or not to make group decisions is not a relevant question. Nurses work in groups and make decisions in groups. How to maximize the group process of decision making is the relevant issue. Obtaining a general understanding of group dynamics and your roles in groups is the first step. Then, being aware of the advantages and disadvantages of group decision making will help you recognize and minimize its pitfalls. Finally, group discussion of your own group process will enhance the process and the decision-making outcome.

REFERENCES

de Bono, E. (1970). *Lateral thinking: Creativity step by step.* New York: Harper & Row, 1970.

Ford J.A., Trygstad-Durland, L.N., & Nelms, B.C. (1979). *Applied decision making for nurses.* St. Louis: C.V. Mosby.

Gelatt, H.B., Varenhorst, B., Carey, R., & Miller, G.P. (1973). *Decisions & outcomes.* New York: College Entrance Examination Board.

Goodstein, L.D., & Pfeiffer, J.W. (1983). *The 1983 Annual for facilitators, trainers and consultants.* San Diego: University Associates.

Hall, J. (1971, November). Decisions, decisions, decisions. *Psychology Today*, pp. 51–53.

Harrison, F.E. (1975). *The managerial decision making process.* Boston: Houghton Mifflin.

Janis, I.L. (1971, November). Groupthink. *Psychology Today*, p. 43.

Knowles, M., & Knowles, H. (1972). *Introduction to group dynamics.* New York: Associated Press.

Mager, R. (1975). *Preparing instructional objectives.* Belmont, CA: Pitman Learning.

Main, E.C., & Walker, T.G. (1973). Choice shifts and extreme behavior: Judicial review in the federal courts. *Social Psychology, 91,* 215.

Raths, L.E., Harmin, M., & Simon, S.B. (1979). *Values and teaching.* Columbus, Ohio: Charles E. Merrill.

Raudsepp, E., & Hough, G.P. (1977). *Creative growth games.* New York: Harcourt Brace Johanovich.

Simon, S., Howe L., & Kirschenbaum, H. (1972). *Values clarification: A handbook of practical strategies for teachers and students.* New York: Dodd, Mead and Co.

Chapter 12

Stress Management

Stress management helps people strike the proper balance between high energy and creativity on the one hand and signs of excessive stress (e.g., fatigue, health problems, role difficulties) on the other. The balance differs for each individual, and finding and maintaining it is a learning process.

The purpose of this chapter is to help you develop your own stress management ability. Nursing is a high-stress profession (Smith, 1978), and knowing how to manage stress will help you be a better leader.

Stress management as an ongoing process involves the following steps:

1. *Develop a personal baseline.* This clarifies your current status.
2. *Identify your specific stressors and signs of stress.* This individualizes the process.
3. *Manage stress.* This involves learning coping behaviors for handling unavoidable stress.
4. *Reduce stressors.* This involves eliminating unnecessary sources of stress.
5. *Develop a balanced lifestyle.* This leads to greater fulfillment and health, which in turn help you keep things in perspective and resist more effectively the negative physical effects of stress.

Once you have developed your own ability to manage stress, you will be better able to extend stress management tools to others, both staff and clients.

STRESS THEORY AND RESEARCH

Since stress is additive (Selye, 1976), the stress experienced both in the personal life of the nurse and at work will become a part of the stress experienced by the nurse at work. Additional stressors experienced at work also become a portion of the total personal stress experienced by the nurse. Stress theory and research aid in understanding the response of the individual regardless of the source of stress. Therefore, in the next two sections, certain critical elements of stress theory are presented and discussed.

Stress theory and research have come from such diverse areas as nursing, medical and health science, organizational behavior, personnel psychology, industrial psychology, psychiatry, clinical and social psychology, sociology, and cultural anthropology. A universally accepted definition of stress does not exist within or among these disciplines. In defining and describing stress, the definitions and paradigms of both Selye and Lazarus are useful.

Selye's Stress and Adaptation Theory

According to Selye (1976), stress is the nonspecific response of the body to any demand. This response of the body is elicited by a variety of different agents or by any demand (stressors). Examples of demands may be for a quick response to a crisis situation, dealing with an angry patient, or dealing with conflict between staff members.

Stressors elicit the General Adaptation Syndrome (GAS). The GAS is the name given to describe all the nonspecific changes occurring throughout the time of continued exposure to a stressor. It is called *general* because according to Selye (1976) it is elicited only by agents having a general effect upon large portions of the body, *adaptive* because it stimulates defenses which help the body adapt, and *syndrome* because the signs are coordinated and partially dependent on each other.

The fully developed GAS consists of three stages: alarm reaction, resistance, and exhaustion. The purpose of alarm is to arouse the body's defenses. When noxious agents continue, there is a fight (resistance) to maintain the homeostatic balance of damaged tissues. Resources are concentrated at the site of the demand. During this time, resistance to the particular agent which produced this stage of the adaption syndrome is at its peak but, at the same time, resistance to most other agents falls below normal. If homeostatic balance is not achieved and exposure to noxious agents continues, the body loses its acquired ability to resist and enters the stage of exhaustion. The outcome of the progression of the GAS through the stages of alarm and resistance may be achievement of organic stability (homeostasis), diseases of adaptation, or exhaustion. Figure 12-1 illustrates Selye's stress and adaptation theory.

There is an element of both stress and adaptation in health and in every disease. While some stress is needed for optimal health, productivity, and morale, excessive stress increases the probability of ill health, low produc-

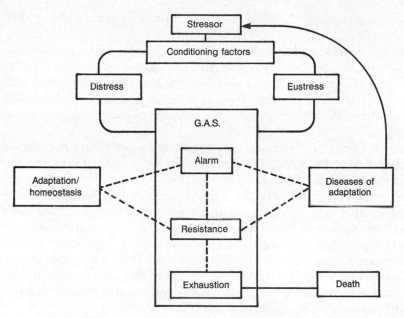

Figure 12-1 Selye's Stress and Adaptation Theory

tivity, and low morale. The relationship between stress and health and stress and productivity is curvilinear (Schmidt, 1978; Selye, 1976).

Resistance and adaptation are dependent on the balance of defense and surrender and are influenced by the direct effect of the stressor on the body. The stressor affects the body directly. Some internal responses to the stressor stimulate tissue defense or help destroy damaging substances; other internal responses cause tissue surrender by inhibiting unnecessary or excessive defense. Either excessive defense or an overabundance of submissive bodily reactions will lead to diseases of adaptation. Disease reflects a fight to maintain the homeostatic balance of tissues despite damage. Diseases of adaptation are consequences of the body's inability to meet stressors with adequate adaptive reactions. If the body uses one organ system preferentially to cope with a stressor, disease can result either from the disproportionate, excessive development of the particular system or from its eventual breakdown from wear and tear.

Diseases in which maladaptation to stress can be a factor include high blood pressure, diseases of the heart and of the blood vessels, diseases of the kidney, eclampsia, rheumatic and rheumatoid arthritis, inflammatory diseases of the skin and eyes, infections, allergic and hypersensitivity diseases, nervous and mental diseases, sexual derangements, digestive diseases, metabolic diseases, cancer, and diseases or resistance in general (Selye, 1976, pp. 169-170).

The relationship between stress and illness in general is further discussed and documented by Pilowsky (1973), Bell (1977), and Pelletier (1977). Dean and Lin (1977) conclude from a review of the stress literature that stressful life events (e.g., bereavement, divorce, job change) are associated with the onset, incidence, and prevalence of a wide range of psychiatric and physical disorders.

Selye's definition of stress as a response of the body does not preclude psychological and behavioral responses; they are simply not his focus. Support for including psychological and behavioral responses in Selye's model is found in Selye's self-observable signs of stress which include impulsive behavior, emotional instability, floating anxiety, stuttering and other speech difficulties, increased consumption of alcohol, tobacco or drugs, neurotic behavior, psychosis, and accident proneness (Selye, 1976). Assuming interactive physical, psychological, and behavioral dimensions in human beings is consistent with a widely held nursing definition: that man is a biopsychosocial being with the biological, psychological, and social or behavioral aspects being interactive and interdependent.

Lazarus' Stress and Coping Paradigm

Lazarus' work focuses on psychological aspects of stress with cognitive appraisal determining one's response to a situation. Lazarus defines psychological stress as "demands that tax or exceed the available resources (internal or external) as appraised by the person involved" (Lazarus, 1981, p. 193). Stress is elicited by the transaction between the demand and the individual's cognitive appraisal of the situation.

According to Lazarus' paradigm (Lazarus, Averill, & Opton, 1974; Lazarus, 1977; Lazarus & Launier, 1978; Lazarus, 1981) transactions between person and environment lead to primary appraisal, the judgment that a situation is irrelevant, benign-positive, or stressful. If the situation is evaluated as stressful, further appraisal establishes harm/loss (damage has already occurred), threat (future potential for damage exists), or challenge (potential for mastery or gain exists). The assessment of stress leads to both emotion and coping and affects secondary appraisal, the evaluation of available coping options, and resources. Emotion affects both the evaluation of coping options and resources and coping responses. Coping responses affect emotion, reappraisal of the situation as irrelevant, benign-positive or stressful, and secondary appraisal, as well as the person-environment transaction.

The purpose of coping is the alteration of the troubled transaction or self regulation of emotion. Both of these purposes are accomplished through the coping modes of information seeking, direct action, inhibition of action, intrapsychic mechanisms, and/or seeking social support. Figure 12-2 illustrates this process.

The emphasis of Lazarus' model is on stress and coping as processes. Stress appraisal and coping continually interact with each other and with the troubled situation; each factor affects and is affected by the other two factors.

Selye states that any demand will produce a response of the body. Lazarus clarifies that not every event is a demand. As illustrated in Figure 12-2, all events are appraised and only those perceived as harm/loss, threat, or challenge act as demands or stressors. In addition, although all demands may produce a response in the body, not all responses are of the same magnitude or duration. There is variation in the intensity of the demand for adaptation or readjustment. The perception of an event as stressful and the magnitude and duration of the response are related not only to what happens but also to the individual to whom it happens. Individual variations have a role in determining the perception of stress, the magnitude and duration of the stress response, and specific coping efforts.

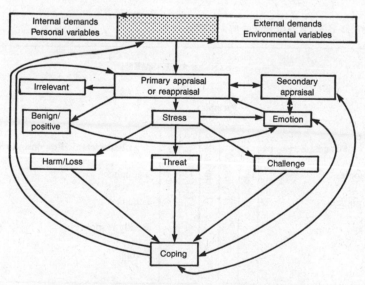

Figure 12-2 Lazarus' Stress and Coping Paradigm

DEVELOPING A PERSONAL BASELINE

Effective management of stress begins with an assessment of current stressors and coping patterns. Recall a particularly stressful incident and use this memory to complete the stress and coping assessment (Exhibit 12-1). Ask yourself the following questions: Where did this particular experience occur? Who were the people involved? What were they expecting of you, and what were you expecting of yourself? What thoughts were going through your mind? What did you feel at the time? How did your body feel? What did you say, and what did you do? Use the chart in Exhibit 12-1 to note your recollections and to complete the coping assessment.

Then identify those variables that are known to maximize the stress response. Put a check in the appropriate column if this particular bout with stress was severe. Although physiological responses to stress are similar regardless of the stressor, the more severe the stressor, the more pronounced the response is likely to be.

The longer an experience lasts, the greater the toll that stress takes. Was the incident prolonged? For example, if the faucet in your bathroom sink drips for a few minutes, it probably will not bother you. If it continues to drip for a couple of hours, it may annoy you, depending on whether it drips during the day or at night. However, if the faucet drips incessantly for 2 weeks, it almost certainly will bother you. In all three examples the situation

Exhibit 12-1 Stress Assessment and Coping Patterns

STRESS ASSESSMENT						
Variables						
Personal Stressors	Severe	Prolonged	Unchangeable	Unfamiliar	Ambiguous	**Characteristic-Responses to Stress**
People:						Thoughts:
Situations:						Feelings:
Expectations:						Bodily responses:
						Action:

Time of day I feel most and least able to cope:

Exhibit 12-1 continued

Influencing Factors
Note the current influence of your:
Maturational level:

Health status:

Cultural heritage:

Physical environment:

Interpersonal relations:

COPING ASSESSMENT

1. What outcome did you desire?

2. What efforts did you make to change the situation, deal with the problem, or achieve this outcome?

3. What feelings did this experience engender in you?

4. What efforts did you make to deal with the feelings?

5. Who was available to you for social support (informational support, emotional support, and/or tangible support)?

6. Did you ask for what you wanted? Did you accept what was offered?

7. What efforts did you make to re-establish physiological equilibrium?

8. Were you pleased with the outcome of the situation? Did you feel less stress as a result of your coping and the outcome?

---

is the same: The faucet drips. Yet, the length of time that you experience the stressor determines whether and to what extent it affects you.

Consider whether the situation was changeable. When we try to alter an unchangeable situation, we needlessly expend energy without being able to affect the situation.

Was the situation familiar? The more familiar we are with an experience or situation, the less likely it is to be stressful.

For instance, recall the first time you gave an injection. Most nursing students find this first experience a stressful one. Yet, giving your 93rd injection was probably not stressful at all. The situation is the same, but familiarity and practice make a significant difference in the outcome of your experience and your feelings toward it (McGrath, 1976).

Consider the degree of ambiguity or clarity of the situation. The more ambiguous the situation, the more likely it is to be stressful. The woman who discovers a lump in her breast may feel stressed not so much by the lump itself as by the uncertainty as to what the lump means. Is it a benign lump? Is it cancer? If it is cancerous, has it already metastasized? Many women awaiting the results of breast biopsy say that knowing the test results ultimately diminishes their stress, even when the test reveals a malignancy. Thus, a person can reduce stress associated with a problem by clarifying the situation and then dealing more knowledgeably with the problem.

Influencing Factors

The degree of stress experienced is influenced by one's maturational level, health status, cultural heritage, physical environment, and interpersonal relationships. The more mature people are, the greater the repertoire of coping skills they are likely to have. Two-year-olds have minimal coping skills. They express themselves verbally and physically, but lack such skills as anticipatory planning, the ability to wait patiently, and problem solving. More mature people have these coping skills and, it is hoped, many more. Because they are better able to cope with a stressful situation, the experience is less stressful than it might be to a less mature person.

Health status influences our vulnerability to stress. Once a person is ill, coping with the illness takes an important portion of his or her limited coping energy. This leaves the person with less energy to cope with other stressors and, therefore, more vulnerable to the negative effects of stress. The person also faces the greater likelihood of additional mental and/or physical health problems caused by stress.

Our culture tells us what is stressful and what is not stressful and sets appropriate guidelines for coping. For instance, someone of Asian background may find that a particular situation causes "loss of face," whereas someone with a different cultural background may have no reaction to the same situation. An American from the Midwest may be concerned about "what the neighbors will think" about a situation, whereas someone of European background may never consider this a concern. Our culture prescribes appropriate actions and feelings, e.g., girls don't fight and boys don't cry. A woman may experience anger as stressful, or a man may experience tears as stressful simply because of this cultural teaching.

The physical environment may add to or diminish the stress experienced in a given situation. A hot, crowded, stuffy environment is likely to make a distressing situation more stressful. The same is true of environments with toxic fumes or irritating lighting. The interpersonal environment can similarly influence the amount of stress experienced. A supportive environment can assist a person in coping with a stressful situation. Conversely, a distressing situation becomes worse when interpersonal problems compound the already difficult situation. See Chapter 3 for a discussion of stressors in the workplace.

You now have a baseline assessment for one stressful situation and a record of how you coped. These data will reveal some of your characteristic patterns of experiencing and managing stress. This knowledge will enable you to identify changes you would like to make in these patterns of behavior.

IDENTIFYING STRESSORS AND SIGNS OF STRESS

Signs of Excessive Stress

When more is required of an individual than the person can handle, stress is the result. When stress becomes excessive, it provides physical and psychological clues; each person has an individualized way of reacting to excessive stress. One person may withdraw from the environment, another may become overly gregarious, others may overeat, and yet other individuals may lose their appetites. Thus, a prerequisite to managing stress is being able to identify these individualized signs of stress in ourselves.

Exhibit 12-2 lists commonly experienced signs of excessive stress. Note those signs that you experience daily or frequently and those that never occur. Write in those additional signs that are indicators of excessive stress for you.

Recognizing your own signs of excessive stress provides you with an early warning that you are experiencing excessive stress. This awareness introduces the possibility of choice. You can respond to these signals with stress intervention, and you can monitor the effectiveness of your intervention by monitoring your signs of excessive stress.

STRESS MANAGEMENT

There are three major approaches to stress management:

1. Practice the essentials of stress management, i.e., what to do when inevitable stress occurs.
2. Manage stressors to reduce the amount of stress experienced.
3. Develop a balanced lifestyle, because optimal wellness is a defense against disease and the negative effects of stress.

Exhibit 12-2 Signs of Excessive Stress

	Constantly or daily	Frequently	Sometimes	Rarely	Never
1. Pounding heart, palpitations, rapid pulse					
2. Rapid breathing, shallow breathing, unexplained shortness of breath					
3. High blood pressure					
4. Tightness in the chest					
5. Muscle tension					
6. Dry mouth, difficulty swallowing					
7. Sweating, sweaty palms, feeling hot or cold					
8. Trembling, nervous tics, twitching					
9. Easily or constantly fatigued					
10. Pain or tension in neck, shoulders, and/or back					
11. Frequent urination					
12. Diarrhea, indigestion, stomach ache, nausea or vomiting					
13. Migraine headaches/other headaches					
14. Premenstrual tension or missed menstrual cycles					
15. Sexual difficulties					
16. Loss of or excessive appetite					
17. Insomnia or excessive sleeping					
18. Grinding of the teeth					
19. Stuttering, other speech difficulties					
20. High-pitched, nervous laughter					
21. Increased number of infections, minor illnesses, rashes					
22. Irritable					
23. Anxious					
24. Depressed					
25. Frustrated or feeling pressured					
26. Feeling emotionally unstable					
27. Angry, jealous, or suspicious outbursts					

Exhibit 12-2 continued

	Constantly or daily	Frequently	Sometimes	Rarely	Never
28. Crying—with or without tears					
29. Feeling worthless					
30. Disinterested or detached					
31. Preoccupation					
32. Difficulty concentrating					
33. Difficulty thinking or disorganized thinking					
34. Foregetfulness, inattention to details					
35. Errors in judgment, distance perception, math, grammar					
36. Thoughts focus on the past constantly					
37. Diminished awareness of external environment					
38. Nightmares					
39. Reduced initiative, productivity, and creativity					
40. Desire to run and hide					
41. Withdrawal—diminished involvement with others					
42. Neurotic behaviors, e.g., phobias, avoidance, regression					
43. Criticizing others, deprecating self					
44. Blaming others					
45. Increased activity level, restlessness					
46. Easily startled					
47. Overly responsive to environmental stimuli					
48. Impulsive behavior					
49. Accident proneness					
50.					
51.					
52.					

Source: From *The Stress of Life,* 2nd ed. (pp. 173–178) by Hans Selye, 1976, New York: McGraw-Hill Book Company. Copyright 1976 by McGraw-Hill Book Company. Adapted by permission.

Approaches 2 and 3 reduce the amount of stress experienced. However, stress cannot be totally eliminated. When it does occur, Approach 1—the essentials of stress management—comes into play. There are four essentials:

1. Deal with the problem.
2. Deal with the feelings.
3. Use available social support.
4. Reduce the physiological arousal of stress.

Deal with the Problem

Problems that tax a person's coping resources will elicit or promote the stress response. As long as the problem persists or for as long as it is perceived to continue, the stress response will continue. Therefore, the person must understand and deal with the problem and make an effort to alter the situation responsible for the problem.

Deal with the Feelings

Feelings or emotions arise in response to both experiences and thoughts. These feelings are a part of the holistic response of the individual, which activates the body purposefully. For instance, anger helps activate the person who perceives a threat to prepare for fighting. Another response to the perception of threat is fear. Fear helps activate the person to flee.

Individuals do not choose their feeling responses; feelings occur in response to the situation or their thoughts. The choice lies in how to deal with the feelings. As with the generalized stress response, feelings arouse the body. If an individual chooses to enact the feelings (e.g., fight or run), the arousal is dissipated through the action. If the individual chooses to suppress the feelings, the activation remains in the body. A number of disorders are associated with (not singularly caused by) unexpressed feelings. For instance, anger activates the upper portion of the body, the portion used to fight. Difficulty expressing anger has been associated with peptic ulcers, arthritis, and headaches of all kinds. Fear activates the lower portion of the body, that portion used to run. Ulcerative colitis has been associated with chronic fear. Thus, the energy of unexpressed feelings eventually finds its escape through these physical outlets, usually to the detriment of physical well-being. For this reason, it is essential to deal not only with problem situations but also with the feelings they engender. If the feelings are not dealt with, chronic activation occurs.

Dealing with feelings is a learned skill. The individual first learns to identify and describe the feelings and then to express them in some way in order to dissipate the activation. It is important to learn to express feelings in ways that are nourishing to the individual but not detrimental to others. Feelings expressed in ways damaging to others usually initiate an upward spiral of increasingly intense feelings.

Physical activity and assertiveness both help in learning to express feelings. Physical activity is a socially acceptable way of dissipating the activation of the body engendered by feelings. Assertiveness training teaches expression of feelings in a way that respects both self and others (see Chapter 5, Assertive Communication and the Nurse Leader).

Use Social Support

Research findings indicate that social support modifies the potentially negative effects of stress and helps people cope with those effects (Schaefer, Coyne, & Lazarus, 1981). People with strong social support have fewer illnesses (Cassell, 1976), experience more positive mental health (Cobb, 1976), and live longer lives (Berkman & Syme, 1979; Cassell, 1976).

Reduce the Physiological Arousal of Stress

Stress elicits a physiological stress response (Selye, 1976). This response can be diminished by (1) burning up excessive arousal with physical exercise and (2) draining off excess arousal through relaxation techniques.

Exercise to Burn Off Excessive Stress

Both the initial and sustained stress responses prepare the body to fight or flee. Because we seldom run or fight, the muscular and biochemical changes meant to stimulate this behavior are unused, and the energy remains stored in our bodies.

Exercise is a healthy way to expend this energy. Exercise that uses large muscle movements sustained over time and that increases the heart rate allows the tension of stress to be released naturally as the physiological effects of stress are channeled outward. Moreover, exercise enhances wellness. A physically sound body is more resistant to stress, and recovers faster from it.

Some of the positive effects of exercise are its ability to:

- strengthen the heart muscle
- decrease the heart rate
- lower blood pressure
- decrease cholesterol and lipid levels in the blood
- increase muscle tone
- strengthen muscles to support the skeletal structures

Moreover, exercise increases respiratory endurance and oxygen intake, stimulates the immune system, improves mental outlook, and helps build confidence. Because it burns calories, exercise decreases the percentage of total body fat. Exercise is also a natural appetite-suppressant. Overall, these changes lead to an enhanced sense of well-being.

Lack of exercise increases the risk of physiological inefficiency, hypertension, coronary artery disease, arteriosclerosis, chronic fatigue, tiredness, poor musculature and inadequate flexibility, demineralization of bones, tension, and such minor body pains as lower back pain. Lack of exercise is also a factor in most chronic, degenerative diseases.

What you do to exercise matters little as long as it increases your pulse rate to the correct amount for your body, generally between 120 and 150 beats per minute, for 20 to 30 minutes at least three or four times a week. To determine your ideal pulse rate during exercise, start with the standard maximum heart rate—220—and deduct your age. The result is your maximum attainable heart rate without passing out. From this figure, deduct your resting pulse rate. To determine the range of pulse rate needed to achieve the benefits of physical exercise, multiply this figure by 60% and 80%. Then add your resting pulse rate. For example, a 40-year-old woman with a resting pulse rate of 70 would determine her ideal pulse rate during exercise as follows:

Maximum heart rate $(220) - 40 = 180$
$180 -$ resting pulse rate $(70) = 110$
$110 \times 60\% = 66$
$110 \times 80\% = 88$
$66 +$ resting pulse rate $(70) = 136$
$88 +$ resting pulse rate $(70) = 158$
Ideal pulse rate range $= 136 - 158$

In addition to vigorous exercise, 15 to 30 minutes of limbering, yoga, or stretching exercises are needed two or three times per week to maintain flexibility, another important component of physical fitness.

Listen to your body for feedback about how quickly to progress in your exercise program and how high to set your aspirations. Sore muscles say, "I was used too much for my current condition—be more gentle with me and/or build me up." By letting your body guide you, you can achieve whatever you desire in physical fitness. When you regularly engage in enjoyable exercise and experience an ongoing sense of improved well-being, then you will incorporate exercise into your life.

Learning to breathe effectively will enhance the pleasure of exercise and relaxation. Our nostrils are meant to filter and moisten incoming air. Therefore, it is especially important to breathe through the nose during exercise when air intake increases. Breathing through the mouth admits air without benefit of filtering and moisturizing.

Relaxation: Draining Off Excessive Energy

The relaxation response is the opposite of the stress response. At the moment of stress, heart rate and blood pressure rise, breathing quickens and becomes shallow, oxygen consumption increases, and blood flow concentrates in the active muscles. During relaxation, heart rate and blood pressure decrease, blood flow concentrates in internal organs, respiration becomes slower and deeper, oxygen consumption decreases, and the maintenance systems (including the immune system) rest, revitalize, and energize. With relaxation, tension drains, and the readiness to fight or flee is replaced by a sense of well-being.

With regular relaxation, an immunization-like effect develops. One 20-minute period of relaxation may affect the body for as long as 24 hours, making it less susceptible to stressors. For example, if a particular co-worker continually upsets you, regular relaxation techniques can help decrease your body's physiological response to this person. If your heart rate, blood pressure, and respiration rise less dramatically, you will feel more in control and more balanced when you encounter this person.

In addition to reducing the effects of stress, relaxation often improves memory and increases creativity. Less sleep may be needed because relaxation is more physiologically refreshing than sleep, minute for minute.

Not only does the physical response to stress diminish with regular relaxation but the recovery time from the effects of stress also shortens. The vital functions of the body return to normal sooner after you become skilled in eliciting the relaxation response. For example, your heart rate returns to normal within 10 or 15 minutes instead of a half-hour after an encounter with the above-mentioned co-worker.

Relaxation can be learned in many forms, and each form has a different set of guidelines or rules. There is no one best way to relax. Try several methods until you find the one best suited to you. You can achieve the physiological response of relaxation through progressive muscular relaxation, relaxation through guided imagery, autogenic training, meditation, yoga, self-hypnosis, or biofeedback. All will help you learn to reverse the physical changes of stress. Moreover, all forms of relaxation increase the alpha brain waves, those associated with mental relaxation.

When practiced regularly, you can induce relaxation in a very short time. Thus, eliciting a relaxation response can help you cope with immediate stress, as well as become a lifestyle practice of stress management. One way to achieve this rapid response is to incorporate relaxation cues into your daily practice routine. For instance:

> Identify the feeling of relaxation with the specific word "RELAX." With your eyes closed, imagine looking up inside your head, at the back of your forehead, and seeing the word "RELAX" written there. Do this while taking a deep breath. Then, as you exhale, imagine and feel the breath and the tension flowing down through your body and out through your feet. Feel the relaxation.

With practice at least 50 percent of the relaxation response can be achieved in 10 or 15 seconds. If you relax before responding to a stressful situation, you will enhance your ability to respond appropriately and effectively.

Most people who teach relaxation techniques suggest daily practice. Some suggest two 20-minute periods a day, although physiological benefits can be demonstrated with one daily 20-minute session. A quiet, uninterrupted time and place to relax are desirable, and morning may be the best time. However, if trying to relax for 20 minutes in the morning creates tension, this is not the best time for you. The worst time is the hour after eating when the blood is involved with digestion. Some people enjoy relaxation as a prelude to sleep or during the night if they awaken regularly. You may sit or lie down to relax. If you choose to sit in a chair, you may find that keeping your feet flat on the floor works best.

Attitude is important in achieving relaxation. The only way to relax is by not trying. Our culture has taught us to believe that, if we really want to achieve something, we only need to try hard. If all of your attention and intention are focused on trying to relax, you will most likely find yourself filled with tension. Rather than trying to make anything happen, concentrate on your technique and let relaxation take care of itself naturally.

Stray thoughts and random noises are noticeable to most beginners who are learning relaxation techniques. Both should be treated like birds in the sky: Do not try to catch or stop the thoughts or sounds. Rather, be aware of their passing and they will pass without disturbing you.

If you practice relaxation when you have a limited amount of time, learn to tell yourself that you will automatically open your eyes and feel refreshed at the end of 20 minutes. While you are developing your inner clock, you may want to set a timer so that watching the clock is not a concern. However, place the timer at a distance from you (e.g., in the next room or under a pillow), so you will not be startled when the alarm sounds.

Not only is relaxation a great technique to reduce stress and promote healing but it is also one method that benefits the healer, as well as the person undergoing care. Each time you teach a person to relax, you will reduce the stress you live and work with and improve your own sense of well-being. Try it. Enjoy it.

One word of caution: As relaxation occurs, you will probably experience certain physical sensations. Warm hands and warm feet—early signs of relaxation—are sometimes preceded by tingling as blood flow increases to the extremities. Many people experience a feeling of heaviness as they relax, whereas others feel as if they are going to float away. With very deep relaxation, the body seems to merge with its environment, and the sense of body boundaries may disappear. This feeling can be frightening to people if it comes unexpectedly. Eventually, people come to enjoy it as they learn to associate it with relaxation. You can reassure concerned persons by telling them to open their eyes if they feel anxious or uncomfortable at any point.

Below are scripts for three relaxation exercises (Trygstad, 1980). Ask someone to read one to you or tape it and listen to the tape of your own voice.

Autogenic Training (Luthe & Schultz, 1969). Autogenic training usually accompanies biofeedback lessons, but it is also useful on its own as a means of easing tension. Each instructive statement is said three times; in the silent period after the instructive statement is said aloud, the relaxing person repeats the statement silently. The relaxing person thus experiences each instruction six times. Use a slow, rather monotonous voice. Begin with a sequence of deep breathing, and then continue with these statements:

> My right arm is heavy and warm (allow the relaxee to repeat this silently, then give the instruction two more times).
> My left arm is heavy and warm (repeat as before).
> My right leg is heavy and warm.
> My left leg is heavy and warm.
> My forehead is cool and my face is relaxed.
> My neck and shoulders are heavy and warm.
> My abdomen is warm and relaxed.
> My breathing is deep and regular.
> My heart beat is slow and steady.
> My entire body is warm and relaxed.

Guided Imagery. The following exercise uses guided imagery. This script should be preceded by instructions to find a comfortable position and practice a sequence of deep breathing. The technique is limited only by your imagination. Although this script uses water images, you can alter the visual image. As you become more and more skilled, new images will occur to you and enrich your teaching.

Breathe out. As you do, feel the support of the chair (or the bed) under you. It will hold you.

Let go of the tension you are using to hold yourself up.

Now take another deep breath, and as you exhale, let go of some of the tension in your muscles.

Take another deep breath—all the way to the bottom of your abdomen—and as you exhale, let your eyes close. Or, if you'd rather, let them focus softly on nothing—just a blur—so you have no visual stimuli.

Now let your awareness follow my voice, and continue breathing softly and deeply.

Start by placing all your awareness in your feet. Feel your feet, and feel the tension that is generated and stored in your feet. You probably weren't aware of it. Now—as you become aware of it, imagine that all that tension can turn to water and drain out through the bottom of your feet.

Now bring your awareness up through your ankles into your calves. Feel your calves and feel the tension that has been created and stored in your calves. Imagine that the tension is turning to water and draining down through your ankles and out through the bottom of your feet.

Now bring your awareness up through your knees and into your thighs. Allow yourself to feel and experience the tension that has accumulated and been stored in your thighs, probably without your ever being aware of it. As this tension comes into your awareness, just pretend that all the tension simply turns to water and drains down through your knees, calves, ankles, and out through the bottom of your feet.

Now bring all of your awareness up into your pelvis, abdomen, and lower back. Experience the tension generated and stored there. As you become aware of the tension, allow it to turn to water and drain down through your thighs, knees, calves, ankles, and out through the bottom of your feet.

Now bring your awareness up through your chest and upper back. Let yourself get in touch with the tension stored there, and as you begin to experience this tension, see—in your mind's eye—all this tension turning to water and draining down through your abdomen, hips, thighs, knees, calves, ankles, and out through the bottom of your feet.

Now place your awareness in your fingers and hands, bring it up through your wrists and forearms, and on up through your elbows and upper arms. Experience all the tension that is generated and stored there, without your ever noticing it. Now, as you become aware of this tension, draw it all upward to join the tension in your shoulders—let it all turn to water, and drain down through your chest, abdomen, hips, thighs, knees, ankles, and out through the bottom of your feet.

Now bring your awareness into your head. Feel the tension across your forehead and around your eyes, in your tongue, and especially in your jaw, and across the top and back of your head. As you get in touch with this tension, let it turn to water and drain down through your neck, chest, abdomen and hips, thighs, and knees, calves, and ankles—and out through the bottom of your feet.

Each time you breathe out, imagine that any tension that is left turns to water and drains out through the bottom of your feet.

Now—feeling a sense of relaxation—imagine that you are in one of your favorite places—outdoors. The sun is shining and it is warm, but not hot. It's soothingly, comfortably warm. Feel the warmth of the sun on your head and neck and shoulders, and see the golden-white glow of the sun around the top of your body. Now feel the warmth of the sun on your chest and back, then on your arms, your legs and feet—on every part of your body. See yourself encompassed by the glow of the sun. Now—as you breathe in—take sunshine into every pore and cell of your body. As you breathe out, feel any remaining tension flow down through your body and out through your feet. Continue to be aware of your breathing for a few more minutes while you breathe in sunshine and breathe out tension.

Progressive Muscle Relaxation (Jacobson, 1974). Very tense people need to teach their bodies to relax. This can be accomplished through progressive muscle relaxation.

Clench the right fist . . . now relax. (Repeat this and all subsequent instructions a second time.)
Clench the left fist . . . now relax.
Now clench both fists . . . relax.
Tighten the right bicep . . . now relax.
Tighten the left bicep . . . now relax.
Now tighten both biceps . . . relax.
Reach with the right arm . . . now relax.
Reach with the left arm . . . now relax.
Now reach with both arms . . . relax.
Wrinkle the forehead . . . relax.
Squint your eyes . . . relax.
Purse your lips . . . relax.
Clench your jaw . . . relax.
Press your tongue against the roof of your mouth . . . relax.
Press the back of your head into the pillow . . . relax.
Bring your right shoulder to your earlobe . . . now relax.
Bring your left shoulder to your earlobe . . . now relax.
Now bring both shoulders to your earlobes . . . relax.

Hold your breath for 10 counts . . . let go.
Tense your abdominal muscles . . . relax.
Tighten the sphincter muscles and hips . . . relax.
Press the right leg into the mattress . . . now relax.
Press the left leg into the mattress . . . now relax.
Now press both legs into the mattress . . . relax.
Point the right toes and stretch . . . relax.
Point the left toes and stretch . . . relax.
Now point both toes and stretch . . . relax.
Stretch the right leg . . . relax.
Stretch the left leg . . . relax.
Now stretch both legs . . . relax.
Flex the right foot . . . relax.
Flex the left foot . . . relax.
Now flex both feet . . . relax.
Tense the right leg . . . relax.
Tense the left leg . . . relax.
Now tense both legs . . . relax.
Now tense the entire body . . . relax.

All three relaxation exercises should end with:

Be aware that you can return to this relaxed state any time you so desire because it is a space inside you. For now, retain as much of the relaxation as you choose as you return your awareness to this time and place. Take a deep breath and as you exhale, wiggle your toes. Take one more deep breath, and as you exhale, know that you are *wide awake*. Open your eyes and move as you are ready.

Biofeedback Training. Biofeedback training uses the concept of feedback to help individuals monitor and control automatic physiological functions, such as blood pressure and heart rate. It is a scientifically planned program that trains selected subjects to control one or more "involuntary" functions. While in the program, the person may learn to regulate blood pressure, heart rate, brain waves, skin temperature, and muscle tension.

The training has four steps: (1) attaching the subject to electronic monitoring equipment; (2) monitoring a particular physiological function (e.g., heart beat); (3) "feeding back" selected information about that function (e.g., increases or decreases in heart rate) to the subject by pictures, sounds, and so on; and (4) rewarding the subject for learning to control that function. Biofeedback training has been used to treat hypertension, lower back pain, tension headache, and insomnia due to anxiety and muscle tension.

MANAGING STRESSORS IN YOUR LIFE

Thus far, the focus of this chapter has been on the essentials of stress management—those things we can do for ourselves once stress occurs. All of these essentials aim to use and channel the energy of stress. The body's nonspecific response to stress is diminished or reversed as energy flows out.

This section emphasizes managing stressors in our lives. Most of the stressors we experience are a product of our choices, and we also have choices about how we respond to stress. This section presents ways to reduce or eliminate stressors to give us more control over the amount of stress we experience. Also described are new responses to existing and inevitable stressors that you can use in your own life and teach to those with whom you work.

Take Responsibility for Self

Managing the stressors in our lives begins with learning to respond to self and assuming responsibility for self. The power of stress management lies in recognizing the choices we make and in discovering our potential for other choices. When we are aware of our choices, we gain the freedom to become more than we are.

The power to make other choices comes with responsibility. The essence of responsibility is often confused with judgment and blame, although it has nothing to do with them. Responsibility deals with personal power, with recognizing that I am response-able for myself, i.e., able to respond to myself and my situation. The more aware I am, the more freedom of choice I have. With more response-ability, I have greater ability to implement choices. Awareness is freedom and responsibility is power, the power to choose and respond.

One way to be in touch with this sense of responsibility is to think about a recent stressful situation. Did you choose to be in the situation that produced the stressor? Could it have been avoided? You may not choose to confront pain and death, but as a nurse you chose to be in the situation where these events occur. You may not choose to be critical of others, but you chose a management position that requires you to give accurate and timely feedback and evaluations. When you recognize that your choices have produced the stressor, you should not feel helpless. Rather, recognize that you can make other choices. For example, you could choose not to be a nurse or nurse manager. If you elect to remain in the stressful situation you will want to consider ways to diminish your stress. Simply knowing that you choose to be where you are and that you can choose responses to the situation helps diminish stress.

Our ability to respond to ourselves is greatly enhanced by awareness. The limitations of our choices are the limitations of our awareness.

A personality trait common to many of us who choose the helping professions is a tendency toward outer directedness. Nurses often know more about what is happening with the people under their care than they know about themselves. Often, we do not take time to develop our self-awareness. It is difficult to respond helpfully to ourselves if we are unaware of our own selves.

Learning about ourselves takes only intention and practice. Awareness exercises are a useful way to begin. Take time now to complete the following sentence as many times as you can in 2 minutes.

> Right now I am (e.g., hungry, tired, bored, fascinated . . .)
> Right now I am . . .

When the 2 minutes have passed, are you still writing? Are you aware of only half a minute's worth of information about yourself, or could you write for 5 more minutes?

How did doing the exercise feel? Strange and awkward are two common responses from those who are unaccustomed to tuning in to self. Interesting and pleasurable are common responses both from those who are tuned to self and from those who typically are not.

It is helpful to be self-aware so we can respond to ourselves in an appropriate way. If I am warm, I might take off my sweater. If I am bored, I may choose to involve myself further in the situation, or I may choose to be elsewhere. I am not able to respond to myself unless I am aware.

Now do another awareness exercise. Make a list of things you cannot do, e.g., I can't fly, I can't lose 5 pounds. When your list is complete, cross out "can't" and substitute the word "won't" wherever it is appropriate.

Does that change your awareness? Your perception? Your ability to respond? I can't fly. That seems to be true. But, I can't lose 5 pounds? Actually, I won't do what I need to do (eat less or exercise more) to lose 5 pounds.

Often, our use of language creates a feeling of powerlessness. When we say "can't" when the truth is "won't," we give away our power—the ability to respond to self. Would we rather feel like victims than acknowledge our power?

Substituting "it" for "I" is another way we give power away. What we attribute to the environment or others, we often cannot change. What we attribute to ourselves, we often can change. If it is cold, I am helpless to change "it." If I am cold, I can put on a sweater or go inside.

How does changing "can't" to "won't" feel to you? Most people feel a greater sense of power. Some also feel guilty with the realization that "I could have but didn't." If you experienced any negative feelings about what you have not done, focus instead on what you can do now. Awareness makes the change possible. If self-criticism accompanies awareness, your interest in becoming more aware will be short-lived. Yet, if you increasingly appreciate the benefits of awareness, awareness will increase, choice will increase, and positive change will come with greater frequency.

Assess Personal Stressors and Characteristic Responses to Stress

You have become more aware of yourself and responsive to self by completing the personal baseline stress coping assessment (Exhibit 12-1). Take time now to note on your stress assessment those additional persons, situations, and expectations that are regularly encountered stressors for you. List additional usual responses to these stressors—thoughts, feelings, bodily responses, actions, and coping responses. Note the time of day when you feel most and least able to cope.

Place a star next to those usual responses to stress that diminish the distress and result in a positive outcome. These are the responses you will want to continue.

Circle those responses that perpetuate the distress and/or result in a negative outcome for you. Describe at least one change in your immediate and/or subsequent response to stress that you believe would be more adaptive for you. For example, you might notice that time commitments and time pressures are an important source of stress for you. What changes can you make in agreeing to time commitments and prioritizing pressures?

Anticipatory planning is an important way to diminish stress. List changes you anticipate in the coming year and put a date next to each:

Change: Date:

If you expect too many changes in too short a time, move back the dates for some. Next to each expected change, note one way to diminish its associated stress.

Now list the activities you must do daily, weekly, or monthly, e.g., pay bills, review charts, shop for groceries. Are these anticipated activities stressful for you? If so, develop a routine for completing these tasks. Having a routine enables you to make fewer decisions and spend less time thinking about when to do the activities. Using routines to minimize decision making and to ensure that needed tasks are accomplished reduces stress, provided the routine itself does not become rigid. If circumstances change, a change in the routine may be necessary.

Consider your ability to manage time (see Chapter 13). Is poor time management a stressor for you? To improve time management, make a daily list of things to do and the expected length of time it will take to do them. Then, number the items to reflect your priorities and do the tasks in numerical order. In this way, you complete the most essential items first. If you consistently cannot complete your list of tasks, you may need to reassess your values, your ability to delegate, and your ability to say no.

Use Knowledge of Variables and Influencing Factors to Diminish the Number of Stressors

Review the variables that may intensify your stressors. Do you regularly encounter stressors that are severe, prolonged, unchangeable, unfamiliar, or ambiguous? To continue your search for more adaptive responses, describe at least one way to lessen the severity, duration, unfamiliarity, or ambiguity in each situation you noted as stressful, e.g., seek more information to lessen ambiguity, shorten the length of time of your encounter, deal with only one problem at a time.

Consider the role of influencing factors. Do these increase or decrease the stress you experience? Now use your knowledge of influencing factors to diminish the stressors you experience. Describe one change you can make to increase your ability to cope, e.g. improve your health, question a cultural constraint, choose a more nourishing physical environment for an encounter.

Hear and Respond to Communication from Your Body

The following exercise is designed to help you become more aware of stress-related symptoms and illness—communication from your body (Exhibit 12-3).

In terms of meeting needs and leading a fulfilling life, disease is not usually considered adaptive. However, there are times when experiencing health disorders may be an adaptive choice. Illness or injury can provide a refuge from otherwise intolerably stressful situations. Sometimes, an illness or accident gives us "time out" when we need it most. It may provide a time of rest and is often the only recognized, legitimate way of shedding roles or obligations for a few days.

From people with cancer, nurses have learned that even a life-threatening disease can have benefits. Many people ill with cancer say that their first

Exhibit 12-3 Communication from Your Body

Recall a past illness, accident, or surgery. Write down what was happening in your life at that time, e.g., your grandmother came to live with you, your first child started school, you went back to school, your husband changed jobs.

1.
2.
3.
4.

Now make a list of all the ways you took care of yourself, made yourself better. If you had a stomachache, did you avoid greasy, highly spiced food? If you sprained your ankle, did you stay off it?

I took care of myself by:

Now write a companion list of the ways you made yourself worse, the ways you interfered with or stopped yourself from getting better. For instance, if you had a stomachache, did you continue to eat highly spiced and greasy foods? If you had bronchitis, did you continue to smoke? If you sprained an ankle, did you continue to walk on it?

I made myself worse by:

To complete this exercise, list the ways you benefited from the illness or accident.

encounter with the illness reorganized the priorities in their lives. Time with significant others became more important than dust under the bed. Time for self, such as watching the sunsets, became valued time. A cancer diagnosis also often precipitates changes in relationships. People who feel estranged from loved ones often say that they do not want to die estranged. Consequently, difficulties in relationships are often mended, resulting in pleasure rather than pain.

Hearing how others have benefited from illness may help increase your personal awareness of the effects of illness in your life. If so, add them to your list.

Consider your response to the exercise in Exhibit 12-3. Then examine the connections between your life experience and the illness or accident you suffered. Could you have heard the message of excessive stress sooner? Could you have received the same benefits without an illness or accident? Sometimes the benefits can be obtained in other ways; sometimes, they cannot.

In our culture, children are relatively powerless. They often do not have the right to say no. If a child says, "I don't want to go on vacation," the usual response is, "Be quiet and pack." If a child says, "I think I'll stay home from school today," the most likely response is, "Get your books and don't be late." Short of sickness, children have little bargaining power. No self-respecting parent would take a sick child on vacation or send a sick child to school. So children learn that sickness brings power and choice. As we become adults, we continue to use the same patterns that worked for us in the past. By considering alternative ways of obtaining what we want, we can learn to achieve our goals and also remain healthy.

Alter Perception and Responses

When stress occurs, we most often want to change the situation or the other person. These are our least available choices. We always have at least two other choices: changing our perception and/or changing our response.

It is our understanding of a particular situation that usually precipitates the stress response in our body. Realistic reappraisal of a situation can decrease our stress. Feedback or input from others also may help.

Consider what you say to yourself about regularly encountered stressful situations. What thoughts do you have that upset you? Do stressful feelings follow unrealistic thoughts?

Examine and acknowledge your belief system. List some of your beliefs about yourself and the nature of the world. Look again at Exhibit 12-1. Describe at least one way you could change your perception of a situation or person you consider to be a stressor, e.g., this person is anxious, rather than this person always has it in for me. Describe at least one way you can respond differently to each person, e.g., expressing feelings, stating wishes, saying no.

Develop Clear, Assertive Communication

Do you consider yourself to be passive, aggressive, or assertive? In what situations and with whom is it hardest for you to express your thoughts, desires, and feelings and to behave congruently with your values?

Select one area for change and practice it consistently. Refer to Chapter 5 for strategies to develop assertive communication.

Create Reality from Imagination

To relaxation, the most powerful stress reduction tool, can be added the technique of guided imagery. Imagery is a way of becoming aware of which mental pictures, expectations, and beliefs direct our choices. Through self-guided imagery we can understand our feelings and experiences and change our expectations and beliefs about ourselves and the world.

The body does not know the difference between pictures in the mind and outer reality. It responds to any stressor, whether real or imaginary. Similarly, it begins to relax or heal if that is the picture in our mind. By becoming aware of and responsive to the pictures in our mind, we can create our desired reality.

Bodily changes act upon mentality and vice versa. A deliberate change in belief systems and expectancy is the goal of guided imagery. In this way, our minds may act positively upon the body. The importance of belief systems has long been known through the placebo effect.

Health care uses for imagery are increasing. Guided imagery is employed to understand illness and to influence self-healing positively. Despite the fact that the link between visualization and neurophysiological alterations remains elusive, a growing body of research findings suggests that subtle mental phenomena can have a profound effect on an individual's entire psychophysiology and are related to affective and behavioral change (Mast, 1986).

Dr. Carl Simonton, a traditionally trained physician who uses chemotherapy and radiation to treat cancer, also employs treatment modalities as (and considers equally important) psychosocial support and the use of relaxation and imagery. He asks people with cancer to practice relaxation three times a day. After they are relaxed, they imagine seeing the weak, disorganized, multiplying cancer cells in the body. Then, the individuals imagine a powerful force (e.g., drugs, faith, white blood cells, guides and helpers, army tanks) coming in, destroying the cancer cells, and transporting them out of the body. Next, they imagine their bodies as whole, healthy, and active once again (Simonton & Simonton, 1978). Simonton claims that this technique is as helpful in the treatment of cancer as chemotherapy and radiation. Practicing imagery is beneficial both in the healing facilitated and in the active role in self-care that it gives the individual.

Imagery has also been used widely in sports. Suinn (1976) taught half of the members of the Colorado State University ski team to use imagery. He taught skiers first to relax and imagine skiing perfectly, then to experience the reality on the slopes, and then to return again to guided imagery. Alternating practice in imagination and physical reality produced superior results. By the time of the competition, the team members to whom he taught imagery were significantly more skilled than the traditionally (physically only) trained team members. Since the 1980 Olympics, all Olympic hopefuls have been trained in relaxation and imagery.

New ways to use imagery are reported regularly. In addition to its use in sports and medicine, imagery reportedly is useful in improving musical ability, weight reduction, academic learning, and eliminating such unwanted habits as smoking. Garfield (1986) has reported that successful people, before achieving success, frequently imagined themselves being successful.

We can use imagery to imagine creating fewer stressors. We also can imagine the energy produced by the body's nonspecific responses to changes being channeled into creative expression. And we can imagine any residual tension held inside the body being released through relaxation.

DEVELOP A BALANCED LIFESTYLE

Many practices, when they become a part of our lifestyle, help improve our health. As stated earlier, optimal wellness is a defense against disease and the negative effects of stress.

Take Care of "Weak Links"

We need to become aware of our genetic frailties and of any bodily systems weakened by our lifestyle. If we know our frailties, we can give our weak links special care. For example, people who are at risk for heart disease are wise to refrain from smoking and to exercise regularly. These practices pay heed to their "weak links."

What are the characteristic health ailments and illness patterns in your family? Do you anticipate experiencing similar problems or illness? If so, would the problems be rooted in learned patterns of behavior? If you became ill next week, what would be your most likely illness? Is the predisposition to this illness based on inherited tendencies, a congenitally weak organ/system, an organ/system that is vulnerable because of health practices (e.g., smoking), or unintentional learning?

Describe one way you can protect/promote the health of this organ/system.

Love Yourself

It is hard to take good care of ourselves if we do not believe we are worth it. Too often, we concentrate on our own or others' negative feedback and become accustomed to this picture of ourselves. Yet, we need to give equal time to self-appreciation. A self-concept in which feelings of appreciation and criticism are balanced is consistent with taking care of ourselves. When we feel good about ourselves, we are more likely to take good care of ourselves.

How many times do you get up in the morning, look in the mirror, smile and say, "Hey, I like you this morning. How are you. What would feel good to you?" Or, how many times have you come home from work or elsewhere and said, "You jerk. That was a dumb thing to do. What's the matter with you?"

Criticize and appreciate in more nearly equal measure. Love yourself. Develop your self-esteem consciously.

Sometimes, self-love is confused with selfishness. Those of us who have chosen the helping professions are often concerned about not being selfish. In contrast, however, loving self prepares us to give. We cannot give what we do not have. If we do not love ourselves, we cannot give love. If we do not know how to take care of ourselves, we can hardly teach others to care for themselves or promote self-care in staff. And if we do not care for ourselves, we deplete our energy and have nothing left to give.

To consciously develop your self-esteem and self-appreciation, list your strengths. If you cannot think of any strengths, consider those characteristics that others like in you and those that you most appreciate in yourself.

Make a habit of acknowledging (preferably with eye contact, looking in the mirror) one of your strengths each day, appreciating yourself for something you have done well, and saying "thank you" to yourself (preferably aloud) for ways you have been good to yourself each day.

Identify one barrier you erect to block your own strength or to minimize one of your greatest assets. Describe a way to overcome this barrier.

Develop Balance

Developing a balance between work and play and between exercise and relaxation diminishes physiological arousal to stress and promotes optimal health.

Are you regular or haphazard, active or passive, in your exercise, relaxation, work, and play? Describe a change you would like to make in your exercise, relaxation, work, and/or play habits.

Eat for Wellness

There are many definitions of optimal nutrition and little agreement. The only real consensus is that white flour, white sugar, salt, and fats are barriers to good health. The less we consume of these substances, the better our bodies will function. Roughage in the form of bran, fresh fruits, and vegetables is a dietary asset needed in greater amounts by most of us.

There is no consensus about vitamin requirements. Some authorities say we need no supplements, whereas others insist that we all need megavitamins. Because there is no consensus, consider what authorities have said, listen to your body, and make your own decision.

Frequently, people interested in vitamin supplements choose to take vitamins B and C. These vitamins are considered "stress vitamins" because our bodies need more B and C when we are under stress. Vitamins B and C are also water-soluble, so any excess is simply excreted. They do not have the potential to accumulate in excess, as can the fat-soluble vitamins A and D.

One way of determining the changes that you might want to make in your diet is to keep a food diary for a week. Look at your total consumption of protein, carbohydrates, fats, vitamins, minerals, and calories. Are these totals congruent with the recommendations of authorities who have a philosophy similar to yours?

Another way to improve eating habits is to pay attention to your body's responses and hear the messages it sends. How does your body respond to the food you eat? Do some foods increase your energy and overall well-being? Do other foods create an unpleasant response? Are your eating habits congruent with what you know and feel about nutrition and your bodily responses to foods?

Emotional associations with food often guide our consumption. Become aware of these associations to determine whether you want to continue or change your eating habits. Does offering food mean you love someone? Does being fed mean that someone loves you? Do you reward yourself with food? Is food a consolation for difficult times? How do your eating habits change as your feelings change?

Describe the single most important change you would like to make in your eating habits.

Develop Nourishing Social Connectedness

The earlier section on social support briefly reviewed some of the research evidence indicating that people need other people. One study demonstrated that the relationship of social connectedness to health was independent of other health practices (Berkman & Syme, 1979).

Who are the nourishing people in your life? Describe one way you could strengthen your connectedness to others.

Engage in Self-Expression

Self-expression is the outward expression of what we feel inside. It is a way to experience ourselves and to transform our feelings into outbound energy.

Because we are all unique, we are all comfortable with different means of self-expression. How we express ourselves is far less important than that we express ourselves. Singing, dancing, drawing, painting, gardening, building, potting, weaving, sewing, and carving are but a few ways we can express ourselves.

How do you most enjoy expressing yourself? Is time for self-expression a priority for you?

Become Environmentally Attuned

Environmental attunement means being aware of personal, social, and physical environments and assuming responsibility for making them more conducive to health.

Personal environmental attunement involves (1) evaluating your immediate living/working space and (2) becoming aware of whether it contributes to or detracts from health. It is important to a person's lifestyle and well-being to have a choice of where to live and work and be personally involved in the physical development and care of these spaces.

Social environment includes interpersonal relationships with significant others, as well as those within the broader community and culture. It also includes social conditions influenced by governmental and private institutions. People experience better health if they are aware of the effects of interpersonal relationships and cultural beliefs in their lives and they are able to choose to maintain or change interpersonal relationships and their belief systems.

Physical environmental sensitivity begins with seeing one's self as part of the ecological system. Because we are part of this system, concern for personal health necessarily includes concern for the environment and other living things—air, water, land, and natural resources.

Do you feel in tune with your personal, social, and physical environments? How can you enhance your environmental connectedness?

Plan for Change

Look now at the stress management summary that follows. There are four essentials of stress management, seven guidelines for managing the stressors in your life, and seven guidelines for developing a balanced lifestyle. Renumber these 18 items according to your priorities.

STRESS MANAGEMENT SUMMARY

Essentials of Stress Management

What to do after stress occurs:

1. Deal with the problem.
2. Deal with the feelings engendered by the problem.
3. Use available social support.
4. Reduce the physiological arousal of stress through exercise and relaxation.

Managing the Stressors in Your Life

What to do to minimize stress:

1. Take responsibility for self.
2. Assess personal stressors and characteristic responses to stress.
3. Use your knowledge of variables and influencing factors to diminish the number of stressors.
4. Hear and respond to communication from your body.
5. Alter perception and responses.
6. Develop clear, assertive communication.
7. Create reality from imagination.

Developing a Balanced Lifestyle

These actions enhance balance and wellness, helping to defend against stress:

1. Take care of "weak links."
2. Love yourself.
3. Develop balance between work and play, exercise and relaxation.
4. Eat for wellness.
5. Develop nourishing social connectedness.
6. Engage in self-expression.
7. Become environmentally attuned.

You now have identified what you most want to do to manage your stress. This summary of stress management can be your personal guideline for making changes. If you made all 18 health changes at one time, you would likely feel stress and perhaps illness from experiencing too much change in

Exhibit 12-4 An Agreement with Myself

I will do _____ (what)

_____ (where)

_____ (when)

_____ (to what extent)

On_____(date) I will evaluate this change and determine whether
or not I want to continue.

I will reward my progress by _____

_____

too short a time. An alternative to massive change is implementing changes
one at a time, in the order of most importance to you.

Each time that you are ready to make a change in your stress management
practices, ask yourself the following:

- What do I most want to do differently in managing stress?
- How do I keep myself from doing that?
- How and when will I start doing what I want?
- How will I reward myself for my progress?

An Agreement with Myself

Now you are ready to make an agreement with yourself (Exhibit 12-4). Be
specific, set a time limit, and build in a reward to help foster change.

An example of such an agreement is: I will run in the park five mornings
out of seven. In 30 days I will evaluate this change. I will reward my progress
with a new pair of running shoes.

You are now on your way to effective stress management.

REFERENCES

Bell, J.M. (1977). Stressful life events and coping methods in mental illness and wellness
behaviors. *Nursing Research, 26,* 136–138.

Berkman, L.F. & Syme, S.F. (1979). Social networks, host resistance and mortality: A nine
year follow-up study of Alameda County residents. *American Journal of Epidemiology, 109,*
186.

Cassell, J. (1976). The contribution of social environment to host resistance. *American Journal of Epidemiology, 104,* 107.

Cobb, S. (1976). Social support as a moderator of life stress. *Psychosomatic Medicine, 38,* 300.

Dean, A., & Lin, N. (1977). The stress-buffering role of social support. *Journal of Nervous and Mental Diseases, 165,* 403–417.

Garfield, C.A. (1986). *Peak performers: The new heroes of American business.* New York: William Morrow.

Jacobson, E. (1974). *Progressive relaxation* (3rd ed.). University of Chicago Press.

Lazarus, R.S. (1977). Cognitive and coping processes in emotion. In A. Monat & R.S. Lazarus (Eds.), *Stress and Coping.* New York: Columbia University Press.

Lazarus, R.S. (1981). The stress and coping paradigm. In C. Eisdorfer, D. Cohen, A. Kleinmann, & P. Mazim (Eds.), *Models for clinical psychopathology* (pp. 177–214). New York: S.P. Medical & Scientific Books.

Lazarus, R.S., Averill, J.R., & Opton, E.M. (1974). The psychology of coping: Issues of research and assessment. In G.V. Coelho, D.A. Hamburg, & L.E. Adams (Eds.), *Coping and adaptation.* New York: Basic Books.

Lazarus, R.S., & Launier, R. (1978). Stress-related transactions between person and environment. In L.S. Pervin & M. Lewis (Eds.), *Perspectives in interactional psychology.* Plenum Publishing Corp.

Luthe, W., Schultz, J.H. (1969). *Autogenic therapy.* Orlando, FL: Grune & Stratton.

Mast, D.Z. (1986). Effects of Imagery. *Image, 18*(3), 118–120.

McGrath, J.E. (1976). Stress and behavior in organizations. In M.D. Dunette (Ed.), *Handbook of industrial and organizational psychology.* Chicago: Rand McNally.

McGrath, J. (Ed.). (1970). *Social and psychological factors in stress.* New York: Holt, Reinhart, Winston.

Newman, J.E., & Beehr, T.A. (1979). Personal and organizational strategies for handling job stress: A review of research and opinion. *Personnel Psychology, 32*(1), 1–43.

Pelletier, K.R. (1977). *Mind as healer, mind as slayer.* New York: Delta Books.

Pilowsky, I. (1973). Psychiatric aspects of stress. *Ergonomics, 16,* 691–698.

San Jose State University Department of Nursing Baccalaureate Program. (1979, Fall). *Self-study report for continued accreditation,* Submitted to the California Board of Registered Nursing.

Schaefer, C., Coyne, T.C., & Lazarus, K.S. (1981). The health related functions of social support. *Journal of Behavioral Medicine, 4,* 381.

Schmidt, W.H. (1978). Basic concepts of organizational stress—causes and problems. In R.M. Schwartz (Ed.), *Occupational stress: Proceedings of the conference* (HEW Publication No. 78-156, NIOSH). Washington, DC: US Department of Health, Education and Welfare.

Selye, H. (1976). *The stress of life.* New York: McGraw-Hill.

Simonton, L., & Simonton, S. (1978). *Getting well again.* Los Angeles: Tarcher/St. Martin's.

Smith, M.J. (1978). A review of NIOSH psychological stress research—1977. In R.M. Schwartz (Ed.), *Occupational stress: Proceedings of the conference* (DHEW Publication No. 78-156 (NIOSH)). Washington, DC: U.S. Government Printing Office, pp. 26–36.

Suinn, R. (1976, July). Psychology for olympic champs. *Psychology Today,* p. 28.

Trygstad, L. (1980). Simple new way to help anxious patients. *RN, 43,* 28.

Chapter 13

Time Management and Delegation

A tool used both to increase the effectiveness of leadership and to decrease stress is time management. It has often been said that time is one of the most frequently discussed yet most misused resources. We know that we all have the same 60 minutes in an hour and the same 24 hours in a day. No more, no less. What is of most importance is how we use the time available to us. Developing a better understanding of our use of time helps us reduce the stress of leadership.

Your personality, education, and culture influence your management of time. The way you view time influences the degree of stress you will feel when you mismanage your time. Are you a high achiever, as are most nurses? Possibly you see time as active, tense, fleeting, or acute. Or, are you more relaxed and see time as quiet, static, maybe even boring? The goal-oriented taskmaster who takes on difficult, sometimes impossible, odds may see time as something to be fought and may feel that there is never enough of it; she usually has high expectations for her use of time.

Consider these symptoms of time mismanagement (Davis, Eshelman, & McKay, 1980):

- rushing
- chronic vacillation between unpleasant alternatives
- fatigue and listlessness, with hours of nonproductive activity
- constantly missed deadlines
- insufficient time for rest or personal relationships
- feeling overwhelmed by details and demands

These symptoms are frequently exhibited by nurses in leadership roles.

Careful assessment and planning can make future activities more rewarding and increase job satisfaction and productivity. Lakein (1980), among others, suggests that 80 percent of our satisfaction and enjoyment comes from 20 percent of our activities! Our problem, however, is we often spend more time in the routine tasks that "have to be done," leaving less time for the 20 percent of our activities that bring us more satisfaction.

TIME MANAGEMENT PRINCIPLES

There are several helpful time management principles we can use in planning time effectively (Mackenzie, 1972).

The *planning principle* refers to anticipating the problems that will arise from actions done without thought. If we fail to plan, we cannot anticipate the crises that may occur or the resources needed to resolve the problems. Every hour spent in effective planning saves 3–4 hours in the execution of the task (American Management Association, 1975).

The *priority principle* refers to time budgeted or allocated to certain tasks in sequence. If we fail to prioritize our tasks, we end up spending time in tasks that are really not important.

The *self-imposed deadline principle* is an excellent form of self-discipline that enables us to have time for ourselves because we set our own deadlines and adhere to them.

The *procrastination principle* indicates that deferring, postponing, or putting off decisions, actions, or activities can become a habit and cause us to lose opportunities and productivity. This can generate personal and interpersonal crises. Learn to understand the reasons why you procrastinate; for example, do you fear failure or are you not challenged enough until the very last minute? By becoming aware you can initiate a plan to deal with and prevent procrastination.

The *delegation principle* gives us the permission to take authority for decision making and to delegate tasks to the lowest level possible consistent with our judgment, facts, and experience. As nurse leaders, we often end up doing something that our assistant head nurse, supervisor, or staff member would be able to do if we could support them doing it. Delegation frees up our time, which can then be spent on other tasks.

In our work with nurse leaders, we have often noted such attitudes as "let me do this," "I must do it all," "I must be totally responsible," or "if I do all these things, surely it will all work out, or it will be acceptable." We must begin to ask for support and let go of the nonproductive belief that only we can effect the necessary change. That applies to our personal lives, as well as our professional lives.

McCay (1973) suggests that problems with time management are not only caused by the failure to delegate and cut corners with techniques but also are derived from the lack of mental alertness caused by the boring routines of work and a lack of creativity. Change your routine, turn off your automatic pilot, and do something new. Choose an activity that is creative. In this way, you can fight the energy sappers of defensiveness, self-criticism, and failure to ask for support. It is also important to know when to stop. Too many of us spend too much time trying to make something perfect or wasting time in developing a new procedure. A colleague recently told the authors that she had developed a unique and innovative procedure and wanted to share it with other hospitals and medical centers, only to find that each organization wanted to act on its own. The procedure could have been modified or adapted, saving many hours of research and development.

It is helpful to analyze how you currently use your time. The following six-part analysis (Exhibit 13-1) will help you determine your objectives for effective time management and collect the necessary data to effect a change in your use of time.

Exhibit 13-1 Time Analysis

PART I

List all of your current professional and personal activities under each heading.

PLANNING

ORGANIZING

DIRECTING

CONTROLLING

COMMUNICATION

DECISION MAKING

HOME, FAMILY, AND PERSONAL RELATIONSHIPS

LEISURE TIME

continues

Exhibit 13-1 (continued)

PART II: TIME ANALYSIS LOG

List all of your activities indicated in Part I. Keep a daily record for 7 days of the time actually spent in those activities. Total the amount of time per week spent on each activity.

ACTIVITY	TIME SPENT						
	Monday	Tuesday	Wednesday	Thursday	Friday	Saturday	Sunday
EXAMPLES:							
Leisure	30 min					3 hr	2 hr
Telephone time	1 hr	2 hr	2 hr	1 hr	3 hr	1 hr	1 hr
Training staff	1 hr			1 hr	1 hr		
TOTAL TIME SPENT	2½ hr	2 hr	2 hr	2 hr	4 hr	4 hr	3 hr

PART III

Circle the greatest amount of time spent in each activity. Then prioritize those activities by indicating HPU (high priority—urgent), HPN (high priority—not urgent), LPU (low priority—urgent), LPN (low priority—not urgent). After you have prioritized your activities, ask yourself the following questions:

1. Is it really important that this activity be done only by me?
2. Can any of these activities be delegated?
3. Am I adhering to realistic expectations for myself in regard to what I can accomplish in one week.
4. Where am I wasting time? Where am I spending time in low priority, nonurgent activities and sacrificing the more important activities?
5. What activities are requiring attention and yet procrastination is evident?

PART IV

Place a checkmark by your most frequently used time wasters.
Common time wasters:

1. lack of personal organization
2. failure to set priorities
3. failure to set goals
4. failure to delegate
5. oversupervision
6. leaving tasks unfinished
7. no daily plan
8. management by crisis or putting out the fires
9. worrying and apprehension
10. trying to do many things at once
11. overcommitment
12. duplicating an effort
13. inability to break things down into subparts or sequencing parts
14. no coordination or teamwork
15. handling papers more than once
16. postponing decisions

Exhibit 13-1 (continued)

17. no self-imposed deadlines
18. failure to say "no"
19. long socialization breaks
20. procrastination
21. confused responsibility and authority
22. doing it all myself
23. too many interests
24. fatigue
25. straightening out your desk
26. turning out trivia
27. slow reading
28. over-reading
29. lack of proper information
30. snap decisions
31. excessive information
32. incomplete information
33. lack of feedback
34. failure to listen
35. lack of clerical staff
36. telephone and visitor interruptions
37. excessive time on the telephone
38. junk mail
39. inability to say no to volunteer requests
40. doing jobs that other family members could do
41. no restoration or relaxation time scheduled

PART V: SELF-ASSESSMENT

These statements refer to time management and organization of your work world. Please read each statement carefully and indicate the number that applies to you.

(1) Never
(2) Sometimes
(3) Frequently

	(1)	(2)	(3)	(4)
(4) Almost always				
1. I organize my work area and office so that information can be found and shared easily.				
2. I keep records of employee performance to use in employee evaluations.				
3. I do "on the spot" counseling to assist employees who indicate difficulty in following standards or policy.				
4. I provide staff with clear and concise information through memos, change of shift reports, and meetings.				
5. I write an agenda for each meeting.				
6. I use a written daily plan.				
7. I use written monthly and yearly plans.				
8. I am satisfied with the way I spend my time.				
9. My use of time reflects goals and priorities.				

continues

Exhibit 13-1 (continued)

	(1)	(2)	(3)	(4)
10. I know when I arrive for work what will be my two or three primary tasks.				
11. I am in control of the time I spend on the telephone and set limits accordingly.				
12. I make it a point to remember names and important associations that go with people's names.				
13. I effectively delegate appropriate tasks and responsibilities.				
14. I take advantage of time windfalls (unplanned free time).				
15. I keep a filing system up to date for all records, memos, evaluations, and learning materials for my use.				
16. I use a tickler system or other system to inform me of projects or tasks due for my particular work setting.				
17. I see that my work unit is informed of upcoming events and duties that affect them.				
18. I deal with my workload effectively.				
19. I have the necessary resources to do my job (assistants, equipment, support, etc.).				
20. I deal with the pressure of work demands and set reasonable limits and expectations.				
21. I provide and meet self-deadlines.				
22. I limit distracting influences in the work environment as much as possible.				
23. I do my hardest tasks when I have the most energy each day.				
24. I plan for organizational and job task changes as much as possible.				
25. I am in good physical condition.				
26. I schedule adequate time for appointments.				
27. I allow "off time" for personal enjoyment and relaxation.				
TOTAL of each column				
TOTAL of all columns				

To score, add up the numbers in each column and then total them.

Explanation of scoring:

85–112   Positive organizational techniques and habits; share your ideas with others.

55–84   Good use of many organizational techniques and habits; you could benefit from gaining additional skills in this area to increase your effectiveness.

Exhibit 13-1 continued

29–54	Planning and organizational skills are needed for you to be more effective in your use of time.
Below 29	Ineffective use of your valuable time and skills.

PART VI: OBJECTIVES FOR MY TIME MANAGEMENT PLANNING
As a result of my analysis my time management objectives are:

My plan to meet these objectives includes:

Resources I need to accomplish this plan are:

I will re-evaluate this plan on:

Source: © 1987 Virginia K. Baillie

If you found you answered "yes" to a great many of the time wasters, that you wasted time on nonpriority items, or that you have a time management problem, then you will benefit from time-saving methods.

Managers spend 70 percent of their day in communications. Of that portion, 9 percent is spent in writing, 16 percent in reading, 30 percent in talking, and 45 percent in listening (American Management Association, 1979). The following time-saving techniques, devices, and methods may afford you better use of that time:

- Set goals and objectives. Be sure to write them down and place them where you will see them.
- Set your priorities. Assign **A** priority to items that are critical and goal related and must be done today. Assign **B** priority to those items that are important and related to goals, but do not necessarily need to be done today. Assign **C** priority to items that may not be related to goals and have no significant time pressure to get them done. They may be easy, quick, or even pleasant.
- Do first things first.
- Delegate.
- Concentrate on one thing at a time.

- Break down a large project into small parts.
- Plan your work with the help of an outline.
- Identify your attention span and the times of the day when you are more vulnerable to stress and poor concentration. For many, the worst time to start an intensely complex problem is the evening. For others, the worst time may be the morning. Choose your best time when you are fully attentive to start a new project.
- Reward yourself periodically.
- Take rest breaks.
- Make good use of spare time.
- Conduct meetings that are short. Consider conducting a brief meeting while everyone stands up!
- Examine your old habits that get in the way of using time well.
- Learn to scan written material for key information.
- Write short letters and memos.
- Find out how you spend your time.
- Identify your time problems.
- Make use of calendars, executive planners, logs, or journals. Use an easy method to keep information concise and organized.
- Color-code your files for easy access.
- Develop effective decision-making skills.
- Limit the time you spend on the telephone and with drop-in visitors.
- Avoid having an "open door" policy during your entire workday; close your door when you need to concentrate.
- Agree on a period of office quiet time.
- Take or return phones calls during specified hours.
- Maintain a telephone log so you can return all calls at one time when possible.
- Plan your calls in writing. Get to the point assertively.
- Listen actively.
- Stand up to talk.
- When talking on the telephone, remember that the way you begin a telephone call affects the way you end it.
- Sort paperwork on your desk according to priority.
- Examine how and when you procrastinate.
- Understand why you are procrastinating.
- In a meeting, define the purpose clearly before starting. Distribute your agenda in advance and control interruptions in the meeting.
- Don't be afraid to say no.

- Organize your work space so it is functional.
- Remove yourself from mailing lists that are not helpful or pertinent to your work.
- Set up a tickler file system.

Determine your time savers and time wasters. Then add a few new time savers to your management plan as you take steps to eliminate the time wasters.

Time is wasted in many ways. The *Wall Street Journal* (1984) reported that the typical worker takes 9 minutes to start work after arrival, 3 minutes to leave for lunch, and 7 minutes to get ready to go home each day. This time adds up to 82.9 hours per year of organizational time per employee.

Now that you have reviewed your own time analysis, ask yourself, "What is my personal view of time management?" Many of us believe in such myths as "time flies," "time is against us," or "there is never enough time!"

- *"Time flies":* Sometimes it seems like our activities are flying through our hands because of inadequate planning and many mistakes in our personal organization. We sometimes give ourselves too much to do in too little time. Decreasing our expectations of what is possible for us to accomplish allows us to manage time more effectively.
- *"Time is against us":* The hurried leader who is never really caught up and is always busy with crisis management and missed deadlines will begin to view time as her enemy. Sometimes that enemy is really us. We set ourselves up for failure by the ways in which we fail to manage our time or set limits on what is expected of us.
- *"There is never enough time":* The myth of time shortage is a popular one. Yet, time shortage is an illusion that results generally from mismanagement of time or attempting to do too much in too little time. We are often unable to say "no" to outside distractions, or we set unrealistic time estimates based on getting everything done when we know that it is impossible.

Doing too much, overorganizing, and compulsive time watching are ineffective as well (Lakein, 1980). Even the "open door" policy, when misused, can interfere with the nurse leader's effectiveness. Let your colleagues and staff know when you are available for questions, trouble-shooting, and advice during the day, but establish clear guidelines about when your door is closed (Winston, 1983). Our first line of defense, then, is learning to eliminate avoidable distractions and reduce the time spent on unavoidable ones.

How we use time is a highly personal matter of choice (Lakein, 1980). You must be the final judge of how to apply the suggestions presented in this chapter and your findings from your time analysis.

EFFECTIVE DELEGATION

Delegation is one of the prime supports to effective time management. A frequently heard maxim in management is to delegate as far down in the organization as you reasonably can (American Management Association, 1979). Only then will you be able to find time for the execution of nurse leadership competencies.

Leaders frequently experience barriers to effective delegation. Which of the barriers in Exhibit 13-2 apply to you? Breaking through your barriers will help increase your ability to delegate effectively.

When delegating, choose personnel who are available and knowledgeable about the tasks. Otherwise you may feel defeated before you start. One of the authors' colleagues in a recent leadership seminar indicated that she once delegated the staff scheduling responsibility to a staff member who did not

Exhibit 13-2 Barriers to Delegation

- Do you feel you can do it better yourself?
- Do you lack confidence in your staff and in their abilities?
- Are you a perfectionist?
- Are you insecure in your own role?
- Do you prefer overmanaging?
- Do you avoid taking the time to train appropriate staff to handle delegated tasks?
- Do you regularly take home a bulging briefcase?
- Do you spend too much time helping others with tasks that they are supposed to be doing?
- When you return from vacation or other extended absence from the office, do you find yourself buried in a backlog of work?
- Are you still doing many of the tasks that you were doing before you were promoted?
- Are you always rushing to meet deadlines?
- Do you have someone who can competently handle your job while you are away?
- Do you frequently do tasks yourself, rather than explain them to someone else?
- Do you sometimes fail to delegate work for fear of not being liked or putting too much on your staff?
- Are you worried about someone taking your job?
- Do you feel that, because you have worked your way up to the position you currently hold, it is hard to let go of certain responsibilities?
- Do you feel it is easier to do everything yourself?

Source: From *Getting Results Through Time Management* by American Management Association, 1975, New York: Education for Management, Inc. Copyright 1975 by Education for Management, Inc. Reprinted by permission.

---

have the skill or knowledge to complete the task. The end result was disastrous! Make sure the staff member is comfortable with more responsibility and is accountable for it. Give the staff member positive reinforcement for learning a new task. Remember that delegation does not mean that the leader gives up responsibility; thus there is the need for frequent feedback, reporting, and legitimate control.

Delegation can be done to different degrees:

1. We can ask the person to make the decision or take action without the need to check back with us.
2. We can ask the person to take action but to let us know what was done.
3. We can ask the person to take action only in part and to confer with us before she goes any farther.
4. We can ask that the person not take action but report on the pros and cons of alternatives.
5. We can ask the person to look into the problem and come up with facts to be considered that will then allow us to make the decision.

It is inappropriate to delegate certain responsibilities. For example, we normally cannot successfully delegate performance appraisal or disciplinary problems. The leader who does so may be considered by staff to be "copping out," denying her responsibility, or failing to consider the importance of her leadership role.

Delegating effectively saves time, increases productivity, and enhances the meaningfulness and challenge of particular job assignments for staff members. Follow these 11 steps to ensure effective delegation:

1. State the plan and identify the task clearly.
2. Allow sufficient time to do the task.
3. Choose the right person for the job.
4. Keep communication channels open.
5. Request feedback and first-hand reports when necessary.
6. Exert control but avoid overcontrol.
7. Consider delegating first the tasks that you do best.
8. Complete a time analysis, and choose any activity on which you spend 30 minutes or more per week.
9. Consider delegating one of those activities per week.
10. Build self-confidence by rewarding those who do the job well.
11. Remember to give people the tools they need to complete the task.

The exercise in Exhibit 13-3 is useful for individual or staff education for effective time management and delegation.

Exhibit 13-3 The Monday Morning In-Basket Exercise

Description: You are a head nurse on a busy medical surgical unit. You arrive to find seven memos and four telephone messages on your desk. Grand rounds are scheduled for 30 minutes from your arrival time, and you wish to participate in them.

Objective: Use time management and delegation principles to manage your time effectively as a nursing leader.

Directions: Take 15 minutes to read the following memos and messages. Rank and prioritize your plan for dealing with each item. Consider how to handle these messages, requests, expectations, and notifications to make the most effective use of your time. Answer these questions.

- What could be delegated and to whom?
- What plan is required?
- What priorities are required?

MEMO #1: Your head nurse indicates that she would like your help in a disciplinary action regarding an incompetent employee on the 11–7 shift.

MEMO #2: The head nurse meeting is scheduled for today at 11 A.M.

MEMO #3: JCAH   will inspect unit policies, treatment plans, and procedures next Friday.

MEMO #4: Two annual performance reviews on staff nurses on your unit are due by Thursday morning.

MEMO #5: A networking dinner will be held tonight at 7 P.M. with your local Congresswoman who is speaking on behalf of nursing legislation.

MEMO #6: The staffing coordinator for the 3–11 shift requests to speak to you about a staffing problem.

MEMO #7: The purchasing department says you are overbudgeted for next month's supplies by $2,000. The Director of Budgeting requests to speak to you immediately.

TELEPHONE MESSAGE #1: An irate physician has called regarding a member of the night staff.

TELEPHONE MESSAGE #2: A family member requests that you return his call. The family member is concerned about a dying relative.

TELEPHONE MESSAGE #3: A colleague working on another unit requests to have lunch with you today.

TELEPHONE MESSAGE #4: The RN from the 3–11 shift called and indicated she is ill and will not report for work that day. She occupies the position of assistant team leader.

Exhibit 13-3 continued

> After delegating, planning, and prioritizing, ask yourself these questions:
>
> - How did I choose to handle the requests, messages, and notifications so as to effectively use my time?
> - Did I assume that I needed to handle all of them?
> - What activities did I eliminate?
> - What requests did I delegate and under what conditions?
> - When did I say "no" and when did I say "yes"?
> - What messages did I choose to respond to personally because of my leadership role and responsibility?
>
> *Source:* V. Baillie.

There will always be some anxiety built into our leadership roles. There is much to be done and only a finite amount of time to get the job done. So as long as we live and work in human organizations, we will have to deal with time constraints (Ashkenas & Schaffer, 1982). Finding time-saving strategies and using them can help us reduce anxiety and become more effective leaders.

REFERENCES

American Management Association (1979). *Getting results through time management.* New York: Education for Management Inc.

Ashkenas, R., & Schaffer, R. (1982). Managers can avoid wasting time. *Harvard Business Review.*

Davis, M., Eshelman, E., & McKay, M. (1980). *Relaxation stress reduction workbook.* Oakland, CA: New Harbinger.

Lakein, A. (1980). *How to get control of your time and your life.* New York: The New American Library.

Mackenzie, R. (1972). *The time trap: How to get more done in less time.* New York: AMACOM.

McCay, J. (1973). *The management of time.* Englewood Cliffs, NJ: Prentice-Hall.

Wall Street Journal (1984, November 18). p. 13.

Winston, S. (1983). *The organized executive.* New York: Warner Books.

Chapter 14

Developing Self and Career

IS THIS A JOB OR A CAREER?

The nursing profession has made many educational and technological advances over the last 50 years. The nurse manager has become an increasingly vital and integral member of the complex health care team. Career planning and development are essential strategies for the effective nurse leader. Today's leaders are required not only to influence the growth potential and development of others but also to evaluate and develop themselves (Stevens, 1978). Productive nurse leaders are able to develop a career philosophy, redefine their values, take professional risks, and seek out mentors.

Many nurse leaders approach their role as a career. These nurse leaders are visionary and articulate, and they make progress along a predetermined career path. They are careerists. Other nurse leaders allow their careers to unfold in a laissez-faire manner, advancing as opportunities present themselves. They are jobbers. Careerists shape the evolving practice of nursing; jobbers maintain the roots and rudimentary characteristics of the profession. Careerists facilitate change; jobbers provide stability. Both exist in and contribute to current nursing organizations. As social organizations change and become more like competitive businesses, the nurse leader must prepare for similar changes in the manager's role (Massie & Douglass, 1981).

Webster's University Dictionary (1984) defines a job as an actively performed task usually for payment, especially a trade, occupation, or profession. In contrast, a career is a lifelong series of different roles and jobs that vary in responsibility, accountability, and professional growth (Moore, 1985). Our attitudes and beliefs about work often determine whether our work is just a "job" or a job within a lifelong career. Do you have a specific career plan? Do you view nursing as a series of jobs or as a career? Your answers will determine if you are a jobber, a careerist, or in transition from one to the other (Exhibit 14-1).

Evaluate your current attitudes, values, needs, and what future role options are available to you as a nurse leader. Review the contrasting attitudes and values shared by careerists and jobbers (Exhibit 14-1) to determine which characteristics best apply to you. If most of your attitudes and values fall in the jobber category, consider yourself a jobber. If most are in the careerist category, consider yourself a careerist. Visualize the jobber and the careerist as opposite ends of a continuum. On some categories, your values may lie close to the center of the continuum, rather than on either end. Personal values and attitudes are influenced by changes in internal and external motivators. If the majority of your beliefs are in the center of the continuum, you may be in transition from one philosophy about work to another.

Exhibit 14-1 Characteristics of Jobbers versus Careerists

JOBBERS tend to be more local (relate primarily to people within the organization).
CAREERISTS tend to be more cosmopolitan (have more outside professional activities, participate in special interest groups).

JOBBERS approach the job day-to-day and have few long-range plans.
CAREERISTS approach the job on a daily basis, but view work as part of a larger plan with a future direction.

JOBBERS believe that they merit compensation for the hours or days worked.
CAREERISTS believe that they merit compensation for the degree of accountability and responsibility they assume and for what they actually accomplish.

JOBBERS are heavily invested in the status quo.
CAREERISTS are interested in progressive changes in the professional environment.

JOBBERS are not change agents by preference and are usually motivated to change by extrinsic factors.
CAREERISTS demonstrate knowledge, skills, and attitudes that facilitate and implement change effectively.

JOBBERS view new opportunities or role enhancement activities as "one more thing to do."
CAREERISTS experience new opportunities as challenges and as creative development activities.

JOBBERS attend developmental activities (inservices and continuing education classes) that are unrelated to a career plan.
CAREERISTS attend developmental activities that contribute to career development and promote their career plan.

JOBBERS complete the minimum number of continuing education units required for relicensure.
CAREERISTS complete continuing education units in excess of licensure requirements and achieve higher degrees or certifications.

JOBBERS view management objective setting as a required task.
CAREERISTS view objective setting as essential and valuable to professional achievement.

Exhibit 14-1 continued

> JOBBERS develop management objectives that meet minimum expected role activities and often include routine role functions.
>
> CAREERISTS develop objectives that are innovative, creative, and visionary and that advance the professional leadership role.
>
> JOBBERS prefer annual salary increases by step or standard percentages, rather than increases based on performance, productivity, or achievements.
>
> CAREERISTS prefer merit compensation based on the individual's unique contributions and effective achievement of objectives.
>
> JOBBERS function in the present.
>
> CAREERISTS deal with the present and plan for the future.
>
> JOBBERS do not have the qualifications or skills to move laterally or upward in another organization.
>
> CAREERISTS are qualified to transfer to lateral or upward roles in a new organization.
>
> JOBBERS are less marketable and cannot risk losing the benefits or salary level they currently receive.
>
> CAREERISTS can easily achieve compensation similar to or greater than present compensation in a new position.

As an additional exercise, evaluate your colleagues to determine if they are predominantly jobbers or careerists. Consider the following six relationships in your organization:

1. the individual (role occupant)
2. the boss (superordinate)
3. the staff (subordinates)
4. peer group members
5. individuals who provide professional resources
6. individuals who provide personal resources, e.g., family and friends

Determining if the nursing division's leaders are jobbers or careerists can help you understand and anticipate potential and actual organizational conflicts, interpersonal conflicts, and role incongruence (Hall et al., 1982; Massie & Douglass, 1981). You will experience role harmony if your career goals match those of your colleagues and role conflict if there is a mismatch. The degree of conflict and its significance depend on whether the role sender has power and influence over you and your position, and vice versa (Douglass, 1984).

Conflict may occur if some nurse leaders approach their position as a career while others approach theirs as a job. For example, in peer groups, repercussions may occur if careerists outnumber jobbers. Competition, infighting, and lack of support are some of the repercussions experienced when peers approach and enact similar roles from divergent perspectives. Careerists perform at a more progressive and professional level. The careerist establishes a standard of practice that most jobbers do not desire and, therefore, choose not to achieve. Jobbers are not necessarily discontent in their role, they are merely underdeveloped.

When jobbers and careerists function in a subordinate (role occupant) and superordinate (role sender) relationship, the potential for role conflict is great (Rheiner, 1982). For example, if a jobber is only performing at a minimal level but still meets organizational expectations, no role conflict occurs. She will be evaluated satisfactorily. However, if the organizational expectations of the role more closely match the characteristics of the careerist, the jobber may feel inadequate and threatened and be evaluated unsatisfactorily. Conversely, a careerist whose boss is a jobber may feel frustrated, underchallenged, and bored in her role. Role conflict between jobbers and careerists may surface through such behaviors as infighting, competition, and resistance to change. This role conflict can impede achievement of organizational goals and adversely affect team-building behaviors.

Exhibit 14-2 is a sample analysis of a nursing division. Use this format in analyzing your own nursing division.

Nurses A and B have personal characteristics that are congruent with most of the nurse leaders and staff with whom they interact. Although they each approach their roles from different vantages, they experience role harmony in their respective settings.

Nurse C experiences role conflict when interacting with other managers, e.g., her boss and peers. She is viewed as competent and supportive by her

Exhibit 14-2 Sample Organizational Analysis of Careerists and Jobbers

	Nursing Division Members					
Individual	Boss	Staff	Peer Group	Professional Resources	Personal Resources	Role Assessment
Nurse A: Careerist(C)	C	C	C + J (Majority = Cs)	C	Supportive	Harmony
Nurse B: Jobber (J)	J	J	J + C (Majority = Js)	J	Supportive	Harmony
Nurse C: Jobber (J)	C	J	C + J (Majority = Cs)	J	Supportive	Conflict
Nurse D: Careerist(C)	C	J	J + C (Majority = Js)	C	Nonsupportive	Conflict

staff and by her professional and personal resources. Nurse C is relatively satisfied with her job and her performance. However, she experiences difficulties in forward planning, in meeting organizational objectives, and doing committee work (depending on the committee participants). Nurse C's boss expects her to perform as a careerist. As a result, Nurse C often experiences conflict when working with her boss.

Nurse D has role harmony with her boss and professional resources. However, she experiences role conflict with her staff and peers and has lost the support of her family in pursuing career goals. This degree of role conflict may adversely affect her ability to promote change in her department. Nurse D must mobilize additional supports or decrease her energy toward her career in order to resolve this role conflict.

It is possible to make some generalizations from the above scenario. A jobber in a jobber organization will experience harmony, at least for the short term. Currently, both the jobber and the careerist can exist in the same organization, but the authors anticipate that this will no longer be possible in the future. As technology advances and present roles are expanded, organizations of the future will recruit nurse managers who are careerists. Despite employee loyalty, these organizations will eliminate managers who are a mismatch with contemporary organizational expectations. The authors recommend that you carefully reassess your career planning style if you are a jobber.

STRATEGIES TO RESOLVE ROLE CONFLICT BETWEEN JOBBERS AND CAREERISTS

Many nurse leaders vacillate between jobber and careerist characteristics depending on role stress. For example, a change in personal resources may preclude someone from allocating the energy needed to perform as a careerist. If your boss, a careerist, is replaced by a jobber, you may become underchallenged because your change agent skills are controlled or obstructed.

As a nurse leader, you can use certain strategies to minimize conflict and enhance harmony between jobbers and careerists. However, these strategies are not without risk as they will disrupt the status quo. Be prepared to go slowly and be supportive of your coworkers as you introduce these new strategies. First, increase your interpersonal contact with those with whom you experience role conflict by:

- inviting your opposite (jobber or careerist) to break or lunch
- repositioning yourself in meetings or committees; sit next to individuals with whom you do not usually interact

- breaking down isolation through interpersonal interactions before and after meetings

Then, increase support of your role by:

- networking actively and developing a professional support relationship with managers who have similar responsibilities in different settings—what are the issues and role expectations that they face?
- conducting discussions about the status of work activities or issues for which you are accountable and responsible
- sharing annual management objectives and action plans with staff and colleagues

Another strategy is to increase your contact with a greater number of nurse leaders by:

- participating in problem-solving groups and volunteering to work on special projects/task forces
- sharing with your superordinate specific areas you would like to develop; request resources for these developmental activities
- sharing achievements and bright ideas, seeking knowledge and skills, and developing contemporary attitudes through the help of a mentor or through reviewing leadership journals
- participating in national or regional conventions or organizations

Most nursing organizations are composed of both jobbers and careerists (Vestal, 1987). Reducing role conflict between them will result in the following benefits:

- Discussions about "real" issues will increase and be conducted by less defensive, entrenched participants.
- Opportunities to clarify issues, gain consensus, seek agreement, and give support to each other will occur more frequently.
- Support will develop among groups, and a sense of "esprit de corps" will evolve.
- A greater sense of trust between working groups will be evident. Diverse issues will be discussed with openness for problem solving rather than interpreted as personal attacks.
- Energy will be directed positively toward achievement and accomplishment, rather than inefficiently used up in infighting between factions and individuals. Energy is finite and must be intelligently spent.

STEPS TO PLANNING A CAREER

Some nurse leaders approach career planning in a very predetermined, focused manner, whereas others approach it in a more laissez-faire fashion. Whatever your approach, a career plan requires focused energy and insight through self-analysis and synthesis of various personal values. Nurses who set career objectives often experience greater intrinsic motivation and productivity. A career plan provides an umbrella of enriching experiences under which the nurse leader can evolve. Career planning leads to career mobility, which can ensure achievement of stimulating work experiences and prevent role stagnation (Vestal, 1987).

Following a career plan does not necessarily require formal achievement of a higher academic degree. Many nurse leaders do not want to or cannot return to school. Additional education is only one approach to career planning. Each job you hold can enhance your career. Use each job to gain knowledge, skills, and expertise in your area of interest. A career will develop as your expertise generates opportunities for you to successfully take on new, more challenging positions.

Nurse leaders with a career plan tend to be more contemporary in their management practice and have a greater commitment to the future of nursing (Vestal, 1987). They are seeking higher levels of expertise and performance. They enjoy change. They experience risk taking as positive and encourage it in others. Role change for most nurse leaders is made in incremental steps, which are determined by their readiness to challenge their own previously held values and role interpretations. Each incremental improvement in the nurse leader's performance brings her management standards to a higher level. The minimum standard of practice becomes what was previously accepted as above average. This upward spiraling of standards has a positive effect not only on the nurse leader and nursing as a profession but also on the health care system and the patients for whom we care.

The career planning process has six steps. Changes in your role and available resources may require frequent modification of this process. Review these steps with the proviso that you can work on more than one step at a time and may have to retrace them as circumstances change.

Step 1: Complete the Data Base Assessment

Complete the Jaffe and Scott Career Explorations and Self-Development Tool (Exhibit 14-3). This assessment will provide sufficient personal data to begin to map out a career plan.

Exhibit 14-3 Career Explorations and Self Development: Important Questions to Ask Ourselves

1. What facets of my career do I enjoy most or find most meaningful?
2. What facets of my career do I like the least?
3. Where in my work do I find the greatest challenge?
4. What skills, talents, and abilities do I bring to my work?
5. What skills, talents, and abilities could my work potentially allow me to develop?
6. What do I want out of my work—what benefits and rewards?
7. What led me to choose the type of work I do? What values and personal feelings led me to this type of work?
8. How has my work been unsatisfying, or how has my satisfaction with my work diminished?
9. What new areas, skills, and types of work would I like to pursue? What prevents me from going in one of these directions?
10. What is the greatest frustration or difficulty in my work? What would I most like to change about my work?
11. What are my current concerns and worries?
12. What are the greatest pressures on me right now? When do I feel them? What must I do about them?
13. What is changing in my life?
14. What are the major values or goals that I would like to achieve in my life?
15. What are the most important payoffs or rewards that I am looking for in my life?
16. What intense, gratifying, and deeply meaningful experience have I had in my life? What sort of peak experiences would I like to have in the future?
17. What are the major constraints or limits that I experience in my life right now, which make it difficult to achieve the rewards, goals, and experiences I seek?
18. What are the major obstacles to getting what I want out of life? (Divide them into obstacles that lie inside you and those that are external. Think of some of the ways that you can change or diminish the force of these obstacles.)
19. What are the things I do well? List them.
20. What are the things that I do poorly? Would I like to improve my ability in these areas or stop doing these things?
21. What would I like to stop doing?
22. What would I like to start doing or learn to do?
23. What are the central goals in my life right now? What were my goals 5 years ago? What do I project will be my goals 5 years from now?
24. Which of the things that I do regularly do I expect to do less often in the following year? What new things do I expect to have to do, or want to do?
25. What is the most important change or crisis that I expect to face in the next decade?
26. What is the most important choice that I will have to make in the next few years?
27. Which domain of my life (work, family, friends, self) is the central one now? In the next 5 years, which domains do I expect to become more or less important in my life?
28. What ideal future can I anticipate? (Imagine what you would like to experience, what you would like to be doing, and who or what kind of people you would like to be doing things with.)

Source: From *From Burnout to Balance* by D. Jaffe and C. Scott, 1984, New York: McGraw-Hill Book Company. Copyright 1984 by McGraw-Hill Book Company. Reprinted by permission.

Step 2: Review Your Present Position and Qualifications

Evaluate whether you exceed or just meet the qualifications for your present position. Project your planned role changes in a variety of scenarios. Are you planning to amplify or to change your position? Explore your career options in the (1) same role/same setting, (2) same role/different setting, (3) different role/same setting, and (4) different role/different setting.

Step 3: Evaluate your Peer Group

Determine how your peers interpret their role. What is their work and educational background? Incorporate career strategies that they have found helpful into your own plan. If you are planning a role change, network with people in the role you would like to assume. Ask them the questions in Exhibit 14-3.

Step 4: Incorporate Any Planned Role Changes

Investigate the possibility of changes in the role you hold, or in the one to which you aspire, over the next 12 to 18 months. Determine what knowledge and skills you will need to meet these changes (Sheridan, 1987).

Step 5: Network with Colleagues and Interest Groups

Determine the expected state-of-the-art performance for the role you plan to assume. Do the following:

- Have business cards made.
- Network with colleagues inside and outside of the organizational setting.
- Participate actively in professional groups and organizations.

Step 6: Develop Your Career Plan

Develop your personal career objectives with action plans and validate these objectives with your professional resources (e.g., peers, mentors, nurses with roles similar to yours but in other settings) to ensure their feasibility. Communicate these plans/objectives to your superordinate, subordinates, peers, and resource group. Implement the plan, allocating special time for it. Stay on course, but adjust as necessary. In addition, perform the following activities:

- Identify and strengthen your personal and professional resources, e.g., human, financial, educational, and available time.
- Develop a professional library.
- Collect and organize journal articles on topics relevant to your clinical and managerial interests.
- Form or join a journal club.
- Review systematically professional journals and publications.
- Achieve professional certification in your specialty; consider an advanced degree as a clinical specialist or a management degree.
- Establish a support group. Identify personal and professional contacts who are supportive to you.
- Enhance and develop your leadership skills. Chair a committee or task force or initiate a new program.

BARRIERS AND SUPPORTS TO CAREER MOBILITY

The nurse leader's ability to change roles is affected by both intrinsic and extrinsic factors. Career planning requires a serious examination of these factors. Placing yourself in the best position to enjoy career mobility is not an easy task. Those supports to career mobility need attention, adjustment, and nurturing to be maintained (Swansburg & Swansburg, 1984).

These factors influence career mobility. Each may serve as a support or barrier to mobility:

- the ability to organize and manage *time*
- the amount of physical stamina and emotional *energy* one has for the job
- *resources* in the form of adequate salary and adequate unit budget to implement objectives, and human resources such as family support, outside diversions, and friendships
- the degree of *commitment* and *motivation* to pursue a career; the existence of those motivators in the work environment
- one's *self-image* and own evaluation of one's role
- *educational qualifications* for the particular role or desired role
- previous *experience* in other roles and the degree of success in those roles
- the degree of effectiveness one has as a *leader*

- the extent of a *career network* that one has with other nurse leaders and the degree of diversity within that network
- how willing one is to take *risks* and extend oneself into new experiences.

In Exhibit 14-4, each factor has been arranged along a continuum, with barriers on one end and supports on the other. This continuum enables you to readily see which factors need to be developed and which are already functioning satisfactorily. Evaluate each factor and determine where you are on the continuum. How many factors have negative answers and are therefore barriers to career mobility? How many are positive and support career mobility? Do your answers fall on the extremes of the continuum? If all factors are "3 + supports," you can pursue your career with few obstacles. Very few nurse leaders have that luxury. Most of us must adjust to the barriers, develop strategies to overcome them, and nurture supports that are sometimes fragile.

Exhibit 14-4 Barriers and Supports for Career Mobility

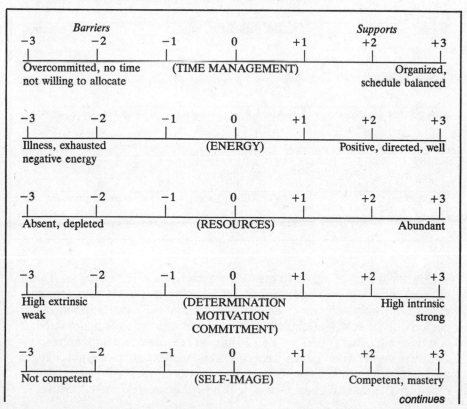

continues

Exhibit 14-4 continued

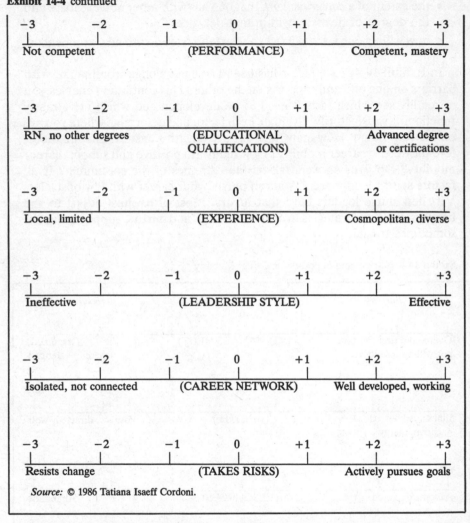

```
-3        -2        -1         0        +1        +2        +3
 |         |         |         |         |         |         |
Not competent              (PERFORMANCE)          Competent, mastery


-3        -2        -1         0        +1        +2        +3
 |         |         |         |         |         |         |
RN, no other degrees       (EDUCATIONAL           Advanced degree
                           QUALIFICATIONS)        or certifications


-3        -2        -1         0        +1        +2        +3
 |         |         |         |         |         |         |
Local, limited             (EXPERIENCE)           Cosmopolitan, diverse


-3        -2        -1         0        +1        +2        +3
 |         |         |         |         |         |         |
Ineffective                (LEADERSHIP STYLE)              Effective


-3        -2        -1         0        +1        +2        +3
 |         |         |         |         |         |         |
Isolated, not connected    (CAREER NETWORK)       Well developed, working


-3        -2        -1         0        +1        +2        +3
 |         |         |         |         |         |         |
Resists change             (TAKES RISKS)          Actively pursues goals
```

Source: © 1986 Tatiana Isaeff Cordoni.

Develop a plan of action to overcome each barrier. For example, if your network is underdeveloped, join an organization that deals with your specialty. Improve your performance knowledge and skills by becoming chairperson of a committee. Remember that supports must also be maintained. If you have high energy and are rich in human resources, adding the responsibility to serve on new committees can tax them. Make incremental changes as you modify those factors that serve as barriers and as you pursue career mobility. Eventually, most factors will be either neutral or supportive.

PRESENTATION OF SELF IN PERSON AND IN WRITING

As part of career planning, the nurse leader must develop certain attributes regardless of the role she holds or area of interest she is pursuing (Brooten, 1984). Effective presentation of self in person and in writing is an essential attribute of the professional, competent nurse leader. Leaders must develop their verbal and written skills because interpersonal communication is a trademark of leadership effectiveness (Vestal, 1987). Often, the effective nurse leader is the one who can persuade others or explain information honestly, clearly, and succinctly.

Nurse leaders communicate by telephone, in groups of varying numbers, and through written communiques. Regardless of the communication method, it is important that you consider the following questions as you prepare for the communication:

- What is the message to be transmitted?
- What is the most effective means to communicate the message? In what arena?
- Who is the receiver?
- What outcomes do you hope to achieve?
- What image do you want to project?

By reviewing these questions before communicating, you will have more control and positive power in interactions.

Presentation of Self in Person

The EASY method is an effective format for presenting information verbally and in person (Linver, 1978). EASY is an acronym for *E*nergy, *A*wareness, *S*trength, and *Y*ou. Whether you are interviewing for a new job, presenting a proposal to an influential group, giving a performance appraisal to a staff member, or teaching in the community, following certain essential strategies will increase your effectiveness in verbal presentations (Kron & Gray, 1987).

The purpose of a verbal presentation is to make something clear, to convince and persuade, to achieve action, and/or to entertain. There are several keys to a successful presentation:

- Use an effective delivery manner.
- Use direct eye contact and project enthusiasm about the subject.

- Assume a posture and poise that command attention.
- Use gestures appropriately.
- Have notes that are readable and numbered by page to ensure their delivery in the correct sequence.
- Modulate your voice, tone, pitch, and loudness.
- Nonverbal communications must be synchronous with the verbal content. For example, if you are talking about a project that interests you, your facial expressions and body position should reflect your interest and complement your verbal comments.
- Allocate enough time to cover the content.
- Organize your entire presentation to fit within the allotted time.
- Put time cues in your material to keep you on track.
- Ensure that the purpose of the presentation is clearly understood. A highlighted overview of the presentation may be appropriate.
- Ensure that your presentation is organized and that you demonstrate a strong desire to communicate what you know.
- Know to whom you are presenting the material. Research your audience before preparing the presentation.
- Demonstrate self-confidence.
- Practice before the delivery.
- Take advantage of any opportunity to present in person.

The opening of your presentation is critical to gain audience interest in what you wish to share. Here are some suggestions to use in opening a presentation:

- Offer a short introduction and overview.
- Do not start with an apology.
- Arouse curiosity.
- Include specific illustrations or examples that are relevant to the group.
- Ask questions of the audience.
- Present a striking quotation.
- Show how the topic of your presentation affects the audience.
- Cite supportive and shocking facts.
- Avoid being either too formal or too casual.

The closing of a presentation is also crucial. It serves to emphasize and summarize the essential points being communicated. Often, speakers have difficulty "wrapping up" a presentation. The following are suggestions to use in closing a presentation:

- Summarize your points.
- Appeal for action.
- Offer alternatives for action.
- Use humor effectively.
- Close with a quotation, if fitting.
- Build up to a climax by using a step-by-step description.
- Be brief, concise, and stop before the audience wants you to stop.
- Allow time for questions.

Presentation of Self in Writing

The nurse leader must frequently use effective writing skills when preparing a resume, developing a proposal, composing a letter of reference, or sending a memorandum (Vestal, 1987). The purpose of written communication is to ensure maximum exposure of ideas, to document critical events, or to transmit information. Written communication usually stands alone without the benefit of immediate verbal feedback, amplification, or clarification. Many bright ideas are either blocked and extinguished or accepted and implemented based solely on how effectively they are written. In this time of rapid change, communication must be clear, accurate, and enhance change, not impede it. You cannot afford to minimize the importance of well-developed writing skills.

Memoranda

A memorandum is an effective format for a short, informal written note to be used as a reminder or as a record of verbal communication. Memos need to transmit a clear message and be well timed. Exhibit 14-5 presents a memo format that organizes the essential information in a succinct manner.

Written Proposal Format

Written proposals are planning tools used to create and facilitate meaningful change. Whether you are doing a feasibility study for a new service, comparing or evaluating products, or recommending solutions for age-old problems, proposals can be your greatest assurance of successful change (Kron & Gray, 1987). A proposal has these components:

- *Heading* (the date, title, presented to, developed by)
- *Background* (and/or the need statement; describe how the proposal supports the departmental, divisional, and organizational goals)
- *Recommendation* (the key options in order of priority; include the top two or three ideas with your recommendation of the most appropriate)
- *Implementation Plan* (describe the implementation plan based on the various options described above; select the most feasible option and develop an implementation plan)
- *Cost Analysis* (include budget for supplies, equipment, salaries of staff, and projected time and educational expenses)
- *Time Line* (provide a visual sequencing of activities, their order of appearance, and the time needed to complete them)
- *Evaluation* (describe the method of evaluation and include time frames)
- *Attachments* (include articles that support your proposal, letters of support, and charts)

Review the following helpful hints to evaluate your written proposal for effectiveness before submitting it for consideration.

- Is the subject clear? The subject should appear in the first sentence.
- Is the purpose clear? Why are you writing the proposal?

Exhibit 14-5 Memorandum Format

DATE:

TO: (Superordinate's name first; all other names alphabetically listed)

FROM: (Name, title, phone extension)

RE: (Topic)

ACTION: _____ Decision needed by: (Date)

             _____ Action: (your reply, ideas) needed by (Date)

             _____ For your information:

             _____ For your records only:

             _____ Please post for your staff to review:

 The body of the memo begins with a clear statement of the purpose. Clearly state the information and what, if any, action you are requesting. Close with a thank you.

CC: (Names delineated)

- Is the conclusion clear? What have you decided? What are you recommending?
- Include headings. Can readers find out what they need to know to make a decision? Is the time line logically organized?
- Use short paragraphs and sentences.
- Use attachments. Attach lengthy background information, charts, articles, and schedules so they will increase reader knowledge but not obscure the intent of the proposal itself. The data in the attachments will lend support for the proposal.

Letters of Recommendation

Letters of recommendation are supportive documents that describe an individual's performance in various roles. The nurse leader periodically secures such letters in order to build a personal professional portfolio. It is difficult either to request or provide an accurate, detailed letter if much time has elapsed since performing the role in question. Therefore, by keeping an ongoing portfolio, you can eliminate potentially frustrating situations when a letter of recommendation is needed.

The following process may help you in securing or preparing letters of recommendation:

- Determine who could speak well about your performance: someone who worked with you on a special project; a committee chair, interdisciplinary colleagues, community contacts; a superordinate's thoughts from your annual evaluation summarized in a letter; or a subordinate's feedback.
- Be clear about what points you would like each individual to emphasize.
- Approach each individual in person if possible and on a one-to-one basis.
- Select a private/semiprivate area to make your request to avoid interruptions.
- Make the request. For example, "Would you be willing to write a supportive letter for my personal file (academic application, new position, etc.) highlighting our work together?"
- Observe the individual's response. If the response is positive, proceed to the next step. If the response is neutral, negative, or perplexed, explore the response.
- Review verbally the specific areas that you would like to have covered in the letter. Have a prepared written summary of these areas to give them, if desired. Many individuals have busy schedules or may be

unskilled writers and would use this summary as an aid to writing the recommendation.
- Reinforce the importance of confidentiality if you are in the preliminary stages of a career change.
- Ask the individual to give you the typed original by a negotiated date.
- Clarify any questions.
- Keep the original in your personal file.
- Make copies of all current letters within the fiscal year and attach to your annual evaluation.

A suggested format for the letter of recommendation is presented in Exhibit 14-6.

Resume

A resume is a brief inventory and summary of one's personal history, educational background, and employment experience. Because it usually precedes the individual's personal appearance, it is a very significant document. It is a document that is submitted unadorned and must be of high enough quality to ensure a follow-up interview. A resume must include sufficient material to convey essential information about who you are (Vestal, 1987). Therefore, include in your resume any special contributions that you have made to your work environment.

Exhibit 14-6 Sample Format for Letter of Recommendation

DATE:

NAME: title, address of the person to whom the recommendation is to be sent

RE: name of the person requesting the letter

RECOMMENDATION:
- introduction
- your working relationship with the person you are recommending, the amount of time you have worked together
- the person's strengths
- the person's attributes that you, as the writer, most admire
- closure

SIGNATURE:

TITLE:

ADDRESS:

Although there is no single best resume format, Exhibit 14-7 presents one sample format. In this example, a summary component of recent accomplishments precedes the traditional resume format. Such a format commands attention because it begins by highlighting achievements.

Most sources advise that a resume be brief, concise, and limited to one page (Swansburg & Swansburg, 1984). However, in the authors' experience, the length of a resume is not an essential factor in deciding either for or against a candidate.

Exhibit 14-7 Resume Format

NAME
ADDRESS
CITY
TELEPHONE NUMBER

PROFESSIONAL OBJECTIVE: (the specific role or career objective you are seeking)
SUMMARY OF ACHIEVEMENTS:
   Clinical Expert: (describe clinical expertise)
   Educator: (highlight experience in designing, developing, teaching, or evaluating educational programs)
   Consultant: (describe role within a specific agency or the community)
   Nurse Leader: (highlight your role in professional organizations, your experience as a preceptor to others or as a community speaker)
   Professional Development: (describe continuing education activities, certifications, and formal degrees)
   Communications: (evaluate working relationships with others from an organizational context)
   Marketing: (highlight your experience in advertising or marketing of programs)
   Publications: (describe current publications)
   Research: (delineate research endeavors and specify your role in relation to each)
ACADEMIC PREPARATION: (most current degree first; include the degree, major, academic institution, city and state, and the dates attended)
EXPERIENCE: (most current job first; include the job title, employing agency, address, dates of employment, and a brief summary that highlights your areas of responsibility and accountability)
LICENSURE/CERTIFICATIONS: (include all professional licenses and certifications and their expiration dates)
PROFESSIONAL AFFILIATIONS: (include professional association memberships, special interest groups)
PROFESSIONAL ACHIEVEMENTS: (public speaking presentations, publications, etc.)
HONORS/AWARDS/SCHOLARSHIPS:
PHILOSOPHY OF NURSING: (this is highly recommended for nurses and can be an attachment to the resume)
REFERENCES: Available on request

BUILDING A PROFESSIONAL FILE FOR YOURSELF

Many nurse leaders keep professional files that document their achievements in their evolving careers. They systematically and on an ongoing basis file data for easy retrieval. There is nothing particularly magical or mystical about a professional file. The authors recommend that you keep in the file the following documents:

- the job description for each position you have held
- each version of your resume
- all proposals you have developed, all letters of recommendation, and all performance evaluations
- a chronological list of all continuing education activities, workshops attended, and continuing education certificates
- a chronological list of all committees, task forces, etc., with the dates and level of participation

REFERENCES

Brooten, D.A. (1984). *Managerial leadership in nursing.* Philadelphia: J. B. Lippincott.

Douglass, L.M. (1984). *The effective nurse: Leader and manager* (2nd ed.). St. Louis: C.V. Mosby.

Hall, D.T., Bowen, D.D., Lewicki, R.J. & Hall, F.S. (1982). *Experiences in management and organizational behavior* (2nd ed.). New York: John Wiley.

Jaffe, D. & Scott, C. (1984). *From burnout to balance.* New York: McGraw-Hill.

Kron, T. & Gray, A. (1987). *The management of patient care: Putting leadership skills to work* (6th ed.). Philadelphia: W.B. Saunders.

Linver, S. (1978). *Speak easy: How to talk your way to the top.* New York: Summitt Books.

Massie, J.L. & Douglass, J. (1981). *Managing: A contemporary introduction* (3rd ed.). Englewood Cliffs, NJ: Prentice-Hall.

Moore, R.C. (1985). A pragmatic view of nursing management. In E.J. Sullivan & P.J. Decker (Eds.), *Effective nursing management in nursing* (pp. 47–66). Menlo Park, CA: Addison Wesley Publishing Co.

Rheiner, N. (1982). Role theory: A framework for change. *Nursing Management,* 13(3), 20–22.

Sheridan, D.R. (1987). Becoming a successful employee. In K.W. Vestal (Ed.), *Management concepts for the new nurse* (pp. 187–197). Philadelphia: J.B. Lippincott.

Stevens, W.F. (1978). *Management and leadership in nursing.* New York: McGraw-Hill.

Swansburg, R. & Swansburg, P. (1984). *Strategic career planning and development for nurses.* Rockville, MD: Aspen Publishers, Inc.

Vestal, K. (1987). Strategies for professional success. In K.W. Vestal (Ed.), *Management concepts for the new nurse* (pp. 201–216): Philadelphia: J.B. Lippincott.

Webster's II New Riverside University Dictionary. (1984) Boston: Houghton Mifflin.

Index

327

About the Authors

Virginia Baillie, RN, MA, CS, is a mental health therapist and educator in human relations and leadership development. She has held positions as director of nursing administration, supervisor, and head nurse in a variety of acute, community, and long term care settings. Currently in private practice in Salinas, California, she has served as a faculty member for three colleges and has taught thousands of workshops for hospitals and businesses.

Louise Trygstad, RN, DNSc, is professor of nursing and associate dean of the School of Nursing at the University of San Francisco. Her practice of psychiatric mental health nursing has been in inpatient and outpatient, community, and private practice settings. She has been a faculty member at four universities and a consultant/educator in stress management and leadership development for numerous colleges, hospitals, health care agencies, and businesses.

Tatiana Isaeff Cordoni, RN, MS, CNA, teaches baccalaureate leadership and the educational track in the masters program at the University of San Francisco School of Nursing. She was formerly director of staff development and quality assurance for nursing at the Merritt-Peralta Medical Center in Oakland, California, and she has also worked as a head nurse and a clinical nurse specialist.